Jon Mayled Jill Oliphant

Consultant: Judith Anderson

GCSE
Religious Studies:
Philosophy and Applied Ethics
for OCR B

through Christianity and secular viewpoints

D0774571

HODDER
EDUCATION
AN HACHETTE UK COM

Glossary terms are emboldened the first time they appear in the main text.

The Publishers would like to thank the following for permission to reproduce copyright material: **Photo credits p.5** *l* (c) P Deliss/Godong/Corbis; *m* © Elio Ciol/CORBIS; **p.7** © Jason Bye/Alamy; **p.8** *tl* © ArkReligion.com/Alamy; *r* Tretyakov Gallery, Moscow, Russia/The Bridgeman Art Library; **p.11** © PictureNet/Corbis; *b* © Matthias Kulka/zefa/Corbis; **p.12** *t* © Stapleton Collection/Corbis; **p.14** Private Collection/© Look and Learn/The Bridgeman Art Library; **p.15** © Kevin Schafer/CORBIS; **p.17** © Isabella Stewart Gardner Museum, Boston, MA, USA /The Bridgeman Art Library; **p.19** Hermitage, St. Petersburg, Russia/The Bridgeman Art Library; **p.21** *l* Cappella Arcivescovile, Ravenna, Italy/Ancient Art and Architecture Collection Ltd./The Bridgeman Art Library; *lm* © P Deliss/Godong/Corbis; *rm* St. Mary's Church, Templecombe, Somerset, UK/The Bridgeman Art Library; *r* © National Gallery of Scotland, Edinburgh, Scotland/The Bridgeman Art Library; **p.22** *l* © P Deliss/Godong/Corbis; *r* © The Art Archive/Corbis; **p.24** © Craig Aurness/CORBIS; **p.25** © Philippe Lissac/Godong/Corbis; **p.26** *t* © Museumslandschaft Hessen Kassel Ute Brunzel/The Bridgeman Art Library; *b* © Philippe Lissac/Godong/Corbis; **p.28** © Bob Thomas/Corbis; **p.29** *t* © Philippe Lissac/Godong/Corbis; *b* © ArkReligion.com/Alamy; **p.31** © Sally and Richard Greenhill/Alamy; **p.32** © Don Hammond/Design Pics/Corbis; **p.33** © imagebroker/Alamy; **p.34** *t* © Angelo Hornak/CORBIS; *b* © Gapys Krzysztof/Alamy; **p.35** *tl* © INSADCO Photography/Alamy; *tr* © Nik Wheeler/CORBIS; *bl* © John Kershaw/Alamy; *br* © Linda Kennedy/Alamy; **p.36** © Antiques & Collectables/Alamy; **p.37** Chris Hondros/Newsmakers/Getty Images; **p.38** © Digital Vision/Alamy; **p.42** Private Collection/The Bridgeman Art Library; **p.43** Fitzwilliam Museum, University of Cambridge, UK/The Bridgeman Art Library; **p.44** © Alinari Archives/CORBIS; **p.45** © Sebastian Pfuetze/zefa/Corbis; **p.46** © 2003 Charles Walker/Topfoto; *b* © INTERFOTO Pressebildagentur/Alamy; **p.48** *t* © James Fielding/Alamy; *b* Mary Evans Picture Library; **p.51** *t* Kunsthistorisches Museum, Vienna, Austria/The Bridgeman Art Library; *b* © Pascal Deloche/Godong/Corbis; **p.54** *tl* © Bettmann/CORBIS; *tm* © Jacques Pavlovsky/Sygma/Corbis; *tr* © Bettmann/CORBIS; *bl* © Bettmann/CORBIS; *bm* © Bettmann/CORBIS; *br* Wallace Kirkland/Time Life Pictures/Getty Images; **p.55** Fitzwilliam Museum, University of Cambridge, UK/The Bridgeman Art Library; **p.56** © Brooklyn Museum/Corbis; **p.57** © Eitan Simanor/Alamy; **p.59** *l* © SHANNON STAPLETON/Reuters/Corbis; *m* © Ibrar Tanoli/Reuters/Corbis; *r* © Alain Nogues/Corbis; **p.60** *t* Private Collection/The Bridgeman Art Library; *b* © Corbis; **p.62** National Gallery, London, UK/The Bridgeman Art Library; **p.64** © Mary Evans Picture Library/Alamy; **p.65** © JUPITERIMAGES/Brand X/Alamy; **p.68** © David Noton Photography/Alamy; **p.70** © Julian Kumar/Godong/Corbis; **p.71** © Look and Learn/The Bridgeman Art Library; **p.72** © Eitan Simanor/Alamy; **p.75** © Keith Leighton/Alamy; **p.76** Mary Evans Picture Library; **p.77** © Louie Psihoyos/CORBIS; **p.78** *tl* Mary Evans Picture Library; *tr* Mary Evans Picture Library; *b* © Maria Grazia Casella/Alamy; **p.81** *t* Mary Evans Picture Library/Grosvenor Prints; *b* © Bettmann/CORBIS; **p.84** Mary Evans Picture Library; **p.87** © Elio Ciol/Corbis; **p.90** © Blaise Mirko/Sygma/Corbis; **p.91** © Reuters/CORBIS; **p.93** © Chase Swift/CORBIS; **p.96** © Jeff Morgan food and drink/Alamy; **p.100** The Fawcett Society/Sophie Louise Kettel, Staffordshire University; **p.101** © The Print Collector/Alamy; **p.103** © Trevor Neal/Alamy; **p.105** © Reuters/CORBIS; **p.107** © Summerfield Press/Corbis; **p.108** © Chloe Johnson/Alamy; **p.109** © Felipe Rodriguez/Alamy; **p.111** Matt Cardy/Getty Images; **p.112** © Keld Navntoft/epa/Corbis; **p.114** © Andrew Wakeford/Alamy; **p.115** © Arclight/Alamy; **p.119** © Gerrit de Heus/Alamy; **p.120** SMC Images; **p.122** Paul Faith/PA Archive/PA Photos; **p.124** SHAUN CURRY/AFP/Getty Images; **p.125** © Lester Lefkowitz/CORBIS; **p.126** © Robert Fried/Alamy; **p.127** © Elisabeth Coelfen People/Alamy; **p.128** © JEFF J MITCHELL/Reuters/Corbis; **p.131** © Peter Hudeck/Alamy; **p.132** © Gary Lucken/Alamy; **p.133** © LISS STEVE/CORBIS SYGMA; **p.134** © Mike Abrahams/Alamy; **p.135** © Malcolm Case-Green/Alamy; **p.137** Philippe Psaila/Science Photo Library; **p.138** Steve Eason/Hulton Archive/Getty Images; **p.141** *t* © Vittoriano Rastelli/CORBIS; **p.141** *m* Zubin Shroff; *b* © Mark Boulton/Alamy; **p.143** Mary Evans Picture Library; **p.145** Sant'Apollinare Nuovo, Ravenna, Italy/Giraudon/The Bridgeman Art Library; **p.147** *t* © Steven May/Alamy; *b* CAFOD/Christian Aid/Leprosy Mission; **p.148** Gerard Whyman/www.cartoonstock.com; **p.149** *t* Charles Hewitt/Picture Post/Getty Images; *b* © Image Source/Corbis; **p.153** Chateau de Versailles, France/Giraudon/The Bridgeman Art Library; **p.154** FPG/Hulton Archive/Getty Images; **p.155** © Bettmann/CORBIS; **p.157** Kunsthistorisches Museum, Vienna, Austria/The Bridgeman Art Library; **p.160** © Ros Drinkwater/Alamy; **p.161** © Bettmann/CORBIS; **p.164** Rolls Press/Popperfoto/Getty Images; **p.167** © ACE STOCK LIMITED/Alamy; **p.168** © Bettmann/CORBIS; **p.170** © Bettmann/CORBIS; **p.171** CHUCK KENNEDY/AFP/Getty Images; **p.173** © Frederic Pitchal/Sygma/Corbis; **p.174** © Hulton-Deutsch Collection/CORBIS; **p.175** FABRICE COFFRINI/AFP/Getty Images; **p.177** © Custom Medical Stock Photo/Alamy; **p.178** © Robert Mullan/Alamy; **p.180** *tl* © LeoniePhoto/Fotolia; *tr* © Lumarmar/Fotolia; *m* © EuToch/istockphoto; *b* © Norman Chan/istockphoto; **p.181** © JUPITERIMAGES/BananaStock/Alamy; **p.182** © MICHAEL DALDER/Reuters/Corbis; **p.183** Bob Thomas/Getty Images; **p.184** *t* © Digital Vision/Alamy; *b* © Bettmann/CORBIS; **p.185** *t* © Mary Evans Picture Library/Alamy; *b* © Screaming Communications; **p.186** © Mark Boulton/Alamy; **p.187** Tim Boyle/Getty Images; **p.188** *t* © Fine Art Photographic Library/Corbis; *m* William F. Campbell/Time Life Pictures/Getty Images; **p.190** © Pictorial Press Ltd/Alamy; **p.191** © Mark Hamilton/Alamy; **p.192** © Pictorial Press Ltd/Alamy; **p.194** SEBASTIAN D'SOUZA/AFP/Getty Images.

Acknowledgements p.13 *The Blind Watchmaker*, by Richard Dawkins, Penguin, 2006; **p.14** *An Essay in Aid of The Grammar of Assent*, by J.H. Newman, Adamant Media Corporation, 2004; **p.66** British Humanist Association.

Every effort has been made to trace all copyright holders, but if any have been inadvertently overlooked the Publishers will be pleased to make the necessary arrangements at the first opportunity.

Although every effort has been made to ensure that website addresses are correct at time of going to press, Hodder Education cannot be held responsible for the content of any website mentioned in this book. It is sometimes possible to find a relocated web page by typing in the address of the home page for a website in the URL window of your browser.

Hachette UK's policy is to use papers that are natural, renewable and recyclable products and made from wood grown in sustainable forests. The logging and manufacturing processes are expected to conform to the environmental regulations of the country of origin.

Orders: please contact Bookpoint Ltd, 130 Milton Park, Abingdon, Oxon OX14 4SB. Telephone: (44) 01235 827720. Fax: (44) 01235 400454. Lines are open 9.00–5.00, Monday to Saturday, with a 24-hour message answering service. Visit our website at www.hoddereducation.co.uk.

© Jon Mayled, Jill Oliphant 2009
First published in 2009 by
Hodder Education,
An Hachette UK company
338 Euston Road
London NW1 3BH

Impression number   8
Year   2013

All rights reserved. Apart from any use permitted under UK copyright law, no part of this publication may be reproduced or transmitted in any form or by any means, electronic or mechanical, including photocopying and recording, or held within any information storage and retrieval system, without permission in writing from the publisher or under licence from the Copyright Licensing Agency Limited. Further details of such licences (for reprographic reproduction) may be obtained from the Copyright Licensing Agency Limited, Saffron House, 6–10 Kirby Street, London EC1N 8TS.

Cover photo © Rubberball/Jupiter Images
Cartoons by Cartoon Studio
Typeset in Usherwood Book 11/13pt and produced by Gray Publishing, Tunbridge Wells
Printed in Dubai

A catalogue record for this title is available from the British Library.

ISBN: 978 0340 985 878

Contents

Introduction

This book is designed to cover the content and skills of the OCR GCSE Religious Studies specifications B J621 (full course) and J121 (short course) Philosophy and Applied Ethics in relation to Christianity and secular viewpoints. However, it is also suitable for use with some of the specifications of other awarding bodies.

It covers the entire content of the course for each of the twelve units. For each unit it covers the specification from the perspective of Christianity, and secular viewpoints on issues are brought in as appropriate. The idea of these secular viewpoints is that they can be used to help in class discussions by posing an alternative point of view.

Each chapter begins with the objectives taken from the specification and these are then repeated for each topic within the chapter. This means you can be sure you are covering the specification requirements for the course, but these may also be helpful when it comes to revision. Anything on the specification for the religion or religions you are studying may appear in the exam.

In each chapter there are exam tips. You will usually find these in the margin of the book like this:

> **Exam tip**
> You need to make sure that you can use these words correctly and understand why Christians use them.

The exam tips are written by very experienced examiners for this course and are designed to help you avoid common mistakes made in the exams and to guide your understanding of what sort of approach exam questions may take on a topic.

In each chapter there are some exam practice questions, which look like this:

Exam practice

'The Bible is a very old book which has nothing to teach people in the twenty-first century.' Do you agree with this statement?

(6 marks)

You might explain that, for Christians, the Bible is the living Word of God and that this means that it is what God wants to say to humanity for all time. Therefore it is still as relevant today as it was when it was first written.

On the other hand you could say that many people disagree over what is in the Bible and do not believe that it should be taken literally. You might also say that for many of the moral and social issues which people face today there is nothing in the Bible to help them.

You can see from this that the exam practice feature in this textbook shows you a typical exam-style question for the topic (this will either be a six-mark question relating to explaining what you know about a topic, or a twelve-mark question discussing what you think about a topic: see below for more on this), and then gives you some pointers on how you might approach answering the question. These should help you prepare for the exam.

Then at the end of each chapter there is a whole page of exam-style questions and guidance on how to answer them, called Looking at Exam Questions. There is a range of question types in the exam, from one mark for an answer up to twelve marks and this end-of-chapter section runs through all the types so you can get used to them all.

Understanding your GCSE exam

In the GCSE examination for OCR Religious Studies (Philosophy and Applied Ethics) you will sit two examination papers if you are studying the short course and four for the full course.

Each paper lasts for one hour and contains three topics.

Paper 1	• Beliefs about deity.
	• Religious and spiritual experience.
	• The end of life.
Paper 2	• Good and evil.
	• Religion, reason and revelation.
	• Religion and science.
Paper 3	• Religion and human relationships.
	• Religion and medical ethics.
	• Religion, poverty and wealth.
Paper 4	• Religion, peace and justice.
	• Religion and equality.
	• Religion and the media.

In each paper there are six questions on each topic, one from each of six religions. If you are studying Christianity on its own, you need to answer the Christianity question from two topics on each paper.

Each question is in five parts:

- Part (a) is a one-mark knowledge question.
- Part (b) is a two-mark knowledge question
- Part (c) is a three-mark knowledge question
- Part (d) is a six-mark question testing your understanding
- Part (e) is a twelve-mark question asking you to evaluate a statement and consider different viewpoints.

You will have 30 minutes to answer each question. You should be able to answer parts (a–c) quite easily and quickly. Once you have answered a question stop and go on to the next one. You do not need to write very much for these questions, you just need to give a correct answer.

For part (d) you will be asked to explain the importance or effect of something such as a particular belief or teaching. You should spend about 8–10 minutes on this part. Remember that you have to explain and not just describe.

For the part (e) question you need to allow 12–15 minutes. You should give a Christian viewpoint and support it with evidence or argument. Then you need to give another view; this can be another Christian view, the view of another religion, or a secular view. Again you need to support it with evidence and argument. Finally, you must give your own viewpoint and support this as well even if it is the same as one of the views you have already given.

When you are studying this course make a list of all the special words and terms used and make sure that you can explain them. You can then use these in your answers.

Although you do not need to learn exact quotations it is helpful if you can refer to biblical texts or other ones in your answers. This book uses the same version of the Bible as the OCR exam, the New International Version (NIV) published by the International Bible Society, but it does not matter if you have used another version in your course.

In the exam the most important thing is that you answer the right number of questions and that you actually answer the question on the paper, not the one you might have revised for particularly.

Remember that some of the marks are for the quality of your written communication so make sure your writing is as clear as possible and try to avoid spelling mistakes.

What is Philosophy?

A dictionary definition of philosophy says: the branch of knowledge or academic study devoted to the systematic examination of basic concepts such as truth, existence, reality, causality and freedom.

This just sounds complicated, even though it is a fairly accurate description of what you will be studying in this part of the course.

At some time all people tend to ask the same questions about life:

- How did we get here?
- Why are we here?
- Did someone or something put us here?
- Who is in charge of everything?
- Why are there good and bad things in life?
- Why do some people suffer more than others?
- Why do some people die in events such as volcanoes and earthquakes?

and finally:

- What happens next?

It would be reasonable to think that when you have read this book you might be able to answer at least some of these questions. In fact, you will still not have any answers but you will have thought about some of the ways in which people have tried to answer them.

Normally we say that we know what the truth is, but actually it is difficult to know what we mean by 'truth'. We could say that truth is something which we can prove by looking at evidence. However, the questions we are asking here do not have any evidence to back up the answers to them. In particular, when we are talking about religion there is nothing we can test to prove something one way or another.

So, there are different types of truth:

- Scientific truth is the most obvious type of truth. Scientific truth means that an experiment can be carried out over and over again and always leads to the same result. We certainly cannot do that when we are talking about religion.
- Historical truth is the sort of truth based on evidence from books or archaeology that shows what actually happened in the past. Although we do have religious books which say they are accounts of what happened, if people do not believe the religion which they are about, they will probably not believe what the books say.
- Moral truth means that people believe that they 'know' whether something is right or wrong although there is no evidence to prove it.
- Artistic or aesthetic truth is when something which people read such as a novel or see in a picture or a film, seems true to them in the sense that it is how things are or it represents the way in which people really behave.

- Finally there is spiritual truth which is generally found in a religion. This means that people follow the religion because in that way they can discover the 'truth' that comes from God.

▲ Can you prove whether this planet exists or not?

In this part of the book you will be looking at several of these major philosophical questions and the way in which people have attempted to answer them, particularly from the view of Christianity.

There are no 'right' or 'wrong' answers or solutions to these problems but you may come to think that some of the arguments are stronger or more convincing than others.

Although spaceships have landed on the moon and on Mars, so far they have not been able to land on the other planets in our solar system. Therefore, if I say that I believe a particular planet in the Milky Way is actually made of cheese and is inhabited by giant mice you have no way of proving or disproving what I am saying and neither do I. Scientists may suggest that their research indicates that this is not true but I can still continue to believe what I have said until I am proved wrong.

Since the beginning of time, humans have asked questions to which they have had no answers. They have developed theories, often based on their religious beliefs, to explain things they do not understand. Today, some of those ideas and beliefs would be dismissed as largely superstition, such as a black cat crossing your path meaning that you will have bad luck. Yet religions have survived and developed for thousands of years and are still a very important part of the lives of many people so this might be an indication that there is some truth in what they teach or that, at the very least, people find them helpful in their lives.

The areas covered in the first half of this book are:

- What people believe about God.
- How some people experience God.
- What people believe will happen when they die.
- What people mean when they say that something is good or is evil.
- How people believe they 'know' about God.
- Whether science has challenged people's belief in God.

Activities

Go back to the list of questions at the beginning of this section.

1 Which do you think are the most/least important?
2 Add any additional questions which you think also need to be answered.

1 Beliefs about deity

This chapter will help you answer questions on:

◆ What Christians believe about the nature of God
◆ What reasons they give in support of this belief
◆ What Christians believe about miracles
◆ How Christians believe God intervenes in the world through miracles
◆ What Christians believe about Jesus and the Holy Spirit
◆ How Christians believe God intervenes in the world through Jesus and the Holy Spirit

Beliefs about the nature of God

This topic will help you answer questions on:

● What Christians believe about the nature of God
● What reasons they give in support of this belief

These are some of the questions people ask about God:

Is there a God?

If there is no God, how did we get here?

What does God look like?

How can we describe God?

Is God male or female?

If there is no God, what is the point of life?

What is God like and how can we describe God?

People find it very difficult to say what God is like because God is beyond human understanding. When people talk about God they tend to use pictures, symbols or symbolic language to describe God. Sometimes people describe God by saying what God is 'not' like: for example, God is not jealous, God is not cruel.

The writers of the **Bible** often used picture images: God is called a shepherd, a warrior, a **judge**, a king, a father and a mother hen. However, these are human images, and so can limit God as God is not a human being or an animal, and to say that he is makes him less than God. This way of explaining God is called **anthropomorphism**.

People also use other words to explain God:

- **Omnipotence**: God is all-powerful.
- **Omniscience**: God is all-knowing.
- **Omnibenevolence**: God is all loving.
- **Omnipresence**: God is present everywhere at the same time.
- **Transcendence**: God is above all.
- **Immanence**: God is within all.

These words can be difficult to understand, and some seem contradictory – an immanent God acts in human history, past, present and future; a **transcendent** God does not, and so humans have to act for God.

Some Christians will talk of God as **impersonal** and somehow mysterious and holy, a sort of force for good, while others will see God as very **personal**, rather like a friend who is concerned about people's needs and feelings.

All these views of God can be found in the Bible, but they all have problems if taken alone. Christians need to combine all these different beliefs about God, but sometimes they stress one belief more than the other. This means that talking about God can lead to misunderstandings, and so Christians use many different ways of talking about God.

Here are some of the ways they use language to describe God.

Analogy

This uses words symbolically to suggest something else. This means that words do not mean quite the same thing when applied to God. For example: to say 'God is good' is different from saying 'My dad is good,' or 'My dog is good'.

Exam tip
You need to make sure that you can use these words to explain God correctly and understand why Christians use them.

Activities

1 Look at the pictures below which show different ways in which artists have tried to represent God – decide which one is most convincing and explain why.

2 Suggest what would be the most suitable way to represent God in art and explain why.

3 Why do you think it is so difficult to describe/imagine/show images of God? Why do you think some people believe it is wrong to show images of God?

▲ Different representations of God. Detail of ceiling fresco painting at Santi Ambrogio e Carlo al Corso by Giacinto Brandi in 1677–9 (left). Fresco detail from Chiesa di S. Pietro e Paolo by Pietro da Vincenza between 1467 and 1527 (centre). Actor Morgan Freeman playing the role of God in the 2007 film *Evan Almighty* (right).

Myth

This is a story which is not factually true, but which has important spiritual truths. We often have to work out the meaning of myths. Many Christians believe the creation stories in Genesis are myths – they teach about God, why the world was created, and God's relationship with the world and creation, but are not actually scientific accounts of creation.

Symbol

A symbol is also a way of explaining the unexplainable, and uses something to represent something else. Christians use many religious symbols, such as the cross, and bread which is not just a food but in a religious context is the presence of Christ.

What Christians believe about the nature of God

God's 'nature' means his *characteristics*, his *attributes*, his *qualities*.

Christians believe in one God – they are **monotheists**. As explained before, Christians say that God is difficult to describe, but they do believe that he has certain characteristics:

- God is outside time and space, he is transcendent and **eternal**.
- God is **omnipotent** (all-powerful), and **omniscient** (all-knowing).
- God is **omnibenevolent** (all-good and all-loving), this means he wants the best for people and gives them rules to live by.
- God will judge everyone.
- God created the universe for a purpose.

Is God male or female?

In answering the question, 'Is God male or female?,' it is important to note that God only appears physically once in the Bible:

Then the man and his wife heard the sound of the Lord God as he was walking in the garden in the cool of the day, and they hid from the Lord God among the trees of the garden.   (Genesis 3:8)

In 1 John 4:12 it says:

No one has ever seen God; but if we love one another, God lives in us and his love is made complete in us.

In Exodus 33:20b God says:

You cannot see my face, for no one may see me and live.

God is Spirit, neither man nor woman. John 4:24 says:

God is spirit, and his worshippers must worship in spirit and in truth.

God is a concept that we understand as being a spirit and so has no form and shape. Therefore, we must have spiritual eyes to 'see' God, yet we as human beings have difficulty attempting to fit an **infinite** concept into our **finite** minds, so we use the term 'him' when talking about God – maybe also because Christian leaders tend to be men.

However, **Jesus** did refer to God as 'Father', and in Christianity, God is called 'Father' in quite a literal sense: besides being the creator and nurturer of creation, and the provider for his children; the Father is said to have an eternal relationship to his only son, Jesus:

All things have been committed to me by my Father. No one knows the Son except the Father, and no one knows the Father except the Son and those to whom the Son chooses to reveal him.   (Matthew 11:27)

This idea of fatherhood is an essential part of God's nature – he is the creator and in that sense is the father of all – but does that mean he is male in the literal sense?

However, many aspects of God do seem to be feminine:

As a mother comforts her child, so will I comfort you.   (Isaiah 66:13a)

St Julian of Norwich lived as an anchoress (a hermit) in a cell attached to the church from which she took her name. She wrote a book *The Revelations of Divine Love*, otherwise known as *Showing of Love* in which she referred to God as a mother.

However, Genesis 1:26 says:

Then God said, 'Let us make man in our image, in our likeness, and let them rule over the fish of the sea and the birds of the air, over the livestock, over all the earth, and over all the creatures that move along the ground.'

The term 'man', in the original Hebrew of the book of Genesis, is used to refer to the whole of humanity – both men and women. Men and women are only patterned after the *image of God* not identical replicas. This does not mean that God has a body like a man or a woman. Being made in the image of God has nothing to do with physical characteristics.

The Trinity

Christians try to explain what they believe about God in different ways.

Christians believe that God is made of three parts or 'persons'. This is called the Trinity. This is a very difficult idea to understand; it gives the impression that there are three gods, but in fact it means that there are three ways of God being God:

- God who is Father – the transcendent creator.
- God who is Son – Jesus who is immanent and personal, who came to earth and lived a human life.
- God who is Holy Spirit – immanent, but impersonal, the way God inspires and guides Christians every day.

One way of understanding this is to consider that a person could be a father, a son and a brother at the same time but still be the same person. Another way is to consider H_2O – it can be a liquid (water), a gas (steam), or a solid (ice) – the same substance in three ways.

▲ St Julian of Norwich. This statue is on the outside of Norwich Cathedral.

Activity

Discuss the view that God has the best qualities of both men and women.

Activity

Use the text of the Nicene Creed to make a picture of a stained glass window.

The main Christian teaching about the Trinity is found in the **Nicene Creed**:

We believe in one God, the Father, the Almighty, maker of heaven and earth, of all that is, seen and unseen.

We believe in one Lord, Jesus Christ, the only Son of God, eternally begotten of the Father, God from God, Light from Light, true God from true God, begotten, not made, of one Being with the Father; through him all things were made. For us and for our salvation he came down from heaven, was incarnate of the Holy Spirit and the Virgin Mary and became truly human. For our sake he was crucified under Pontius Pilate; he suffered death and was buried. On the third day he rose again in accordance with the Scriptures; he ascended into heaven and is seated at the right hand of the Father. He will come again in glory to judge the living and the dead, and his kingdom will have no end.

We believe in the Holy Spirit, the Lord, the giver of life, who proceeds from the Father and the Son, who with the Father and the Son is worshipped and glorified, who has spoken through the prophets. We believe in one holy catholic and apostolic Church.

We acknowledge one Baptism for the forgiveness of sins. We look for the resurrection of the dead, and the life of the world to come. Amen.

Christians accept that God is the ground of our being, the **First Cause**, the reason behind the existence of everything. They believe that God is the designer and creator of the universe. This is the same God who is written about in both the **Old Testament** and the **New Testament**. This is the same God that Jesus prayed to as Father. Not only did God the Father create the universe, but he sustains it. He continues to rule and control everything. God is almighty.

▲ Images representing the Trinity. Clockwise from top left: the Trinity symbol from St Nicholas' Church in Amsterdam, the Netherlands. The Holy Trinity by Andrei Rublev, 1420s. A modern graphical representation of the Trinity symbol.

It is natural to want to know about the character or nature of God. If there is one God who created the universe, what is this one God like? Is God really so distant and so remote that people can never know? It is important to Christians that God is identified as Father even before acknowledging him as creator. Jesus taught his disciples to begin their prayers with the words '**Our Father**'. Jesus taught that God cares about everything and everybody; that God the Father is a loving Father who is kind and merciful, but also just and fair. Christians affirm that we can know these things because God has revealed himself to humans in many ways and continues to do so. One way in which Christians believe God reveals himself is in the world which he created. Christians believe not only in the transcendence of God but also in the immanence of God. This means that he is close to and cares for even the smallest part of his creation. Christians believe that the natural world can point people to God.

Activities

1 Draw or write your own way of representing and explaining the Trinity. Think how you could use shape, colour, words and space to get your idea across.

2 Record in your own words what each of the words used to describe God means (see page 5), and why they are important to Christians. Make a table like this:

Key word	Meaning	Importance to Christians	Example	Secular view
Omnipotence	All-powerful	God is more powerful than anything else we can imagine.	God created the world 'ex nihilo' – from nothing	There is no evidence for this.

Exam practice

'There is no way of knowing what God is like.'
Discuss this statement. You should include different, supported points of view and a personal viewpoint. You must refer to Christianity in your answer. *(12 marks)*

This is a typical question you might find on an exam paper.

You could say that it is difficult to know what God is like as he is infinite. You could discuss some of the language people use to explain what God is like. You could say that we cannot prove that God exists, and that any description is limited by our own human experience, for example the idea of God as a father.

You might discuss some of the characteristics of God. You could also discuss the fact that there are so many inconsistencies in how people understand God, simply because he is beyond our understanding.

You could also refer to what the Bible says about God, and this is why Christians might think they know what God is like.

The reasons Christians give in support of their belief in God

Here are some things that people have said about belief in God:

> *If there is a God, whence proceed so many evils? If there is no God, whence cometh any good?*
> **Boethius**

> *If God did not exist, it would be necessary to invent him.*
> **Voltaire**

> *The question, 'How can you believe in a God who permits suffering on this scale?' is therefore very much around at the moment, and it would be surprising if it weren't – indeed it would be wrong if it weren't [after the 2004 Asian tsunami].*
> **Rowan Williams – Archbishop of Canterbury**

> *A god who let us prove his existence would be an idol.*
> **Dietrich Bonhoeffer**

Activities

1 What do you think these people mean in the quotes above, and do you think the Christian beliefs about God that you have looked at so far help you understand?

2 Why do people believe in God? How many reasons can you list?

3 Why do people not believe in God? How many reasons can you list?

Exam tip
You need to make sure you can use the following key words correctly: atheist, theist, agnostic.

It is not always easy to explain beliefs, but it is important to challenge them in order to see how well they stand up, and to look for the flaws in the arguments both for and against belief in God.

Philosophers have tried for centuries to present arguments for God's existence, and Christians have used these to support their belief in God.

Argument 1: the ontological argument

This argument is unlike any of the others – it does not rely on our observations of the universe or the world around us, but uses logic and words (a linguistic argument). The ontological argument was first put forward by **St Anselm of Canterbury** (1033–1109).

Anselm was writing to convince **believers** that they were right in their beliefs, and declared that anyone should accept his definition of God. He defines God as, 'That than which nothing greater can be conceived'. In other words, God is the most perfect being imaginable, and he must exist otherwise we could not produce this description.

Although the ontological argument is based on some valid reasoning, it does have some problems as it seems to say that we can know the nature of an unknowable God.

Argument 2: the cosmological argument

Why is there something rather than nothing?

This argument says that the universe must have come from somewhere – Christians believe it came from God. This is the message of the first creation story in Genesis:

In the beginning God created the heavens and the earth.   (Genesis 1:1)

St Thomas Aquinas (1225–74) devised several arguments to prove God's existence. He argued that something cannot come from nothing. Therefore the universe must have a cause and everything in the universe must have a cause – something or someone must have brought it into existence. He said that everything can be traced back to a First Cause, and this is God.

It is just like the first domino in a row toppling that causes all the rest to fall. Aquinas also said that God is a **necessary being** – by this he means that God must exist: he cannot not exist. He was not created as we are, and there was no time when he did not exist.

The **Big Bang theory** backs up the idea that the universe had a beginning. The Big Bang was not something that happened *in* the universe – it *created* the universe. The essential idea is that the universe has expanded from a primordial hot and dense but minute mass at some finite time in the past and continues to expand to this day. The Big Bang theory proposes the universe was extremely hot and dense when it was created around 14 billion years ago, and that it cooled as it expanded. There is evidence for the Big Bang in the background radiation in the universe left over from the cooling after the Big Bang.

Although scientific explanations tell us how something came about, or how it works, they cannot go further. They cannot tell us whether there was a creator or a plan.

The question that we cannot answer is: what caused the Big Bang? **Atheists** and **agnostics** would say it was just chance, theists would say it was God.

Argument 3: the teleological argument or argument from the design of the universe

Another common argument is that the world shows that it has been designed and so must have been created or designed by someone: it could not have come about by chance.

There are two famous Christians who proposed versions of the design argument: Newton and Paley.

Isaac Newton (1642–1727) was one of the first modern scientists and he thought that the human thumb, so intricately designed and unique to each person, had to have a designer:

> In the absence of any other proof, the thumb alone would convince me of God's existence.
> God created everything by number, weight and measure.

The discovery of the uniqueness of everybody's DNA is a more modern way of looking at this.

William Paley (1743–1805) used the idea of a watch to explain that the world did not appear by chance. In the eighteenth century a watch was one of the most complicated pieces of machinery that had been made.

Paley said that if someone was walking across a field and came across a large rock, they would just assume that it had always been there. But if they found a watch lying on the ground, they would assume it was the product of a designer as its many moving parts

▲ Everything in the universe must have a cause: just like the first domino in a row toppling causes all the rest to fall.

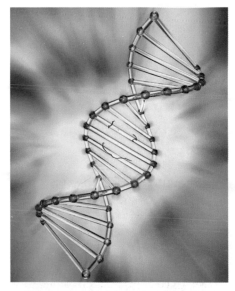

▲ Could DNA be evidence of design? This is a photograph of a model representing the double-helix structure of a DNA molecule.

Research task

Research the Fibonacci series in nature. Do you think it supports the Teleological Argument or not?

Discussion point

Can you see any problems with the idea that the world is designed? Is it a good design?

would not have come together by chance. Paley argued that the world was also like a machine, so complicated that it could not have come into existence by chance – it must have been designed and that designer was God.

Natural selection

Charles Darwin (1809–82) challenged the Teleological Argument with his theory of evolution. He said that all life developed through **natural selection** – tiny differences and genetic mutations between creatures of the same species can sometimes make one individual slightly better suited to their environment than others. This means that it survives longer and has more offspring who inherit that trait. In this way, over millions of years, a tiny difference is enhanced and developed into a whole new species or sub-species. Those species who have not adapted die out. The 'survival of the fittest' means the survival of those who are best fitted to their environment. There is no design in this process; if the evolution of life started again from the beginning, it would not produce anything like the same results.

However, Darwin never tried to explain where everything originated – just how life changed and adapted once it was here. The mainstream churches, including the **Roman Catholic Church** and the Church of England, accept evolution.

▲ Charles Darwin: does his theory mean the Bible is wrong?

> **Exam tip**
> Remember that although evolution is driven by random genetic mutations the process of evolution is not itself random – the individuals that are better adapted to the demands of their environment will always be more successful than those that are not, in the competition for food and for breeding partners. Evolution could be, like gravity, something designed by God as a framework for how the universe works. Where evolution comes into conflict with belief is where belief states that God created all life on earth just as it is, and where people argue about how life on earth began in the first place.

Intelligent design

In reply to Darwin's theory some Christians suggested the theory of **intelligent design**. The theory of intelligent design says that life is so complex that it must have been designed by a higher intelligent being, and not evolved by natural selection – as Charles Darwin argued and the vast majority of scientists now believe.

Followers of intelligent design see evidence of an 'intelligence' behind all the changes in organisms.

Despite developing the theory of evolution Charles Darwin continued to believe that God was behind it all:

> Another source of conviction in the existence of God … follows from the … impossibility of conceiving this immense and wonderful universe, including man with his capacity for looking far backwards and far into futurity, as the result of blind chance or necessity.   (Charles Darwin, *The Autobiography of Charles Darwin*)

▲ The Creation Museum in Kentucky, USA features displays based on the belief that the earth was created exactly as described in the Bible, some 6000 years ago.

The Goldilocks effect

However the universe began, it appears to be 'fine-tuned' for our existence. If certain physical properties were minutely different, even by about one in ten to the power of 60, we would not be here. The physical constants and laws of nature, like Baby Bear's bed and porridge, are 'just right' for us.

This does not provide a perfect argument for the existence of God but it is fully consistent with a universe planned by God, say some Christians.

However, atheists would argue that of course the universe appears to be just right for humans because we have also evolved to meet its conditions:

> Imagine a puddle waking up one morning and thinking, 'This is an interesting world I find myself in, an interesting hole I find myself in, fits me rather neatly, doesn't it? In fact it fits me staggeringly well, must have been made to have me in it!' This is such a powerful idea that as the sun rises in the sky and the air heats up and as, gradually, the puddle gets smaller and smaller, it's still frantically hanging on to the notion that everything's going to be alright, because this world was meant to have him in it, was built to have him in it; so the moment he disappears catches him rather by surprise. I think this may be something we need to be on the watch out for.'   (the author Douglas Adams)

Richard Dawkins wrote in the *Guardian*:

> There is no evidence in favour of intelligent design: only alleged gaps in the completeness of the evolutionary account.

And he also argued against Paley in his book *The Blind Watchmaker*:

> Paley's argument is made with passionate sincerity and is informed by the best biological scholarship of his day, but it is wrong, gloriously and utterly wrong. The analogy between telescope and eye, between watch and living organism, is false. All appearances to the contrary, the only watchmaker in nature is the blind forces of physics, albeit deployed in a very special way. A true watchmaker has foresight: he designs his cogs and springs, and plans their interconnections, with a future purpose in his mind's eye. Natural selection, the blind, unconscious, automatic process which Darwin discovered, and which we now know is the explanation for the existence and apparently purposeful form of all life, has no purpose in mind. It has no mind and no mind's eye. It does not plan for the future. It has no vision, no foresight, no sight at all. If it can be said to play the role of watchmaker in nature, it is the blind watchmaker.

Argument 4: the argument from experience

Some people have argued that God can be experienced; this may be through miracles which we will look at in more depth later, it may be through having prayers answered, or through meditation or prayer. People have said that they have felt God's presence, or heard him speak to them, and so he must exist. Or it may be a conversion experience, whereby a person's whole life is changed by some powerful event, like St Paul's conversion:

As he neared Damascus on his journey, suddenly a light from heaven flashed around him. He fell to the ground and heard a voice say to him, 'Saul, Saul,

Activity

How many examples of the Goldilocks effect can you think of?

▲ *The Road to Damascus* by Clive Uptton (1911–2006).

why do you persecute me?' 'Who are you, Lord?' Saul asked. 'I am Jesus, whom you are persecuting,' he replied. 'Now get up and go into the city, and you will be told what you must do.'

The men travelling with Saul stood there speechless; they heard the sound but did not see anyone. Saul got up from the ground, but when he opened his eyes he could see nothing. So they led him by the hand into Damascus. For three days he was blind, and did not eat or drink anything. In Damascus there was a disciple named Ananias. The Lord called to him in a vision, 'Ananias!' 'Yes, Lord,' he answered. The Lord told him, 'Go to the house of Judas on Straight Street and ask for a man from Tarsus named Saul, for he is praying. In a vision he has seen a man named Ananias come and place his hands on him to restore his sight.'

'Lord,' Ananias answered, 'I have heard many reports about this man and all the harm he has done to your saints in Jerusalem. And he has come here with authority from the chief priests to arrest all who call on your name.' But the Lord said to Ananias, 'Go! This man is my chosen instrument to carry my name before the Gentiles and their kings and before the people of Israel. I will show him how much he must suffer for my name.'

Then Ananias went to the house and entered it. Placing his hands on Saul, he said, 'Brother Saul, the Lord – Jesus, who appeared to you on the road as you were coming here – has sent me so that you may see again and be filled with the Holy Spirit.' Immediately, something like scales fell from Saul's eyes, and he could see again. He got up and was baptised, and after taking some food, he regained his strength.   (Acts 9:3–19)

Rudolf Otto (1869–1937) used the word **numinous** to describe religious feelings and experiences: it is the idea of awe and wonder that we sometimes feel during emotional moments in life or when we feel the presence of something greater than ourselves. This means different things to different people: it could be walking into a religious building, standing on a cliff, a piece of music or many other things.

A more secular view would say that real experiences that have a deep effect on a person can have completely natural sources without any divine connections.

Argument 5: the moral argument

This argument simply says that people have a basic understanding of 'good' and 'bad', 'right' and 'wrong' and this knowledge must have come from God.

Cardinal John Henry Newman also said that the reason why we have a conscience is because God has given it to us so that we know how to do good. He argues that the presence of the conscience shows God's existence. It implies a personal God and our sense of guilt, moral responsibility and obligation is a sense of God:

> We feel responsibility, are ashamed, are frightened at transgressing the voice of conscience, this implies that there is one to whom we are responsible.   (J.H. Newman, *The Grammar of Assent*)

All of these arguments have people who support them and people who do not. However, they are only arguments and cannot actually prove the existence of God in a way that scientists, atheists and agnostics would accept. They are statements but not refined scientific arguments.

Activity

Go over all the arguments for the existence of God again. Which of the arguments do you think are convincing? Why? Which are the least convincing? Why?

Why people do not believe that God exists

Some people (atheists and agnostics) would reject all these arguments. They think there is no evidence for God's existence, or at least no reliable evidence. They argue that a person should only believe in things for which they have good evidence.

Atheists argue that because everything in the universe can be explained in a satisfactory way without using God as part of the explanation, then there is no point in saying that God exists. They would argue that a God is not necessary for the universe to exist, as it could just as easily have come about by chance. Life on earth could also just have evolved because the conditions here on earth just happen to be suitable. There is no need for some great design plan, as everything has come about by pure chance and there is no ultimate purpose to it all. Also, the world cannot have been designed by God (who is perfect) as it is full of design flaws, such as earthquakes, floods and so on.

A further argument against God's existence would say that if God is in control why did he make us imperfect and incomplete in some way? Why not just make us perfect the first time, instead of us struggling to reach perfection? God cannot be all-good and all-powerful as Christians say because evil exists and he does nothing about it. They would also argue that there is no need of God for people to be moral and to make good moral decisions.

Many people would add that faith is blind and not rational: God was once the explanation for things we did not understand, but now it is God who needs explaining.

◄ If God can prevent natural disasters, why doesn't he? If he chooses not to, what sort of a God is he? Arenal volcano, Costa Rica, erupting in 1998.

Exam practice

Explain why Christians believe in God. *(6 marks)*

There is a lot you can write in answer to this question. You might use the many different arguments for the existence of God. You might write about people having experiences of God or events which have changed their lives and made them believe in God.

You might want to include the influence of their upbringing, the example of other people or being part of a Christian community.

Miracles

This topic will help you answer questions on:

- What Christians believe about miracles
- How Christians believe God intervenes in the world through miracles

The concept of miracles

A miracle is:

- Something out of the ordinary that catches the attention.
- Intended by God as a sign of his love and/or power.
- A marvellous event which cannot have been brought about by humans or by nature and so is said to be performed by God.
- Usually a miracle shows control over the laws of nature. (The laws of nature are scientific generalisations, arrived at by experimentation and/or observation, that try to explain how nature works, or how scientists expect nature to work.)

Miracles are not optional extras to Christianity. Indeed, Christianity is founded on the beliefs that God became human (**incarnation**) and that he has power over death, shown in the **resurrection** of Jesus Christ. Jesus said:

I lay down my life – only to take it up again. No-one takes it from me but I lay it down of my own accord. I have authority to lay it down and authority to take it up again.   (John 10:17b–18a)

Do miracles break scientific laws?

Scientific laws are shorthand descriptions of how nature normally behaves. They do not force nature to behave that way. Unlike the legal use of 'law', scientific laws do not legislate that something must happen, only that on the basis of previous experience we can expect it to happen. So it is misleading to talk about scientific laws being 'obeyed' or 'broken'.

Scientific laws can be looked on as reflecting the orderly and regular ways God works: the 'customs of God'. However, if God wishes to act differently for a particular purpose, and perform a miracle, Christians believe that he is free to do things differently.

God intervening in the world through miracles

Thomas Aquinas defined miracles as 'those things done by divine power apart from the order usually followed in things', in other words something done by God which is different from that way things usually happen. So, when, at the wedding in Cana, Jesus turned water into wine, this was something done by the power of God which does not usually happen. Aquinas identified three types of miracle:

1 First, he considered those things that God did that nature could not do. This is the most traditional approach to defining a miracle: it is

effectively a breach of a law of nature, which contradicts our regular experience about how the world works. Aquinas used the example of the reversal in the course of the sun as such a miracle. Walking on water or the raising of the dead are other things which nature cannot do or cause.

2 Secondly, Aquinas identified those acts that God did that nature could do, but not in the same order, for example a recovery from paralysis, or perhaps from a terminal illness. It is not logically impossible for these things to happen, but they are not usually expected. Nature can bring about a spontaneous remission or recovery, but we would not expect this to happen and so if it does, it may be attributed to the direct intervention of God.

3 Finally, he defined as miracles those things done by God that nature could do, but that God did without using the forces of nature. An example of this type of miracle might be recovering from a cold or flu. We would expect this to happen naturally, but if it happened more quickly than usual, perhaps after someone had prayed, then we might call it a miraculous intervention by God.

Aquinas therefore allowed for a range of possible events that we could call miracles, and did not limit them to breaking natural laws. A miracle, according to Aquinas, is seen above all as God's intervention. It is an act of God that has beneficial consequences for the recipient and that may include breaking a natural law, but does not necessarily have to do so.

The miracles of Jesus

There are many examples in the New Testament of Jesus performing miracles: he turned water into wine, walked on the sea, he healed the sick, raised the dead, calmed a storm and **exorcised** demons.

That day when evening came, he said to his disciples, 'Let us go over to the other side.' Leaving the crowd behind, they took him along, just as he was, in the boat. There were also other boats with him. A furious squall came up, and the waves broke over the boat, so that it was nearly swamped. Jesus was in the stern, sleeping on a cushion. The disciples woke him and said to him, 'Teacher, don't you care if we drown?'

He got up, rebuked the wind and said to the waves, 'Quiet! Be still!' Then the wind died down and it was completely calm.

He said to his disciples, 'Why are you so afraid? Do you still have no faith?'

They were terrified and asked each other, 'Who is this? Even the wind and the waves obey him!'   (Mark 4:35–41)

It may also be described as miraculous for someone to be born of a virgin and come back from the dead:

The Word became flesh and made his dwelling among us. We have seen his glory, the glory of the One and Only, who came from the Father, full of grace and truth.   (John 1:14)

Some Christians have argued that it does not matter whether the miracles of the New Testament really happened or not. What is important is the spiritual message about God's love for humanity which lies behind these miracles.

Activity

Look at Aquinas' three types of miracle and decide which one you find most convincing.

▲ *The Storm on the Sea of Galilee* by Rembrandt van Rijn, 1633.

17

Discussion point

1 Some Christians do not believe that the miracles in the Bible actually happened but are stories to symbolise important concepts: that Christians should keep faith despite what happens (calming the storm) or that God's love is for everyone (feeding of the 5000).

What do you think of this view?

Exam tip

Remember when writing about miracles that the Church has authenticated very few events as actually being miracles. Also, you need to be able to explain why some Christians do not believe in miracles.

Activities

1 Why are miracles important to Christians? What difference might they make to a Christian's life?

2 What might the fact that there are miracles tell us about God?

The New Testament writers used the Greek word 'seimeion' ('a sign') to refer to the healing miracles of Jesus. They were signs that he was the **Messiah**, signs of God's love in practice, signs of God's intervention in the world. Miracles in the New Testament are meant to gain the attention of the unbeliever and show who Jesus really is.

Miracles today

All miracles are seen as the work of the Holy Spirit. Some people believe that there are Christian faith healers who can use the power of the Spirit to heal people of illnesses. However, many diseases are cyclical and symptoms come and go: joint pain, headaches, and so on often disappear for no apparent reason. Has God made our bodies in such a way that they heal themselves? Even spontaneous remission of cancer is well documented. Doctors cannot explain everything yet – some things are just a mystery.

Lourdes is a town in south-western France. In 1858, a 14-year-old girl called Bernadette Soubirous had a series of visions of the Virgin Mary who requested that a church should be built on the rock over the grotto where the visions took place. Today its **sanctuary** stands over the alcove in which Mary appeared. Beneath it, the spring welling up from the floor at the back of the grotto has become central to the beliefs and activities of pilgrims from the Catholic Church who come to wash themselves in its waters, just as Mary told Bernadette to do.

In 1862 Pope Pius IX ruled that the visions were genuine. More than five million pilgrims visit Lourdes every year in the hope of a cure for themselves or someone close to them.

Many people are said to have recovered from illnesses after visiting Lourdes, but the Roman Catholic Church has only accepted 66 cases as miracles. The most recent miracle acclaimed was that of Jean-Pierre Bely, a Frenchman with a 15-year history of multiple sclerosis. At the age of 51 he was cured in October 1987 and authenticated as a miracle in February 1999.

Discussion points

2 If a miracle is God's action in the world why does he not do it all the time?

3 Why does he even need miracles to show himself?

4 If the miracles at Lourdes are true, why does God not heal all the sick people who go there?

Exam practice

Explain why some Christians might not believe in miracles. *(6 marks)*
In your answer you need to consider the reasons which some Christians give for not believing in miracles. This might be that they can be seen as arbitrary and that a good God would not perform miracles for some people who need them and not for others. You might also say that they believe that because God created the universe and the laws which govern it then he would not do things which break his own laws.

Beliefs about Jesus and the Holy Spirit

This topic will help you answer questions on:

● What Christians believe about Jesus and the Holy Spirit
● How Christians believe God intervenes in the world through Jesus and the Holy Spirit

Christian beliefs about Jesus

Jesus is central to Christian faith. One of the earliest statements of Christian faith seems to have been 'Jesus Christ is Lord'. The word 'Christ' in Greek stands for the word 'Messiah' in Hebrew. To the Jews the word 'Messiah' referred to a leader whose coming had been prophesied in the Jewish Scriptures. Messiah means '**Anointed One**'. Kings, prophets and priests were anointed in the Jewish religion.

There were many people claiming to be the Messiah at the time of Jesus, when Jews were living under Roman rule and wanted their freedom. The Romans saw any claim to be the Messiah as treason, because Jews should obey the Roman Emperor above all else. However, the majority of Jews did not believe that Jesus was the Messiah, especially after he was executed.

When Jesus was crucified in Jerusalem, the accusation over the cross read 'Jesus of Nazareth King of the Jews'.

The main reason that the followers of Jesus accepted their crucified leader as their Lord and King was that they believed that Jesus rose from the dead after his crucifixion. The New Testament describes him being seen by a number of different people during the next 40 days. Among the witnesses of the Resurrection were the apostles. These were disciples who had been chosen by Jesus during his ministry (teaching) to be 'sent out' to spread his message, which was the gospel (which means 'good news') about the Kingdom of God.

▲ *The Crucifixion* by Alonso Cano, c.1635.

Jesus as fully human and fully divine

Christians believe that Jesus was God in a human body. They use the word incarnation to describe this: Jesus was God incarnate. This means God was Jesus and Jesus was God – human and divine at the same time. God became flesh and blood. For Christians, the doctrine of the incarnation means that the theological idea of the immanence of God has a new dimension as he becomes human. God really does know what it is like to be human, and so can take an active role in people's lives. Jesus is also known as '**Immanuel**' which means 'God with us'.

Jesus as teacher and guide

Jesus was a teacher and his life is seen by Christians as the perfect example of God-like behaviour and attitudes.

The Sermon on the Mount in Matthew 5–7 has many of Jesus' teachings all gathered together in one place so that new Christians could learn how to live like him.

Discussion point

Consider what the phrase 'God with us' means to Christians.

Here are some of the teachings.

The Beatitudes

Now when he saw the crowds, he went up on a mountainside and sat down. His disciples came to him, and he began to teach them saying:

Blessed are the poor in spirit,
for theirs is the kingdom of heaven.

Blessed are those who mourn,
for they will be comforted.

Blessed are the meek, for they will inherit the earth.

Blessed are those who hunger and thirst for righteousness,
for they will be filled. Blessed are the merciful,
for they will be shown mercy.

Blessed are the pure in heart,
for they will see God.

Blessed are the peacemakers,
for they will be called sons of God.

Blessed are those who are persecuted because of righteousness,
for theirs is the kingdom of heaven.

Blessed are you when people insult you, persecute you and falsely say all kinds of evil against you because of me. Rejoice and be glad, because great is your reward in heaven, for in the same way they persecuted the prophets who were before you.   (Matthew 5:1–12)

You have heard that it was said, 'Love your neighbour and hate your enemy.' But I tell you: Love your enemies and pray for those who persecute you, that you may be sons of your Father in heaven. He causes his sun to rise on the evil and the good, and sends rain on the righteous and the unrighteous. If you love those who love you, what reward will you get? Are not even the tax collectors doing that? And if you greet only your brothers, what are you doing more than others? Do not even pagans do that? Be perfect, therefore, as your heavenly Father is perfect.   (Matthew 5:43–48)

Jesus' parables, miracles and actions also show Christians how they should live.

The Parable of the Lost Sheep

Now the tax collectors and 'sinners' were all gathering around to hear him. But the Pharisees and the teachers of the law muttered, 'This man welcomes sinners and eats with them.'

Then Jesus told them this parable: 'Suppose one of you has a hundred sheep and loses one of them. Does he not leave the ninety-nine in the open country and go after the lost sheep until he finds it? And when he finds it, he joyfully puts it on his shoulders and goes home. Then he calls his friends and neighbours together and says, "Rejoice with me; I have found my lost sheep." I tell you that in the same way there will be more rejoicing in heaven over one sinner who repents than over ninety-nine righteous persons who do not need to repent.'   (Luke 15:1–7)

Jesus heals the sick

Jesus went through all the towns and villages, teaching in their synagogues, preaching the good news of the kingdom and healing every disease and sickness.   (Matthew 9:35)

Exam tip
There are no special texts which you need to know for the examination but it is worth remembering texts you have studied to illustrate your answers.

Activities

1 What do you think the following phrases mean?
   - Thirst for righteousness.
   - They will be filled.
   - Blessed are those who mourn.
2 What does the word 'sinners' mean in the Parable of the Lost Sheep?
3 Explain what the Parable itself has to do with the tax collectors and the sinners.

Activity

4 Using these ideas of atonement and Jesus as saviour, try to explain why Jesus' last words on the cross, as reported in the Gospels, were: 'It is finished' and 'Why have you forsaken me?'

Discussion point

What do the pictures below mean and how do they show the following beliefs about Jesus?

a Jesus as fully human and fully divine.

b Jesus as teacher and guide.

c Jesus as Saviour.

d Jesus as eternal.

Research task

Research some of the symbols of Jesus: the cross, the crucifix and the fish. Find out when and how they were used, how they are used today and what they mean.

Jesus as saviour

As Christians see Jesus as God in human form his death has a particular importance, but it also creates another puzzle: God is eternal, so cannot die. Jesus is God, so why did he die? One explanation that Christians give is that Jesus died to take away sin.

Christians believe that Jesus died to make it possible for people's sins to be forgiven. All people fall short of God's standards and the result is separation from God. The New Testament teaches that the death of Jesus was part of God's plan for reconciling the world to himself. Christians believe that Jesus Christ took the punishment for the sins of the whole world so that God and humanity could be made as one, and God's forgiveness is open to anyone.

This teaching is called the **Atonement** – Jesus' death on the cross makes people at one with God. This is what Christians mean when they say that Jesus is the **Saviour** or **Redeemer** of the world.

When Christians experience forgiveness of sin and commit themselves to following Jesus, some say that they have been saved.

Jesus as eternal

Jesus did not remain dead, but rose from the dead and returned to his Father for eternity.

The Resurrection has always been central to the Christian message. For Christians, the Resurrection proves that Jesus is the promised Messiah and that there is life after death. Easter is the festival when Christians celebrate the Resurrection but it is celebrated every Sunday and at every **eucharist**.

The resurrected Jesus was not a ghost. According to the accounts in the New Testament he was so real that the disciples ate and drank with him. The New Testament recounts various resurrection appearances which occurred during the next 40 days. Then Jesus appeared for one final time before he returned to his Father in the mystery of the Ascension. The Acts of the Apostles gives a description of the Ascension of Jesus (Acts 1:1–11). Christians believe that they also will have eternal life like Jesus.

Christians also believe that Jesus will come again to judge the living and the dead – God created the world and sustains the world and so will be in control at the end of the world. The return of Christ is called the **Parousia**, the Appearing. Christians believe that this dramatic event will automatically bring Judgement because people will no longer have the opportunity to choose to believe.

▲ Representations of Jesus from different sources and countries. From left to right: Warrior Christ, a fifth-century mosaic from Ravenna, Italy; an image on the Shroud of Turin; the head of Christ from a panel painting in St Mary's Church, Templecombe, Somerset, c.1280; *Cristo Salvator Mundi* (*Christ Saviour of the World*) by El Greco, c.1600.

Christian beliefs about the Holy Spirit

Christians believe that after his resurrection Jesus told his disciples that when he left them he would send the Holy Spirit to them. This coming of the Holy Spirit is first shown in the Bible when the disciples are all together on the day of Pentecost:

When the day of Pentecost came, they were all together in one place. Suddenly a sound like the blowing of a violent wind came from heaven and filled the whole house where they were sitting. They saw what seemed to be tongues of fire that separated and came to rest on each of them. All of them were filled with the Holy Spirit and began to speak in other tongues as the Spirit enabled them.   (Acts 2:1–4)

The experience had such an impact that their lives were totally changed. Christians celebrate the giving of the Holy Spirit at Whitsuntide.

Christians believe that the Holy Spirit continues to work in the world. In John's gospel Jesus calls the Holy Spirit the paraclete, which is a Greek word for the 'comforter'. Christians believe that the Holy Spirit gives them guidance, faith, hope, understanding and the spiritual strength to live up to the teachings of Jesus. The power of the Holy Spirit, they believe, is what inspires people and gives special charismatic gifts, such as the ability to preach, teach, heal, prophesy and speak in tongues like the disciples did after Pentecost. Most important of all, the Holy Spirit helps them to spread love in the world.

But the fruit of the Spirit is love, joy, peace, patience, kindness, goodness, faithfulness, gentleness and self-control.   (Galatians 5:22–23a)

Christians believe that the Holy Spirit has always been at work in the world. The Holy Spirit referred to in the Apostles' Creed is the same Spirit of God which hovered over the waters at creation in the book of Genesis, the Bible's account of the creation of the world. It is also the same Spirit which spoke the **Word of God** through the Old Testament Prophets. The word for spirit in Hebrew is 'ruach'. It can also be translated as 'breath' or 'wind'.

Discussion points

1 Why is Pentecost regarded as the birthday of the Christian Church?

2 The Bible uses the symbols of fire and wind to represent the Holy Spirit. Why do you think this is, and do you consider them to be good symbols?

3 A dove is a symbol of peace. It is also used as a symbol of the Holy Spirit. Do you think it is a good symbol?

▲ Representations of the Holy Spirit. A detail from the baldacchino (the canopy that covers the altar) in St Peter's Basilica, Rome, Italy (left). Detail from *The Annunciation* by Fra Angelico, 1430–45 (right).

Beliefs about deity: Looking at Exam Questions

Each question has **five** parts (a–e), and you need to answer all the parts.
You will only answer **one** question on each topic. There is a total of
24 marks for each question.

(a) What is a god? *(1 mark)*

You could simply write that a god is a divine being, or a god is a supreme being who is worshipped, or you might say that a god is the creator of the universe.

(b) Name two things that Christians might believe about miracles. *(2 marks)*

You might write that a miracle is an amazing event that could not be brought about by humans or by nature, and so is said to be performed by God. You might say that people see miracles as a way God shows his love for people.

Or you might say that Jesus' miracles showed to his followers that he was the Messiah and Son of God. You might say that Christians today believe miracles are work of the Holy Spirit.

The question asks you to name two things so make sure that in your answer you make the two different statements clear.

(c) Describe Christian beliefs about God. *(3 marks)*

You might explain that Christianity is a monotheistic religion. You might say that Christians believe in God as Trinity: God the Father, God the Son and God the Holy Spirit.

You may say that Christians believe God is eternal, omnipotent and omniscient, an almighty creator who is both transcendent and immanent, personal and impersonal.

You may say that Christians believe that God is Love, but that he wants us to live morally and will judge everyone. You might write that Christians believe that God wants people to have a relationship with him, and that he shows what he is like in Jesus.

(d) Explain why Christians believe in God. *(6 marks)*

In answer to this question you might use all the different arguments for the existence of God, and write in some detail about each one. You might write about people having experiences of God or events which have changed their lives and made them believe in God.

You might include some of the work you have done on miracles.

You might want to include the influence of people's upbringing, the example of other people or being part of a Christian community.

You might include the secular view that Christians believe in God because they are deluded or want some sort of comfort.

(e) 'If God existed we would know it.'
Discuss this statement. You should include different, supported points of view and a personal viewpoint. You must refer to Christianity in your answer. *(12 marks)*

You might consider some of the different ways that Christians would say they know of the existence of God: the Bible, the evidence in creation, the evidence from their conscience, their own personal experience of God in their lives.

You might also write about the influence of other Christians and the Christian community.

On the other hand you might say that existence of so much suffering and evil in the world shows that God does not exist.

2 Religious and spiritual experience

This chapter will help you answer questions on:

◆ How Christians experience God as a community or as an individual through worship

◆ The concept of worship

◆ Worship in a Christian place of worship or at home

◆ The symbolism in worship: how it is used and what it means

◆ The use of art and music to express beliefs about God

◆ The concept and purpose of prayer and contemplation

◆ How food is used in Christian festivals

◆ Fasting as a response to God

Introduction

What does it mean to have a religious experience?

It is something that most people experience, but do not always call 'religious'; it is perhaps that 'tingly feeling', that experience of something 'other'. It may be when we hear a particular piece of music, see the view from the top of a mountain, visit a big cathedral: it is a feeling that reminds us of our own smallness.

It is hard to put these feelings into words. We might try by using an expression such as 'a sense of awe' or 'a sense of wonder'. Rudolf Otto (1869–1937) said that in these situations we were experiencing God and he used the word 'numinous' (the presence of God which inspires awe and reverence), calling this feeling the 'wholly other': something which is totally different from any other experience, and which we do not always have the words to explain.

Many religious people might say that they are having a religious experience when they are feeling something which is different from the ordinary everyday feelings. For some people this spiritual feeling gives them certainty in their belief: they feel that they 'know' God exists because of this spiritual feeling or religious experience.

People express their belief in God following their religious experience in different ways:

- some may pray, and want to spend time talking to God
- others may **meditate**, they sit quietly, try to empty their minds of ordinary thought and, they would say, listen to their spiritual feelings
- others may attend religious services, to worship God with others.

There are also different ways in which belief in God can be expressed: in art; in religious buildings; in music; and in the religious ceremonies and **liturgy** (the way in which people worship, including the order of the service and what happens during it).

Activity

Think of a time in your life when something gave you this feeling of the 'wholly other'. What was it and why do you think you felt like that?

▲ The Grand Canyon, Arizona, USA creates a sense of awe in many visitors. Its vastness perhaps reminds people of their own smallness.

As well as these ways of expressing spirituality, these beliefs and feelings are also expressed in the sacred writings of religions and the ways in which these are regarded and treated. The ways in which spirituality is expressed varies between and also within religions.

Worship

This topic will help you answer questions on:

- How Christians experience God as a community or as an individual through worship
- The concept of worship
- Worship in a Christian place of worship or at home

For many Christians **worship** is one of the most important ways of expressing belief and is centred on their local Christian community, which in turn is part of a worldwide community of Christians. This is called the Church.

Throughout both the Old and New Testaments worship is seen as one of the most important things people can do. Worship was seen as a priority for the early Church; the apostles and the new converts saw worship as central:

They devoted themselves to the apostles' teaching and to the fellowship, to the breaking of bread and to prayer. Everyone was filled with awe, and many wonders and miraculous signs were done by the apostles. All the believers were together and had everything in common. Selling their possessions and goods, they gave to anyone as he had need. Every day they continued to meet together in the temple courts. They broke bread in their homes and ate together with glad and sincere hearts, praising God and enjoying the favour of all the people. And the Lord added to their number daily those who were being saved.   (Acts 2:42–47)

Christian worship grew out of Jewish worship. Jesus was a religious Jew who went to the synagogue and celebrated Jewish festivals, and his disciples also followed Jewish ritual and tradition. The first obvious difference from Judaism was making Sunday the Christian holy day instead of the Jewish Sabbath on Saturday. This was done because Christians believe that Jesus rose from the dead on a Sunday.

Jesus' promise to stay with his followers, in the person of the Holy Spirit, influenced the development of Christian worship from early times:

When the day of Pentecost came, they were all together in one place. Suddenly a sound like the blowing of a violent wind came from heaven and filled the whole house where they were sitting. They saw what seemed to be tongues of fire that separated and came to rest on each of them. All of them were filled with the Holy Spirit and began to speak in other tongues as the Spirit enabled them.   (Acts 2:1–4)

This is the Spirit which Jesus promised would come to the disciples after he had left them and gone to heaven:

When the Counsellor comes, whom I will send to you from the Father, the Spirit of truth who goes out from the Father, he will testify about me.   (John 15:26)

▲ A celebration of the eucharist.

Activity

What does a Christian believe? Write down as many things as you can and then discuss these with other people.

Christians believe that this Spirit has continued to guide the Christian Churches since that time. Christians also believe that when they worship they may receive guidance from the Holy Spirit. So Christians regard worship as something that they do not do only for God, but that God is also at work in worship through Jesus' example and the presence of the Holy Spirit.

Christians may worship on their own (private worship) or together with other people (public or communal worship).

Public worship

There are as many different types of public worship as there are different **denominations** of Christians. Different churches, even within the same denomination, will use very different styles of worship. Some will be elaborate, with a choir singing complex music, others will leave the music to the congregation, who sing simpler **hymns** or worship songs. In fact you could say that the *way* Christians worship is as much a part of their Christian identity as *who* they worship.

Church services on a Sunday divide into two general types: eucharistic services and services of the Word. Both types of service will include hymns, readings and prayers. The eucharistic service will be focused on the act of Holy Communion. The **service of the Word** does not include communion, but instead features a much longer sermon, in which the preacher will speak at length to explain a biblical text and bring out its relevance to those present.

The eucharist

The eucharist (from a Greek word meaning 'thanksgiving') is common to all Christians and even those who usually worship with a service of the Word will celebrate it from time to time. It is often called by other names such as: Holy Communion, Mass, Lord's Supper, Breaking of Bread and Liturgy. However, the event with which it is concerned is the same:

The Lord Jesus, on the night he was betrayed, took bread, and when he had given thanks, he broke it and said, 'This is my body, which is for you; do this in remembrance of me.' In the same way, after supper he took the cup, saying, 'This cup is the new covenant in my blood; do this, whenever you drink it, in remembrance of me.' (1 Corinthians 11:23b–25)

This took place at the Last Supper that Jesus ate with his disciples before he was crucified. He shared bread and wine with them and said that this made a new covenant to replace the covenants which God had previously made with the Jews. This account by Paul in 1 Corinthians is the earliest we have. There are also accounts in the gospels.

One of the major differences between Christians has been, and continues to be, in what sense Christ is 'present' in the eucharist:

- **Orthodox churches** and the Roman Catholic Church hold that Christ has a 'real presence' in the bread and wine and that in some mysterious way the bread and wine, while continuing to look and taste like bread and wine, are truly Christ's body and blood. This is called **transubstantiation**.

▲ *The Descent of the Holy Spirit* by (Hans or Johann) Rottenhammer, 1594–5, is one artist's view of the Pentecost.

▲ Bread and wine on the altar.

Fact box

The three major divisions or denominations in the Christian Church are:

- Roman Catholic Church: Roman Catholics believe that the Pope is God's representative on earth and that they must follow what he says. The first Pope is said to have been St Peter.
- The Orthodox Churches: which include the Russian and Greek Churches. The Roman Catholic and Orthodox Churches split in 1054 over their beliefs about the Trinity (see page 7).
- Protestant Church: the split between the Roman Catholic and Protestant Churches came in 1517.

A monk called Martin Luther (1483–1546) taught that people could only be accepted by God because of their faith, not by doing good deeds or money. Luther nailed a document containing 95 statements about this to a church door in Wittenberg, Germany. The 'protesters' formed into the Protestant Church, separate from the Roman Catholic Church. The Church of England or Anglican Church is a Protestant Church.

- The **Protestant traditions**, generally, regard the service as a memorial meal where Christ is spiritually present but there is no effective change in the bread and wine. This is called **memorialism**. However, some Protestants believe that the bread and wine become the body and blood of Jesus when they are received by a Christian. This is called **receptionism**.
- The **Anglican tradition**, as is often the case, moves between these beliefs depending on the tradition of the parish and the parish priest. In this sense Christ has a 'real presence' in the eucharist but the bread and wine are not 'transformed'. This is sometimes called **consubstantiation**.

For many Christians, the celebration of the eucharist and receiving Holy Communion is at the centre of their worship: it is a **sacrament**, which means that it is a special way of receiving grace. A sacrament is defined as an outward, physical sign of an inward, invisible grace.

Believers would say that the eucharist unites them with Christ. In all Churches the bread and wine are blessed using the words of Jesus, and then given to the congregation by the priest or a specially appointed person. In some Churches the eucharist is a very simple ceremony, but in others it is much more elaborate, with special prayers, hymns and Bible readings before the words of Jesus are said.

In the Roman Catholic Church and some Anglican Churches the eucharist or mass is celebrated every day. It is considered so important that in some churches a portion of the consecrated bread is kept in a **tabernacle** in the church so that communion can be taken to the housebound and the ill. For some other Christians attending the eucharist may be a daily, weekly or monthly event.

> **Exam tip**
> You do not need to know all these special terms about the eucharist for the examination but if you can use them correctly they may help your answers.

> **Exam practice**
> **Explain why the Last Supper is so important to Christians.**
> *(6 marks)*
>
> In your answer you need to include:
>
> - what actually happened at the Last Supper
> - why it took place when it did
> - how Christians continue to remember the Last Supper and why.

▲ An open Bible and lit candle.

Activities

1 Many school assemblies include the Lord's Prayer, and many people in Britain can repeat it from memory, but what does it mean?

2 Explain each line of the Lord's Prayer in your own words.

3 How do you think it helps Christians experience God?

Other services of worship

As well as the eucharist, many Christians attend other services of worship. This usually consists of prayers, Bible readings, hymns and a sermon. These services stress the importance of the **Word** and of hearing the teachings of the Bible and of worshipping and praying to God. This form of worship is central in most Protestant Churches such as Methodists and Baptists. The sermon is an important part of many services; the priest or minister will talk about one of the Bible readings, linking it to people's everyday lives and what is happening in the world:

All Scripture is God-breathed and is useful for teaching, rebuking, correcting and training in righteousness. (2 Timothy 3:16)

In the church public prayers are often led by one person, who may read a set prayer or pray their own prayer out loud. Usually this is the priest/vicar or a church leader, but sometimes others may do this. Everyone joins in by thinking about what is being prayed, and then saying 'Amen' ('so be it') at the end. Sometimes everyone will say a prayer together. One of the best known is the prayer Jesus taught his followers, called the Lord's Prayer:

> Our Father in heaven,
> hallowed be your name,
> your kingdom come,
> your will be done,
> on earth as in heaven.
> Give us today our daily bread.
> Forgive us our sins
> as we forgive those who sin against us
> Lead us not into temptation
> but deliver us from evil.

Many churches have special prayer services, when everyone who attends is invited to take part in a prayer.

There are four main types of prayer and the easiest way to remember them is by using the letters A.C.T.S:

- **A** = **Adoration**: worshipping God for who he is and what he has done.
- **C** = **Confession**: people saying sorry for things that they have done wrong and asking God's forgiveness.
- **T** = **Thanksgiving**: people thanking God for what he has done for them.
- **S** = **Supplication**: people asking God for their own needs and those of others.

Charismatic worship

Another form of Christian worship is called **charismatic** and can be found across all Christian denominations. Here people try to open themselves to the Holy Spirit and be inspired by it. The style of worship is very free and could be described as joyous. The term 'charismatic' comes from the Greek word for 'gifts', and refers to the gifts of the Holy Spirit, including healing, prophecy, and **speaking in**

tongues ('glossolalia'). Various Christian denominations and groups practise forms of charismatic worship, such as clapping, raising hands, speaking in tongues and informal leading of prayers. The idea of glossolalia or speaking in tongues is found in the Acts of the Apostles:

When the day of Pentecost came, they were all together in one place. Suddenly a sound like the blowing of a violent wind came from heaven and filled the whole house where they were sitting. They saw what seemed to be tongues of fire that separated and came to rest on each of them. All of them were filled with the Holy Spirit and began to speak in other tongues as the Spirit enabled them.

Now there were staying in Jerusalem God-fearing Jews from every nation under heaven. When they heard this sound, a crowd came together in bewilderment, because each one heard them speaking in his own language.

Utterly amazed, they asked: 'Are not all these men who are speaking Galileans? Then how is it that each of us hears them in his own native language? Parthians, Medes and Elamites; residents of Mesopotamia, Judea and Cappadocia, Pontus and Asia, Phrygia and Pamphylia, Egypt and the parts of Libya near Cyrene; visitors from Rome (both Jews and converts to Judaism); Cretans and Arabs – we hear them declaring the wonders of God in our own tongues!'   (Acts 2: 1–11)

Many Christians through history have been so moved by worshipping that they have started saying words and sounds that they do not understand, which is taken to be speaking in tongues.

▲ Worship in a Pentecostal Church in Miami, Florida, USA.

Quaker meetings

In contrast, the group of Christians called the **Religious Society of Friends** or **Quakers** have a totally different form of worship. In a Quaker meeting for worship the group sits in a room in silence for an hour. From time to time someone may speak briefly, but sometimes the entire hour may pass without a word being spoken. Quaker worship is very different to the worship of most Christian Churches in that it does not follow a set liturgy or code of rules: a service has no structure and there is no leader.

Quakers do without a liturgy because they believe that worship happens when two or three people come together to worship – nothing more is needed:

For where two or three come together in my name, there am I with them. (Matthew 18:20)

Quaker meetings for worship take place in meeting houses, not churches. These are simple buildings or rooms. The people usually sit facing each other in a square or a circle. Everyone waits in shared silence until someone is 'moved by the Spirit' (has a strong religious feeling) to do something as part of their worship.

A person will only speak if they are convinced that they have something that must be shared, and it is rare for a person to speak more than once. The words spoken are usually brief and may include readings (from the Bible or other books), praying or speaking from personal experience. Each speaking is followed by a period of silence. Quakers believe that God speaks through these words, which should come from the soul (the inner light) rather than the mind and could

▲ Quaker worship.

Activities

1 What do you understand by the following key words:
   ◆ belief
   ◆ worship
   ◆ prayer?
2 Make a chart showing the different types of Christian worship.
3 Imagine you are a Christian believer and write a paragraph explaining *why* you worship.

Exam tip

Remember not all Christians worship in the same way, and that there as many different types of worship as there are Christians and many different types of buildings are used for worship.

carry a message from God to anyone in the meeting. The meeting ends when the elders shake hands.

If asked what they are actually doing in a meeting for worship, many Quakers would probably say that they are waiting, waiting in their utmost hearts for the touch of something beyond their everyday selves. Some would call it 'listening to the quiet voice of God' – without trying to define the word.

Worship in the home

Many Christians may also worship on their own in private or with their family at home. They may choose readings from the Bible and then pray to worship God. Prayer is a very important aspect of Christian life and worship. As well as there being many different prayers there are different types of prayer. Some are formal set prayers such as the Our Father and the prayers which are said during services in church.

Some prayers are spontaneous when a person wants to speak to God at a particular moment. When some people pray they may be asking God to intervene in the world. They are asking God to change things in the world such as to end a drought or floods. Sometimes people may pray for another person who is ill. Many prayers are said to thank God for what has happened or for life and existence in general.

Sometimes Christians may meditate; they sit quietly and try to empty their minds of ordinary thought and listen to their spiritual feelings. Many Christians will have a time when they can sit quietly and spend time with God.

The use of the rosary in worship

One of the commonest forms of prayer, particularly in the Roman Catholic Church, is the use of the rosary. The rosary is said to have been developed by St Dominic in the thirteenth century and consists of a string of beads with a crucifix. The beads are divided into five sets of one large bead and ten smaller ones. Each set of ten beads is called a decade.

At the beginning of saying the rosary, the worshippers bless themselves with the crucifix and then say the Apostles' Creed, the Our Father and three Hail Marys:

Hail, Mary, full of grace the Lord is with thee;
Blessed art thou among women,
And blessed is the fruit of thy womb, Jesus.
Holy Mary, Mother of God
Pray for us sinners,
Now and at the hour of our death. Amen.

Followed by the 'Glory be':

Glory be to the Father
And to the Son
And to the Holy Spirit;
As it was in the beginning
Is now, and *ever* shall be
World without end.
Amen.

Then, meditating on one of the sets of five mysteries (see below), worshippers say one 'Our Father', ten 'Hail Marys' and one 'Glory be' for each decade of their rosary. At the end of saying the rosary, the prayer 'Hail Holy Queen' is said:

Hail, Holy Queen.
Mother of Mercy,
Our life, our sweetness,
And our hope
To you do we cry,
Poor banished children of *Eve*.
To you do we send up our sighs,
Mourning and weeping
In this valley of tears.
Turn, then, Most Gracious advocate,
Your eyes of mercy towards us,
And after this, our exile,
Show unto us
The blessed fruit of your womb, Jesus,
O clement, O loving, O sweet Virgin Mary.
Pray for us, O Holy Mother of God.
That we may be made worthy of
The promises of Christ.
Amen.

▲ Praying the rosary.

There are four sets of Mysteries:

The Joyful Mysteries

1 The Annunciation: Luke 1:26–38
2 The Visitation: Luke 1:39–45
3 The Nativity: Luke 2:6–19
4 The Presentation in the Temple: Luke 2:22–40
5 The Finding in the Temple: Luke 2:41–52.

The Sorrowful Mysteries

1 The Agony in the Garden: Luke 22:39–53
2 The Scourging at the Pillar: John 19:1
3 The Crowning with Thorns: John 19:2–3
4 Carrying the Cross: Luke 23:26–32
5 The Crucifixion: Luke 23:33–46.

The Glorious Mysteries

1 The Resurrection: Luke 24:1–8
2 The Ascension: Acts 1:6–12

3 The Descent of the Holy Spirit: Acts 2:1–4
4 The Assumption of the Virgin: Psalms 45:10, 14, 15
5 The Coronation of the Virgin: Revelation 12:1–2, 5.

The three sets of mysteries were established by the sixteenth century. In 2002, Pope John Paul II added a fourth set of mysteries.

The Luminous Mysteries

1 1 The Baptism of Jesus in the Jordan: Luke 3:21–22
2 The Wedding at Cana: John 2:1–11
3 Jesus' Proclamation of the Kingdom of God: Luke 4:43
4 The Transfiguration: Luke 9:29–36
5 The Institution of the eucharist: Luke 22:19–20

Activities

4 Choose two mysteries from each set and research them using a Bible.
5 Explain why you think they are called Joyful, Sorrowful, Glorious and Luminous.
6 Consider possible reasons why Pope John Paul II decided to add a fourth set.

Activity

1 Make a list of as many features of churches as you can. Now arrange the features into two groups: those associated with the Word of God and those showing a connection between people and God through rituals and ceremonies.

▲ A stained glass window in Canterbury Cathedral.

▲ A font in a French church.

Protestant traditions tend to emphasise the **lectern** and **pulpit**. Some, such as the Quakers, may have neither.

In churches of the Orthodox traditions where does the main action take place? The building will have a screen to hide the main sanctuary, which is accessible only to the priests, like the ancient Jewish temple in Jerusalem.

Stained glass windows are an ancient way of telling Bible stories but were seen by some after the Reformation as too 'Catholic'.

The shape of the building itself has meaning. Many are built in the shape of a cross, traditionally pointing to Jerusalem where Jesus was crucified and where he rose from the dead, but some are round and others are just a square room. Again the shape can point to the beliefs of the Christian community and how they like to worship God.

Church furniture will also tell a good deal about what a group of Christians values. Are there statues, and if so do they have candles around them? Candles are usually a symbol of prayer. Is the furniture all facing in one direction or is it arranged in a circle? The more candles there are in a church, the 'higher' the church is likely to be ('High Church' is a name given to Anglican traditions whose practices are closer to Roman Catholic ones).

Inside most churches is a **font** which holds the water for baptisms, sometimes near the door as this is the place where people enter the church and enter the Christian faith, sometimes at the front near the **altar** to show that baptism leads to Holy Communion. In a Baptist church there is a large tank under the floor at the front of the church. When an adult is ready to be baptised this is uncovered so that he or she can receive baptism by total immersion under the water.

For many hundreds of years it has been traditional for the altar to be placed at the east end of the church, in a part of the church called the sanctuary. When the priest stood at the altar he then had his back to the people, 'facing God'. Recently many churches have moved the altar away from the east wall so that the priest is facing the people.

The altar may be of stone or wood and is usually covered with a coloured cloth which shows the season in the church's year and then has a linen cloth on top. The altar may have large candlesticks on it, usually two or six, which are lit during services. In the past these always served a practical purpose of providing light but are also a reminder that Jesus was the 'Light of the World'.

In the sanctuary can also be found the Paschal candle which is lit at Easter from new fire, and then every Sunday until the feast of the Ascension. During the rest of the year it is lit at baptisms, marriages and funerals. The candle has symbols on it:

- at the centre is a cross
- the Greek letters alpha and omega
- the date of the current year which indicates God's presence
- five grains of red incense representing the five wounds which Jesus received.

In the wall behind the altar or to the side is often a box called a tabernacle. Here the consecrated bread is placed after the eucharist.

This bread is called the 'host'. It can then be taken to anyone who is too sick to attend church. Near the tabernacle there will be a light burning to show that the consecrated bread is inside. Sometimes the host is placed in a special container called a pyx, which hangs over the altar.

Either side of the altar in many Anglican and Roman Catholic churches are the pulpit (from where the sermon is preached) and the lectern (from where the Bible is read). Some churches, particularly Roman Catholic ones, have statues of the Saints around the church and people may light votive candles and place them in front of the statues, asking the particular saint to pray for them. There will also be crosses and crucifixes. A crucifix is a cross with the image of Jesus on it.

Many Protestant churches may be much plainer than this. The Protestant churches tend not to have statues or images in them. In the Ten Commandments it says:

You shall not make for yourself an idol in the form of anything in heaven above or on the earth beneath or in the waters below. You shall not bow down to them or worship them; for I, the Lord your God, am a jealous God, punishing the children for the sin of the fathers to the third and fourth generation of those who hate me, but showing love to a thousand generations of those who love me and keep my commandments. (Exodus 20:4–6)

Protestants believe that having statues in a church would break this Commandment. Protestant churches have an altar and font, but the altar may not be given the same importance as it is in a Roman Catholic church. Instead the pulpit may be central to the building. In some chapels the pulpit is placed on the centre of the east wall above the table on which the eucharist is celebrated. This shows the importance which they give to the Ministry of the Word – the preaching of the Bible.

Orthodox churches are also of a different design. At the west end is the narthex. This may contain pictures of the Last Judgement and of scenes from the Old Testament. The font is placed in the narthex. In the nave (the main part of the church) there are very few seats, just ones for the old or sick. People stand during services. At the front of the nave is the iconostasis. This is a screen covered in **icons** (pictures) of the saints. In the centre of the iconostasis are the royal doors which are opened during certain parts of the liturgy. In front of the doors is a small platform called the amvon on which the priest stands. Behind the doors, the whole area of the sanctuary is called the altar. It contains the holy table where the liturgy (eucharist) is celebrated.

Whatever the design, however, all Christian places of worship are designed to praise God and to provide a place where Christians can come together and worship.

The place of worship itself is, therefore, symbolic, and a first glance will tell whether the Word or the sacrament of the eucharist has the most important place: where is the altar? Where are the pulpit and the lectern? Which of these three is the most obvious? How does it look as if the building is used? Look back to earlier in this chapter to remind yourself of details of these.

Activity

2 Knowing specialist vocabulary is very important for this course. Make a table with two columns. Down the first column list the following words: altar (Holy Table), cross, crucifix, font, host, iconostasis, lectern, narthex, pulpit, pyx, sanctuary, tabernacle, votive candle, paschal candle. Then write definitions of these key terms in the second column.

Research task

Find out about the triple Paschal candle used in the Orthodox Church.

▲ Clockwise from top left: a tabernacle, a pulpit, a paschal candle and a lectern.

Activity

Two new churches are being built in your community, one Roman Catholic and one Protestant. Write a brief for the architect to explain why the design needs to be different for each.

Exam practice

'People do not need symbols to worship God.'

Discuss this statement. You should include different, supported points of view and a personal viewpoint. You must refer to Christianity in your answer.

(12 marks)

You are free to answer either way. You might argue that all religions use symbols in different ways but that some believers may feel that worship should be personal between the worshipper and God and that symbols are a potential hindrance.

You could refer to the approaches of the different Christian denominations, and may give examples from the different types of buildings to illustrate your answer.

You may refer to a secular view that considers symbols to be of artistic merit, but not relevant to worshipping God.

You need to make sure that you state clearly what you think and why you think it.

The use of art and music to express beliefs about God

This topic will help you answer questions on:

● The use of art and music to express beliefs about God

▲ A Russian-made icon of the Madonna and child.

The use of art to express beliefs about God

The place of art in the transmission of the Christian message and culture is very important. Except for some Protestant churches, most Christians use pictures to convey messages about their beliefs.

From the very earliest times, mosaics showing Christ in majesty in heaven, such as that in Ravenna, were used in churches. The early symbols came from Roman art, for example Christ was symbolised by a fish, a cross, or a lamb, or by the combined Greek letters chi and rho (XP, the first two letters of the Greek spelling of 'Christ', see page 33) as a monogram. Christ the Good Shepherd was often shown as a beardless young man, derived from Roman pictures of Apollo. Since that time there have been countless representations of Christ in art, most of which are also representative of the artist and his culture, showing religion as part of the everyday world, but also something different.

For centuries, when the Bible was not read in a language that most people could understand, its message was conveyed largely by visual means. Stained glass windows are one of the most popular means in the UK. This tradition of stained glass to help in worship continues to this day.

In Orthodox churches there are usually many icons (pictures) of the saints and Jesus. In religion, icons act as a bridge between a person and a religious figure: Jesus, Mary or a saint. It is not the picture, the wood or the paint that is being worshipped, it is the concept: the figure beyond the icon. This is slightly more complex than the icon simply being a representation of a figure. In fact an icon painter will say that they do not paint the icon, they write it.

Worshippers say that an icon seeks to evoke an experience of stillness. The gaze of the icon seems directed at the viewer in an intimate and personal way. Many people find that this helps them to identify qualities which for them are eternal.

Some churches, particularly Roman Catholic ones, will have the **Stations of the Cross** around the walls. These may be pictures or plaques. The stations were developed by the Franciscans and each one recalls an event in the last days of Jesus' life. Some are from the Gospels and some are traditional:

1 Jesus is condemned by Pilate (Matthew 27:15–26)
2 Jesus receives the cross (John 19:17)
3 Jesus falls under the weight of the cross
4 Jesus meets Mary
5 Simon of Cyrene carries the Cross for Jesus (Matthew 27:32)
6 Saint Veronica wipes Jesus' face
7 Jesus falls again
8 Jesus speaks to the women of Jerusalem (Luke 23:27–31)
9 Jesus falls for a third time
10 Jesus' clothes are removed (Matthew 27:28)
11 The crucifixion
12 Jesus dies (Matthew 27:45–56)
13 Mary receives Jesus' body
14 Jesus is buried (Matthew 27:57–61).

Particularly during Lent people may walk from one station to the next, stopping and praying at each one.

The use of music to express beliefs about God

From the earliest days of Christian worship believers have sung hymns of praise and thanksgiving to God and used music to express their feelings. Music can have a powerful effect on people and it is not surprising, then, that music played an important part in the worship of biblical communities. It was a way in which people could feel closer to God. Many of the first Christians would have been Jewish and familiar with the psalms as used in Jewish worship.

▲ Praying at the thirteenth Station of the Cross in St Patrick's Cathedral, New York, USA.

Discussion point
Do you think that art helps Christians to worship?

Activities
1 Consider what makes music special to you.
2 Have you ever found that a particular song expresses a feeling or memory that it would be very hard to put into words?

Research task
Research some different types of Christian art and show how it may help people to worship. (Different types could be divided among a class to research and present as a display or a PowerPoint® presentation.)

Activity

Write down three examples of music you know that:

◆ praises someone or something
◆ is relaxing or mood-changing
◆ is designed for a specific event.

The main strands in Christian music are:

- communal praise, expressed largely in hymns
- music for reflection
- music for specific occasions.

These often overlap. For example, a requiem may be performed as a memorial for a specific occasion, or may be used for general reflection. The Passion set to music in a concert performance is used in one way but the same music could be used in a church as part of a Good Friday service.

Hymns are the most common use of music in worship, and there have been many great writers of hymn tunes throughout the ages, but there is also a very strong tradition of using folk music and the popular melodies of the time as a basis for religious music. Today the tradition of turning popular music to religious use continues and includes everything from Christian rock bands and folk groups through new forms of plainchant to abstract musical compositions.

Hymns, especially in Anglican churches and, above all, cathedrals are usually led by a choir and often contain religious teachings. Anglican cathedrals, some Catholic cathedrals and some university colleges have a strong choral tradition and choir schools which keep this traditional music alive.

However, contemporary worship songs tend to use simple, repetitive lyrics (and as a result are often called a 'praise chorus' or 'worship chorus') and are often guitar-based and led by a small group of musicians. These are particularly popular in Protestant Evangelical churches and in charismatic worship.

In the twentieth and twenty-first centuries, music from all over the world has been used in churches in Britain. Exciting liturgical settings from Africa and South America, for example, provide new vitality and insights for worship, and remind Christians that Christianity is a world religion.

Gospel music has also become very popular as a way of expressing belief. This is very emotional and evangelical vocal music that first appeared around 1870 in the USA. It began in the southern states among African-American Christians. One of the earliest examples is 'I Love to Tell the Story' (1869) by William Fischer. However, there are some Protestant denominations which believe that singing is fine, but that musical instruments should never be used in worship.

▲ Hymn singing is an important aspect of many Christian services.

Exam practice

'Music helps people to worship God.'

Discuss this statement. You should include different, supported points of view and a personal viewpoint. You must refer to Christianity in your answer.   *(12 marks)*

Your discussion could include reference to differences between Christian groups, and the ways in which some use music as a focus for worship whereas others find silence a better aid to worship.

Your answer might also consider the different type of music used in different styles of worship and consider whether these are helpful.

Prayer

This topic will help you answer questions on:

● The concept and purpose of prayer and contemplation

Prayer is an expression of a Christian's relationship with and dependence on God. It is a conversation with God. In prayer believers may offer praise, make a request of God, or simply express their thoughts and emotions. Prayer is a two-way spiritual relationship in which the Christian should not only talk to God but also listen to what God might be saying to them.

We have seen many different ways in which Christians pray – for believers prayer deepens their faith and makes them feel more at one with God – just as Jesus did when he prayed. Christians know that prayers are not always answered – the person who is sick does not get better – but they accept that when they pray they ask that God's will be done. However, they also believe that prayer is very powerful and is a channel to God, part of the way Christians believe that they do God's will on earth.

When Christians pray they hope that God will answer their prayer. However, in many instances their prayers will not be answered. Christians believe that this does not mean that God has not heard their prayers but that he has a reason for not granting their request which humans may not be able to understand.

Food and fasting

This topic will help you answer questions on:

● How food is used in Christian festivals
● Fasting as a response to God

Unlike many other religions Christianity does not have strict rules about food and fasting. Christians may eat any sort of food, and although some Christians may choose to be vegetarian there is no Christian rule about this. However, some Christians do eat certain foods at certain times, for example some people will follow the old tradition of not eating meat on a Friday (often fish was substituted) in memory of Jesus' crucifixion.

Food in Christian festivals

There are also traditional foods that are eaten at certain festivals, for example mince pies at Christmas, hot cross buns on Good Friday and pancakes on Shrove Tuesday; although as society has become more secularised, these foods are now available in the shops throughout the year. Food, however, is still an important part of celebrating Christian festivals in the home and much of it is symbolic, such as eggs at Easter which symbolise new life.

▲ Easter eggs, pancakes, hot-cross buns and mince pies are all associated with Christian festivals.

Christians also celebrate Harvest Festival in the autumn when God is thanked for the successful gathering in of the harvest. This service is especially important in rural areas and the churches are decorated with flowers, sheaves of corn and vegetables. The food collected usually is distributed to the elderly and house-bound in the area. At this time many Christian churches also have special collections for countries in the world that do not have a plentiful food supply and collect money to support aid agencies such as the Catholic Agency for Overseas Development (CAFOD) and Christian Aid.

Fasting

Fasting is usually when people go without food or drink for a period of time. For Christians there are two main periods in the year when this is done: Lent, which is the time of preparation for Easter, and Advent, which is the time of preparation for Christmas. Today people no longer fast during Advent, but Lent is still observed.

Lent starts on Ash Wednesday and continues until Easter Saturday. Fasting was one of the many disciplines that Christianity inherited from Judaism. In the first two centuries of the Christian Church, believers would fast for two or three days before Easter. By the time of the council of Nicaea in 325CE however, fasting had been extended in some churches to 40 days, probably in recognition of the 40-day fast by Jesus in the wilderness, as well as the 40-day fasts of Moses (Deuteronomy 9:9) and Elijah (1 Kings 19:8):

Jesus, full of the Holy Spirit, returned from the Jordan and was led by the Spirit in the wilderness, where for forty days he was tempted by the devil. He ate nothing at all during those days, and when they were over, he was famished. (Luke 4:1–2)

By the seventh century a 40-day fast was kept in the Western and Eastern churches, with one meal only allowed each day, and meat, fish and eggs forbidden.

The Eastern Orthodox Church has retained a strong Lenten discipline, but in the Western Church the rules were relaxed from the Middle Ages. The Roman Catholic Church now prescribes fasting on Ash Wednesday at the start of Lent and Good Friday at the end. On these days, which are called Family Fast Days, Catholics collect the money they would have spent on food for the poor; it is usually donated to CAFOD.

Churches, including the Church of England, still require observance of the season however, and many Christians still fast on Fridays by eating one meal and donating the money saved to charity, or by giving up such things as chocolate and alcohol for 40 days. Many Christians will keep Lent by devoting more time to religion and charitable works. Fasting during Lent is not allowed on Sundays.

Apart from these important times in the Christian year it was also customary for **Roman Catholics** to fast for twelve hours before receiving communion. Now this has been reduced to just one hour.

Activity

Why do you think that many religions encourage believers to give up things for special events or periods of time?

Religious and spiritual experience: Looking at Exam Questions

Each question has **five** parts (a–e), and you need to answer all the parts.
You will only answer **one** question on each topic. There is a total of
24 marks for each question.

(a) What is prayer? *(1 mark)*

You could simply write that a prayer is a spoken or unspoken way of communicating with God.

(b) Name two places in which Christians might worship. *(2 marks)*

You may answer that they worship in a church, a chapel, a meeting house, a cathedral or at home. Remember the question asks for two places.

(c) How do Christians worship? *(3 marks)*

Your answer will depend on whether you decide to write about worship in the home, in public, or both. Your answer could include:

- daily private Bible reading and prayer
- family times of worship such as grace before meals
- the sharing of Christian festivals in the home
- house groups
- clergy taking the eucharist to those who cannot get to church
- formal or informal church services; various types of services such as the eucharist and the different forms of worship such as prayer, hymns, readings and sermons.

(d) Why do some Christians fast? *(6 marks)*

In answer to this question you might start by saying that fasting is not a very important part of worship for Christians.

You may talk about the fasting during Lent, how it has changed and what it now means. You might write about fasting on certain days and of giving the money to the poor.

You could include the short period of fasting before communion that reminds Christians of its importance and meaning.

You might even include the secular view that Christians simply fast or give up something during Lent because of tradition and it has no real meaning.

(e) 'Everyone should thank God for their food.' Discuss this statement. You should include different, supported points of view and a personal viewpoint. You must refer to Christianity in your answer. *(12 marks)*

You might agree with this statement and discuss the idea of God as creator and sustainer of the universe, including the provider of food. You may give examples such as Grace at meal times and Harvest Festival.

You may disagree from a secular viewpoint and say that food production is down to humans and nothing to do with God.

3 | The end of life

Activity

Make a list of as many aspects of a person which you might think were part of their soul. Then compare it with the definitions below:

◆ consciousness
◆ thoughts
◆ feelings
◆ decision-making
◆ emotions
◆ how people decide right from wrong
◆ private thoughts and feelings
◆ the part of a person which lives on after death.

This chapter will help you answer questions on:

◆ **What Christians believe about the concept of soul**
◆ **The relationship between the body and soul**
◆ **Concepts of life after death**
◆ **Christian beliefs about heaven, hell, purgatory, salvation, redemption and the suffering of Christ**
◆ **God as judge**
◆ **The relationship between God the judge, life on earth and the afterlife**
◆ **Funeral rites and the ways funeral rites reflect belief and aim to support the bereaved**

The concept of the soul and the relationship between body and soul

This topic will help you answer questions on:

● **The concept of soul**
● **The relationship between the body and the soul**

The soul is described as the non-physical part of a person while the body is the physical part. Christianity teaches that all humans have an immortal soul. This means that it is a part of them which does not die when their physical body dies, but lives on and goes with them when they die.

For Christianity, it is the soul which separates humans from animals. Most Christians do not believe that animals have souls. However, some people, such as St Francis of Assisi, disagreed with this view. This is part of his part of a sermon he is said to have preached to a flock of birds:

> My sister birds, you owe much to God, and you must always and in everyplace give praise to Him; for He has given you freedom to wing through the sky and He has clothed you … you neither sow nor reap, and God feeds you and gives you rivers and fountains for your thirst, and mountains and valleys for shelter, and tall trees for your nests. And although you neither know how to spin or weave, God dresses you and your children, for the Creator loves you greatly and He blesses you abundantly. Therefore … always seek to praise God.

According to the Bible, God created humans in his own image:

> So God created man in his own image, in the image of God he created him; male and female he created them.   (Genesis 1:27)

▲ St Francis of Assisi preaching to the birds, by an unknown artist, twentieth century.

What is not clear is what 'in his own image' – *imago dei* – actually means.

Does it mean that humans were made in the physical image of God? Since we have no idea what God actually looks like and whether it is possible to describe God in physical human terms this is unlikely.

Does it mean that spiritually we are made in the image of God: knowing good from evil for example? This seems more likely and perhaps it is our soul which does make us like God.

This also seems to fit with the verse in the second biblical account of the creation:

the Lord God formed the man from the dust of the ground and breathed into his nostrils the breath of life, and the man became a living being. (Genesis 2:7)

Christianity teaches that this 'breath of life' is God breathing the soul into the first human.

The idea of a soul or non-physical part of the body which lives on after death is found in other religions. In Hinduism, for example, it is the atman (self or soul) that is reborn into a new body.

So Christians came to the belief that the soul and the body were separate and that the soul continued to exist after the body had died. A very similar teaching can be found in the works of the Greek philosopher Plato who believed that the soul came from and belonged to a purer place and returned there when the body died.

By the time of the writing of the New Testament, the apostle Paul was teaching that the soul and the body were often opposed to each other and that the soul tries to follow what God teaches and wants while the body is looking for pleasures that can be found on earth. Paul said that when someone died, it was a new 'spiritual body' that went to heaven. It seems probable that he meant this spiritual body to be the soul but it is not completely clear from his writing:

The body that is sown is perishable, it is raised imperishable; it is sown in dishonour, it is raised in glory; it is sown in weakness, it is raised in power; it is sown a natural body, it is raised a spiritual body. If there is a natural body, there is also a spiritual body.   (1 Corinthians 15:42b–44)

Unlike Judaism, Christianity teaches that when Eve picked the fruit from the Tree of the Knowledge of Good and Evil in the Garden of Eden, she introduced **'original sin'** into the world.

According to the teaching of the Roman Catholic Church, original sin is the way in which humans are born with a lack of holiness about them, and this is different from any actual sins that people commit themselves:

When the woman saw that the fruit of the tree was good for food and pleasing to the eye, and also desirable for gaining wisdom, she took some and ate it. She also gave some to her husband, who was with her, and he ate it. Then the eyes of both of them were opened, and they realised they were naked; so they sewed fig leaves together and made coverings for themselves.

▲ The philosopher Plato, c.424–347BCE.

Exam tip
Remember that the Christian teaching about the soul is different from other religions and philosophies.

43

▲ *Adam and Eve* by Tintoretto, c.1550–3.

Activity

Make a list of things you, or someone else, has done wrong which might be considered to be sins. Now put them in order according to which you think are the most serious ones. Do you think a Christian would agree with the order you have put these in?

Exam practice

Explain Christian teaching about original sin. *(6 marks)*

In your answer you will need to explain what is meant by the idea of original sin. You might explain that the Roman Catholic teaching is that it is the way in which humans are born with a lack of holiness about them and this is different from sin that a person commits themselves. You might also explain the origins of the idea in the story of Adam and Eve in the Garden of Eden.

Then the man and his wife heard the sound of the Lord God as he was walking in the garden in the cool of the day, and they hid from the Lord God among the trees of the garden. But the Lord God called to the man, 'Where are you?'

He answered, 'I heard you in the garden, and I was afraid because I was naked; so I hid.'

And he said, 'Who told you that you were naked? Have you eaten from the tree that I commanded you not to eat from?'

The man said, 'The woman you put here with me – she gave me some fruit from the tree, and I ate it.' …

To the woman he said,
'I will greatly increase your pains in childbearing;
with pain you will give birth to children.
Your desire will be for your husband,
and he will rule over you.'

To Adam he said, 'Because you listened to your wife and ate from the tree about which I commanded you, "You must not eat of it,"
'Cursed is the ground because of you;
through painful toil you will eat of it
all the days of your life.
It will produce thorns and thistles for you,
and you will eat the plants of the field.
By the sweat of your brow
you will eat your food
until you return to the ground,
since from it you were taken;
for dust you are
and to dust you will return.'   (Genesis 3:6–12, 16–19)

Some people believe that being made in the image of God, humans would have been immortal but that they lost their immortality when they ate the fruit.

The phrase 'original sin' does not appear in the Bible but the idea is found in Paul:

Therefore, just as sin entered the world through one man, and death through sin, and in this way death came to all men, because all sinned.
(Romans 5:12)

For as in Adam all die, so in Christ all will be made alive.
(1 Corinthians 15:22)

It is the second quotation that explains Christian teaching about the importance of the crucifixion of Jesus. Jesus, as part of the Trinity, was the Son of God, God in human form. When Jesus died and was resurrected three days later he atoned for the 'original sin' of Adam and Eve and overcame the power of death. In this way humans were forgiven their sins because Jesus' death, which he chose willingly, cleansed humanity which meant that people's immortal souls were now able to survive death and reach heaven.

Jesus said, 'I am the resurrection and the life. He who believes in me will live, even though he dies; and whoever lives and believes in me will never die.'
(John 11:25–26a)

According to the first letter of Peter in the New Testament, after the crucifixion, Jesus went down to hell:

For Christ died for sins once for all, the righteous for the unrighteous, to bring you to God. He was put to death in the body but made alive by the Spirit, through whom also he went and preached to the spirits in prison. (1 Peter 3:18–19)

This is also found in the Apostles' Creed:

I believe in Jesus Christ, his only Son, our Lord,
who was conceived by the Holy Spirit,
born of the Virgin Mary,
suffered under Pontius Pilate,
was crucified, died, and was buried;
he descended to the dead.

When he descended to hell, Jesus freed the people who had been there since the times of the Old Testament. According to medieval Christian thinking, these people such as Abraham were in a place called the 'Limbo of the Fathers'. It was only when Jesus overcame 'original sin' that these people were able to reach heaven.

In Christianity today it is original sin which is washed away by the sacrament of baptism when a baby or an adult are first welcomed into the Church.

A non-believer would probably not agree that people had a soul. However, many people link the idea of soul with that of conscience. Many non-believers do believe that they have a conscience although they would not agree that it comes from God.

▲ An infant baptism.

Research task

Because this book is about Christian Philosophy and Ethics it does not go into detail about topics like baptism. Find a copy of 'Common Worship' or look it up on the internet and write an account of an infant baptism showing how the idea of washing away original sin is found in the service.

Life after death

This topic will help you answer questions on:

- Concepts of life after death
- Beliefs about heaven, hell, purgatory, salvation, redemption and the suffering of Christ
- God as judge and the relationship between God the judge, life on earth and the afterlife

Concepts of life after death

The American writer and philosopher Benjamin Franklin (1706–90) wrote:

In this world nothing can be said to be certain, except death and taxes.

In this book we do not need to consider taxes, but the statement can certainly be seen to be true. We may not be able to predict anything about our lives except that one day we will die. In one year approximately 659,000 people die in the UK. However, the questions which remain are: what happens when we die? What happens to us next? Is there anything after death?

These are very important questions even though we cannot answer them. Perhaps one of the things which does distinguish us from animals is that they do not appear to worry about what will happen next. We cannot know this for sure, but they show no signs of having any real concerns apart from eating, breeding and avoiding pain. Yet,

Activity

Make a list of as many different beliefs about life after death as you can find.

▲ People using a ouija board to contact the spirit world.

Exam tip
Christians do not believe in reincarnation. The Christian church teaches that people have 'one soul and one life to save it in'.

▲ An angel with the trumpet of the last judgement. A fourteenth-century fresco in a Swedish church.

probably since the first human being died, people have been trying to understand or work out what will happen to them after death.

Of course, many people do believe that death is simply the end of life and that everything, including their consciousness will also come to an end. They will simply cease to exist. Most non-believers are therefore not afraid of death in the way in which some believers are. For people with a religious belief there can be a fear that, however hard they may try, they will not be judged good enough to go to heaven after death. If someone does not belief in any afterlife then this fear is removed.

The popularity of TV programmes and films about the supernatural suggests that many people believe that there is a form of life after death in the sense of ghosts, poltergeists and psychic experiences. Some people, particularly under hypnosis, believe that they can recall events from their previous lives but no one has ever been able to prove this.

Other people such as Hindus and Sikhs believe that the soul or self of a person is reincarnated many thousands of times and that it is only when a person has lived a truly good life in every respect that they will be united with God.

Heaven, hell and purgatory

As we have already seen (page 44), because of Jesus' crucifixion Christians believe that they are freed from the punishment of original sin and now have the chance to go to heaven depending on the way in which they live their lives.

Christian teaching is that one day Jesus will return to earth. This event is called the 'Parousia' or 'second coming'. At this time God will judge everyone. Those who have ignored the teachings of Jesus and the Bible will be sent to hell where they will receive eternal punishment, while those who have accepted Jesus as their saviour and followed his teachings will go to heaven. Some Christians believe that this judgement takes place as soon as someone dies, while others may believe that there will be a Day of Judgement in the future. Although these views seem very different that is perhaps just because we are thinking in a human time frame and not as God who is outside of time:

Listen, I tell you a mystery: We will not all sleep, but we will all be changed – in a flash, in the twinkling of an eye, at the last trumpet. For the trumpet will sound, the dead will be raised imperishable, and we will be changed. (1 Corinthians 15:51–52)

The Roman Catholic Church teaches that there is also another place called **purgatory**. People who have been good Christians but have still committed some sins go to purgatory where they are fully cleansed until they are in a state ready for heaven. Some people believe that almost everyone will have to spend time in purgatory.

Heaven

Views of heaven have changed over the centuries since the beginning of Christianity. In the medieval world heaven was described as a magical place with angels sitting on clouds and playing harps. However, this is probably just an attempt to represent an idea which is too complex for human language. It may, in part, be based on Old Testament passages such as the description of God's throne in Ezekiel:

Then there came a voice from above the expanse over their heads as they stood with lowered wings. Above the expanse over their heads was what looked like a throne of sapphire, and high above on the throne was a figure like that of a man. I saw that from what appeared to be his waist up he looked like glowing metal, as if full of fire, and that from there down he looked like fire; and brilliant light surrounded him. Like the appearance of a rainbow in the clouds on a rainy day, so was the radiance around him.   (Ezekiel 1:25–28)

Another description of heaven is found in the Book of Revelation:

After this I looked, and there before me was a door standing open in heaven. And the voice I had first heard speaking to me like a trumpet said, 'Come up here, and I will show you what must take place after this.' At once I was in the Spirit, and there before me was a throne in heaven with someone sitting on it. And the one who sat there had the appearance of jasper and carnelian. A rainbow, resembling an emerald, encircled the throne. Surrounding the throne were twenty-four other thrones, and seated on them were twenty-four elders. They were dressed in white and had crowns of gold on their heads. From the throne came flashes of lightning, rumblings and peals of thunder. Before the throne, seven lamps were blazing. These are the seven spirits of God. Also before the throne there was what looked like a sea of glass, clear as crystal.
   In the centre, around the throne, were four living creatures, and they were covered with eyes, in front and in back. The first living creature was like a lion, the second was like an ox, the third had a face like a man, the fourth was like a flying eagle. Each of the four living creatures had six wings and was covered with eyes all around, even under his wings. Day and night they never stop saying:
"Holy, holy, holy
is the Lord God Almighty,
who was, and is, and is to come."   (Revelation 4:1–8)

One of the ideas about heaven is that when people arrive there they will see the 'Beatific Vision': this is an eternal and direct view of God which gives people total happiness:

How great will your glory and happiness be, to be allowed to see God, to be honoured with sharing the joy of salvation and eternal light with Christ your Lord and God … to delight in the joy of immortality in the Kingdom of Heaven with the righteous and God's friends.   (St Cyprian, third century CE)

Some Christians believe that the statement in the Apostles' Creed means that when people get to heaven they will be in their physical bodies:

I believe in the Holy Spirit,
the holy catholic Church,
the communion of saints,
the forgiveness of sins,
the resurrection of the body,
and the life everlasting.

Activity

Look at the teachings about heaven on pages 46–7. Explain, as a person living in the twenty-first century, what you believe heaven might be like.

Exam tip
Christians believe in the 'resurrection of the body'. Never confuse this with reincarnation.

For this reason some Christian groups still do not allow cremation and insist on burial.

The ancient Greeks also believed that in the afterlife, people lived in the same physical body and in the condition in which they died. In some ways it is also similar to the symbolic way in which death is portrayed in this poem by Laurence Binyon which is read every year at Remembrance Day services in the UK:

> They shall not grow old, as we that are left grow old:
> Age shall not weary them, nor the years condemn.
> At the going down of the sun and in the morning
> We will remember them.

Christian belief is that death is not something which people should be frightened of but that they should look forward to a life in heaven when there will be no more suffering and where they will live happily with God for ever. Today, many Christians believe that heaven is something like a state of mind and is not a physical thing which can be described.

Hell

Original Christian teaching is that people who did not accept Jesus as their saviour and follow his teachings would be sent to hell after death and would be punished there for eternity. Hell is described as a place of torture with everlasting fires burning. Pictures of hell were often painted on the chancel arches of churches to remind the congregation of what could happen to them. These were called doom paintings.

Although there are still some Christians who believe in this ancient idea of hell, most would probably say that hell is a state of mind or that it is the denial of the Beatific Vision.

Christian teaching has always been that if people have had the opportunity to hear about Jesus and then chosen not to accept and follow him, they cannot enter heaven. However, the Roman Catholic Church has, in recent years, said that heaven is not necessarily closed to those who have never encountered Christianity:

> Those who, through no fault of their own, do not know the Gospel of Christ or his Church, but who nevertheless seek God with a sincere heart, and, moved by grace, try in their actions to do his will as they know it through the dictates of their conscience – those too may achieve eternal salvation. *(Ad gentes [To the Nations] 7)*

Purgatory

The Roman Catholic Church teaches that very few people are ready to go to heaven when they die. Although they have lived good Christian lives they are still not free from sin. In particular, they may be guilty of sins such as envy or **avarice** which are very difficult to control. Therefore they go to purgatory rather than to heaven. They stay here until their souls are ready for heaven. However, people who go to purgatory will reach heaven eventually and are not at risk of going to hell.

Teachings about purgatory are found in the writing of the Church Fathers including St Augustine, Gregory I, Origen and St Gregory of Nyssa.

▲ A medieval doom painting from Wenhaston church in Suffolk.

▲ An illustration from *Purgatorio* by Dante first published between 1307 and 1321.

The Church taught that living relatives could help shorten the time that souls stayed in purgatory by prayers for the dead. In the Middle Ages people bought indulgences which were supposed to give them time off purgatory by giving money to the Church. However, this system was open to abuse and eventually was stopped.

Modern teaching about purgatory is found in the *Catechism of the Catholic Church*:

> 210. What is purgatory?
> Purgatory is the state of those who die in God's friendship, assured of their eternal salvation, but who still have need of purification to enter into the happiness of heaven.
>
> 211. How can we help the souls being purified in purgatory?
> Because of the communion of saints, the faithful who are still pilgrims on earth are able to help the souls in purgatory by offering prayers in suffrage for them, especially the eucharistic sacrifice. They also help them by almsgiving, indulgences, and works of penance.

Salvation, redemption and the suffering of Christ

Christianity teaches that after death God will judge people for the way in which they have lived their lives. In particular, Christians believe that they are judged on the concern they have shown for others. Jesus' teaching on this is found in the Parable of the Sheep and the Goats which shows that people who care for others will receive eternal life, but people who simply ignore the suffering of others will be punished in hell:

> When the Son of Man comes in his glory, and all the angels with him, he will sit on his throne in heavenly glory. All the nations will be gathered before him, and he will separate the people one from another as a shepherd separates the sheep from the goats. He will put the sheep on his right and the goats on his left.
>
> Then the King will say to those on his right, 'Come, you who are blessed by my Father; take your inheritance, the kingdom prepared for you since the creation of the world. For I was hungry and you gave me something to eat, I was thirsty and you gave me something to drink, I was a stranger and you invited me in, I needed clothes and you clothed me, I was sick and you looked after me, I was in prison and you came to visit me.'
>
> Then the righteous will answer him, 'Lord, when did we see you hungry and feed you, or thirsty and give you something to drink? When did we see you a stranger and invite you in, or needing clothes and clothe you? When did we see you sick or in prison and go to visit you?'
>
> The King will reply, 'I tell you the truth, whatever you did for one of the least of these brothers of mine, you did for me.'
>
> Then he will say to those on his left, 'Depart from me, you who are cursed, into the eternal fire prepared for the devil and his angels. For I was hungry and you gave me nothing to eat, I was thirsty and you gave me nothing to drink, I was a stranger and you did not invite me in, I needed clothes and you did not clothe me, I was sick and in prison and you did not look after me.'
>
> Then they will go away to eternal punishment, but the righteous to eternal life.   (Matthew 25:31–43, 46)

Christians believe that they will receive salvation and redemption through devotion to Jesus. This teaching can be found in Paul's Epistle to the Romans:

Research task

Find out more about one of the Church Fathers discussed in the text and what they said about purgatory.

Activity

Look back at the list of sins you made earlier (page 44). Which of these do you think might be dealt with in purgatory and might stop someone going straight to heaven?

Exam tip
Purgatory is a belief of Roman Catholic Christians but many other Christians do not believe in it.

Therefore, there is now no condemnation for those who are in Christ Jesus, because through Christ Jesus the law of the Spirit of life set me free from the law of sin and death. For what the law was powerless to do in that it was weakened by the sinful nature, God did by sending his own Son in the likeness of sinful man to be a sin offering.   (Romans 8:1–3a)

Christianity teaches that God has set standards for people's behaviour. These are found in the teachings of the Bible, in particular in the teachings and example of Jesus. Many, if not most, people will not be able to reach these standards, but if they continue to pray for forgiveness and have faith in Jesus they will not be sent to hell.

Roman Catholics, and some Anglicans, believe that people can help themselves lead better lives by confessing their sins to a priest who will forgive them. This is based on Jesus' teaching:

And I tell you that you are Peter, and on this rock I will build my church, and the gates of Hades will not overcome it. I will give you the keys of the kingdom of heaven; whatever you bind on earth will be bound in heaven, and whatever you loose on earth will be loosed in heaven.   (Matthew 16:18–19)

If you forgive anyone his sins, they are forgiven; if you do not forgive them, they are not forgiven.   (John 20:23)

The service of confessing sins is known as the Sacrament of **Reconciliation**. After the Christian has confessed their sins to the priest they are given absolution:

God, the Father of mercies, through the death and resurrection of his Son has reconciled the world to himself and sent the Holy Spirit among us for the forgiveness of sins; through the ministry of the Church may God give you pardon and peace, and I absolve you from your sins in the name of the Father, and of the Son, and of the Holy Spirit. Amen.

Judgement

There are two kinds of judgement in Christian teaching. One is known as **General Judgement** or the Last Judgement when God will pass his final sentence on the whole of humanity as well as on the soul and body of each individual. This shows that the soul is held responsible for the behaviour of the body.

There is a description of what one early Christian thought would happen at the Last Judgement in the Book of Revelation:

Then I saw a new heaven and a new earth, for the first heaven and the first earth had passed away, and there was no longer any sea. I saw the Holy City, the new Jerusalem, coming down out of heaven from God, prepared as a bride beautifully dressed for her husband. There will be no more death or mourning or crying or pain, for the old order of things has passed away.' (Revelation 21:1–2, 4b)

Particular Judgement is the judgement given to every soul when a person dies. According to Roman Catholic teaching this judgement will allow every soul to go immediately to heaven, purgatory or hell. This view is based on two biblical passages:

- The Parable of the Rich Man and Lazarus:

  There was a rich man who was dressed in purple and fine linen and lived in luxury every day. At his gate was laid a beggar named Lazarus, covered

Exam practice

'People should confess their sins to God not to a human being.'
Do you agree?   (12 marks)

In your answer you need to explain the Roman Catholic Sacrament of Reconciliation (confession) and say why this happens. You can then explain what you feel is good or bad about this idea. Also, give your own opinion and arguments about the statement.

with sores and longing to eat what fell from the rich man's table. Even the dogs came and licked his sores.

The time came when the beggar died and the angels carried him to Abraham's side. The rich man also died and was buried. In hell, where he was in torment, he looked up and saw Abraham far away, with Lazarus by his side. So he called to him, 'Father Abraham, have pity on me and send Lazarus to dip the tip of his finger in water and cool my tongue, because I am in agony in this fire.'

But Abraham replied, 'Son, remember that in your lifetime you received your good things, while Lazarus received bad things, but now he is comforted here and you are in agony. And besides all this, between us and you a great chasm has been fixed, so that those who want to go from here to you cannot, nor can anyone cross over from there to us.'

He answered, 'Then I beg you, father, send Lazarus to my father's house, for I have five brothers. Let him warn them, so that they will not also come to this place of torment.'

Abraham replied, 'They have Moses and the Prophets; let them listen to them.'

'No, father Abraham,' he said, 'but if someone from the dead goes to them, they will repent.'

He said to him, 'If they do not listen to Moses and the Prophets, they will not be convinced even if someone rises from the dead.'   (Luke 16:19–31)

- The other passage comes from Jesus' words on the cross:

But the other criminal rebuked him. 'Don't you fear God,' he said, 'since you are under the same sentence? We are punished justly, for we are getting what our deeds deserve. But this man has done nothing wrong.'

Then he said, 'Jesus, remember me when you come into your kingdom.'

Jesus answered him, 'I tell you the truth, today you will be with me in paradise.'   (Luke 23:40–43)

▲ *The Rich Man and Lazarus* by Bassano, c.1550.

Activity

Rewrite the story of the Rich Man and Lazarus in a modern setting and make sure that you explain the teachings clearly.

Funeral rites

This topic will help you answer questions on:

- Funeral rites
- The ways funeral rites reflect belief and aim to support the bereaved

When a Christian is dying a Christian minister will try to visit them to help them prepare for their death. The person may wish to confess their sins to the minister and, for Roman Catholics, they may wish to receive a sacrament which is known as the Anointing of the Sick:

Is any one of you sick? He should call the elders of the church to pray over him and anoint him with oil in the name of the Lord. And the prayer offered in faith will make the sick person well; the Lord will raise him up. If he has sinned, he will be forgiven.   (James 5:14–15)

The person is anointed with the Oil of Unction, which is consecrated every year by a bishop at the Chrism Mass on Maundy Thursday.

Usually a funeral service takes place in a church and the body is then either buried or cremated. At the ceremony some Christians may have a Requiem Mass. This is a eucharist service where special

▲ Oil of Unction.

prayers are said for the soul of the dead person. Although black is a traditional colour for mourning, churches are often decorated with white flowers to represent the new life with God which the person is now entering. Candles are lit as a reminder that Christians are saved because Jesus was the 'Light of the World':

When Jesus spoke again to the people, he said, 'I am the light of the world. Whoever follows me will never walk in darkness, but will have the light of life.' (John 8:12)

The smoke of the candles, as with the incense often used in funerals, is said to represent the soul and prayers going up to heaven.

The opening of a funeral service is usually the reading of this passage from John:

I am the resurrection and the life. He who believes in me will live, even though he dies; and whoever lives and believes in me will never die. (John 11:25b–26a)

Jesus said these words when he raised Lazarus from the dead and so it reminds Christians that those who have faith in Jesus will live with him in heaven. As the coffin or the casket of ashes is placed in the ground the minister or priest says:

We commit this body to the ground, earth to earth, ashes to ashes, dust to dust.

A gravestone is placed at the site later. This contains details of the person's life and often a prayer or quotation from the Bible. Relatives and friends may put flowers on the grave particularly at Christmas and Easter and on the date of the dead person's birthday.

For a non-believer a funeral service might be something quite different. Usually these services are held at a crematorium and may consist of particular pieces of poetry or music which were chosen by the person who has died. Then one or more people will speak about the person. Usually these ceremonies are seen as a celebration of the person's life. Sometimes, instead of a service at the crematorium the family and friends of the dead person may choose to have a separate memorial service at a later date. The service is something important for those still alive as a way of showing respect for the person who has died, but it is not believed that it helps the dead person in any way.

Research task

To save space everyone should be cremated. Do you agree or disagree?

Activity

Using a copy of a Christian funeral service, look carefully at what is said and done. Which parts of the service do you think are helpful to the mourners? Are there any parts which you think are unhelpful?

Exam practice

'Funerals are for the living not the dead.' Give different views on this statement. *(12 marks)*

In writing a response to this question you need to consider the intended purpose of a funeral. You will need to consider what people believe about life after death and whether they think that a church ceremony may help the dead person get to heaven. You should also then consider whether the ritual ceremonies are there so that friends and relatives are helped to come to terms with the death because they believe that the person has gone to be with God. You might also consider the view of a non-believer about this.

The end of life: Looking at Exam Questions

Each question has **five** parts (a–e), and you need to answer all the parts.
You will only answer **one** question on each topic. There is a total of
24 marks for each question.

(a) What is death? *(1 mark)*

You might simply say that death is the end of all physical and mental life.

(b) What is meant by 'soul'? *(2 marks)*

The spiritual or non-physical part of a person. You might write that the soul is the other half of a person to the body or that it is the spiritual or non-physical part of a person.

(c) What do Christians believe about life after death? *(3 marks)*

You might write about Christian beliefs about heaven, hell and purgatory. You may give a brief description of these but there are only three marks available and you do not have a lot of time.

You might say that Jesus overcame death at his crucifixion so that Christians could go to heaven. You might also say that some people believe that heaven and hell are states of mind rather than physical places.

(d) How may Christian funeral rites reflect beliefs about life after death? *(6 marks)*

In answering this question you might explain the main elements of a Christian funeral service, with the emphasis on the promise of resurrection and comforting images of the dead at rest and in the hands of God. You might say that death is something which takes a person forward into eternal life; you might also explain that funeral services might be seen as comforting as death is not the end and the separation from loved ones is temporary.

(e) 'When people die that is the end.'
Discuss this statement. You should include different, supported points of view and a personal viewpoint. You must refer to Christianity in your answer. *(12 marks)*

In your answer you might say that ghosts and near-death experiences do provide evidence for life after death and that some people would say that Jesus' resurrection is evidence. You might argue that faith and belief are more reliable as proof for life after death than any factual evidence.

On the other hand you could argue that, without any evidence to the contrary, death must be the end. You could simply write that a god is a divine being, or a god is a supreme being who is worshipped, or you might say that a god is the creator of the universe.

4 Good and evil

This chapter will help you answer questions on:

- ◆ Christian concepts of good and evil
- ◆ God and the Devil (Satan)
- ◆ The Fall, original sin and redemption
- ◆ Concepts of natural and moral evil
- ◆ Approaches to why there is evil and suffering in the world
- ◆ Responses to the problem of evil
- ◆ Understanding ways of coping with suffering
- ◆ Sources and reasons for moral behaviour: the Bible, faith in Christ, conscience

Christian beliefs about good and evil

This topic will help you answer questions on:

- ● What Christians believe about the concepts of good and evil
- ● God and the Devil
- ● Beliefs about the Fall, original sin and redemption

Activities

1 In two columns write down as many things as you can in five minutes, one column for good things and the other for evil.
2 Look at the columns; what general comments can you make about what makes something 'good' and what makes something 'evil'?

Concepts of good and evil

Sometimes we use the words 'good' and 'evil' without really thinking what we mean by them. We might say that someone is a 'good' person or perhaps that someone is 'evil'. However, what do we actually mean when we say this? We may find it reasonably straightforward to say what we mean when we describe someone as evil – we do not like them or they do or think things which we do not like. On the other hand, 'good' is a word we use so often in daily

Clockwise from top left: Adolf Hitler, Saddam Hussein, Genghis Khan, Gandhi, Martin Luther King Jr and Blessed Mother Teresa. ▶

conversation that it might not be so easy to say what we mean by a 'good' person.

When we look at the words themselves we need to consider the sort of things which they mean. 'Good' might describe a holiday, winning the lottery, a pizza or just someone who is kind. 'Evil' is not as simple because it could mean something which we actually think might harm us or other people. We might use the words 'right' and 'wrong' instead as being things which we do or do not approve of. The question is, how do we make these judgements about what is 'right' and 'wrong' or 'good' and 'evil'? We might say that we just 'know' but for philosophers the question needs more consideration.

It might be true that we learn basic sets of rules from our relatives and friends and these cover things such as:

You shall not murder.
You shall not commit adultery.
You shall not steal.
You shall not give false testimony (lie).
You shall not covet.

These, of course, are the second five of the Ten Commandments.

Most religions have similar sets of basic rules and followers of these religions believe that they come from God. They are there to teach people how God wants them to behave.

God and the Devil (Satan)

For Christians, God is the beginning of everything and everything which God created is good.

God saw all that he had made, and it was very good. (Genesis 1:31a)

If this is true then it leads us to another question: 'If God is good and everything which God made is good – where does wrong or evil come from? How is it that some people behave in ways which go against what God says?' Some Christians would say that if there is evil in the world then there must also be a power of evil as well as a power of good. This power is often referred to as the Devil. So, although God is encouraging people to be good and behave as he wants them to, the Devil is trying to persuade people to be evil.

The question which this does not answer is why does God allow the Devil, or this power of evil, to exist and why does God allow us to be tempted to do evil when we are supposed to follow God's teachings? According to the Bible, it is God who will judge us at the end of our lives and the decision will be made on whether we have followed God's teachings in which case we will go to heaven or whether we have followed evil when we may go to hell.

Some people would say that there is no such thing as the Devil and that it is just people who chose to be evil. For example: they might say that Blessed Mother Teresa chose to be good and Saddam Hussein chose to be evil. However, this still leaves the question as to why God created something which was good and yet part of this creation appears to be evil. It does not seem a good enough argument just to say that some people are weak and chose the wrong thing.

▲ *Satan Addressing his Potentates*, an illustration from *Paradise Regained* by John Milton, drawn by William Blake, c.1816–18.

Exam tip

Some students write in their examination answers that it says in the Bible that Lucifer was a fallen angel. This is untrue and therefore a weak answer. There are some references to the fall of Lucifer in the Bible but the story is actually in the Apocrypha. To explain this would be a very good answer.

Activity

Read the story of the Temptation of Jesus in Luke 4:1–13. Explain the temptations that Satan gave to Jesus and why it was so important that he resisted them.

Exam tip

Remember, many Christians do not believe in the idea of a physical heaven and hell.

▲ *The Temptation in the Wilderness* by James Tissot, 1886–94.

The Devil (Satan)

The story of the origins of the Devil is not found in the Bible but in other religious books called the Apocrypha, which were not thought suitable to include in the Bible itself.

The story says that Lucifer was one of the archangels. When God created the first human he ordered the archangels to bow down to him, but Lucifer was proud and refused. God threw him out of heaven and he fell to hell where he became the Devil. There is a reference to this story in Luke's gospel where Jesus says:

I saw Satan fall like lightning from heaven.   (Luke 10:18)

There are also references to Satan in the Apocalypse or Book of Revelation:

And there was war in heaven. Michael and his angels fought against the dragon, and the dragon and his angels fought back. But he was not strong enough, and they lost their place in heaven. The great dragon was hurled down – that ancient serpent called the devil, or Satan, who leads the whole world astray. He was hurled to the earth, and his angels with him.

Then the dragon was enraged at the woman and went off to make war against the rest of her offspring – those who obey God's commandments and hold to the testimony of Jesus.   (Revelation 12:7–9 and 17)

There are very few references to Satan in the Bible, although he does appear at the beginning of Jesus' ministry when he tempts him in the wilderness for 40 days.

Christianity teaches that God is much more powerful than the Devil and that therefore good is much stronger than evil. However, it also says that God created people with **free will** so that they could decide what to do for themselves. This means that people are free to choose bad over good even though they know the probable consequences of their actions.

Although some Christians today might say that they do not believe in the figure of the Devil and that it is people who chose to be evil without any power of evil influencing them, for many Christians Satan is still very real. Because of this belief some people think that people and buildings can be possessed by the Devil and they have special ceremonies carried out to 'exorcise' or remove the Devil.

There are occasions in the New Testament when Jesus drives out demons:

Jesus was driving out a demon that was mute. When the demon left, the man who had been mute spoke, and the crowd was amazed. But some of them said, 'By Beelzebub, the prince of demons, he is driving out demons.' (Luke 11:14–15)

Other Christians might say that Jesus performed these exorcisms because it was what people expected at the time and that today we would regard these people as having mental diseases not having the devil in them. Some might also say that belief in the Devil and the punishments of hell were used in the Middle Ages to frighten people into going to church regularly.

The Fall, original sin and redemption

According to the Bible, Eve picked the fruit from the Tree of the Knowledge of Good and Evil in the Garden of Eden when this had been forbidden by God. When she did this she introduced 'original sin' into the world (see Chapter 3, page 43). Some people believe that being made in the image of God, humans would have been immortal but that they lost their immortality when they ate the fruit. Although the actual phrase 'original sin' does not appear in the Bible the idea is found in Paul:

Therefore, just as sin entered the world through one man, and death through sin, and in this way death came to all men, because all sinned.
(Romans 5:12)

For as in Adam all die, so in Christ all will be made alive.
(1 Corinthians 15:22)

In this first letter to the Corinthians the importance of the crucifixion of Jesus is explained. Jesus was the Son of God and allowed himself to be crucified by the Romans. He died and three days later came back from the dead. In this way he 'atoned' for the 'original sin' of humanity and overcame the power of death. People were redeemed from their sins because he died. This teaching is found in the following hymn:

> There is a green hill far away,
> outside a city wall,
> where our dear Lord was crucified
> who died to save us all.
>
> We may not know, we cannot tell,
> what pains he had to bear,
> but we believe it was for us
> he hung and suffered there.
>
> He died that we might be forgiven,
> he died to make us good,
> that we might go at last to heaven,
> saved by his precious blood.
>
> There was no other good enough
> to pay the price of sin,
> he only could unlock the gate
> of heaven and let us in.
>
> O dearly, dearly has he loved!
> And we must love him too,
> and trust in his redeeming blood,
> and try his works to do.   (Cecil Frances Alexander)

In Christianity today it is original sin which is washed away by the sacrament of baptism when a baby or adult is first welcomed into the church. In the Anglican Church the Priest says:

> We thank you, Father, for the water of baptism.
> In it we are buried with Christ in his death.
> By it we share in his resurrection.
> Through it we are reborn by the Holy Spirit.
> Therefore, in joyful obedience to your Son,

Exam tip
Make sure that you know what is special about 'original sin'. You need to be able to explain that many Christians believe that it was sin introduced into the world by Adam and Eve in the Garden of Eden and that since then everyone has been born in a state of original sin. For Christians this is removed by the sacrament of baptism.

▲ The site where many Christians believe Jesus was crucified in the Church of the Holy Sepulchre in Jerusalem.

Discussion point

'Children should not be baptised until they are old enough to decide for themselves.' Do you agree or disagree? Why?

we baptise into his fellowship those who come to him in faith.
Now sanctify this water that, by the power of your Holy Spirit,
they may be cleansed from sin and born again.
Renewed in your image, may they walk by the light of faith
and continue for ever in the risen life of Jesus Christ our Lord;
to whom with you and the Holy Spirit
be all honour and glory, now and for ever.

The congregation then responds:

Fight valiantly as a disciple of Christ
against sin, the world and the devil,
and remain faithful to Christ to the end of your life.

Exam practice

Explain Christian teachings about God and the Devil. *(6 marks)*

In your answer you need to explain that, for Christians, God is omnipotent, omniscient, omnipresent and omnibenevolent: God is total goodness. God is also the creator and protector of all life. The Devil is seen as a force for evil, trying to tempt Christians away from following God's teachings and the example of Jesus. You might also say that Christians believe that the Devil is far less powerful than God and can never win the struggle for souls.

The problem of evil

This topic will help you answer questions on:

● Concepts of natural and moral evil
● Approaches to why there is evil and suffering in the world
● Responses to the problem of evil

It is an undeniable fact that there is evil in the world and this inevitably causes problems for Christians. If God is omnipotent (all-powerful), omniscient (all-knowing) and omnibenevolent (all-good), how can God allow evil to exist?

Concepts of natural and moral evil

Christians say that there are two kinds of evil:

* Moral evil: this is the deeds or behaviour of people which are seen to be cruel and uncaring.
* Natural evil: this covers natural events such as volcanoes, floods and hurricanes, which may harm or kill people but do not appear to be caused by human beings. Nowadays people might say that some of these are caused indirectly by humans because they could be the effect of global warming and environmental destruction. However, many of the people who are the victims of these events are known to have lived good lives so the question remains as to why God would allow them to be punished in this way.

Exam tip
When you are writing about natural and moral evil make sure that your examples are for the correct kind.

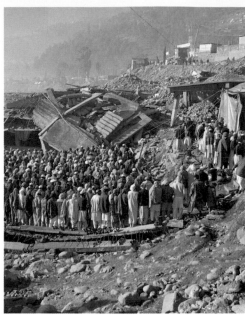

▲ Natural disasters: a firefighter in the floods of New Orleans, USA, 2005 (left); earthquake survivors in Balakot, Pakistan, 2006 (centre); victims of a drought in Selbo, Burkina Faso, 1973 (right).

Approaches to why there is evil and suffering in the world

Some people might argue that a good God would not allow evil and suffering in the world. If this is the case then there are a number of options:

- God does not exist.
- God is not all-powerful.
- God is actually responsible for everything so is responsible for evil and suffering as well as good.

Non-believers, such as humanists, might say that all human beings have the choice of how to behave. They can either choose to live their lives and behave in a way which is good for themselves and for other people, or they can live in a way which might seem good for them but which is damaging for others.

Christians are still left with two major questions about evil:

- They believe that God is good so how can God let evil exist in the world.
- In the story of creation, God created humans last and placed them in charge of the whole of creation. It is clear that God loves humans so how can he let natural disasters happen to them?

At this point it is important to consider the story of Job in the Old Testament. Job is a good man who worships God and lives a good life. A figure called the 'Adversary' (in some translations of the Bible such as the New International Version he is called Satan) asks God's permission to test Job to see just how devoted he is to God. God is confident of Job's devotion and gives permission. Over a period of time Job loses his wife, his children, his animals, all his wealth and

Activity

What examples can you think of where someone might live in such a way that they are happy but other people suffer?

59

his health. He has three friends called his 'Comforters' who argue with him and each other about what he ought to do. Despite everything which happens to him, Job does not lose his faith in God.

Finally, the Adversary realises that nothing will shake Job's faith and God speaks to Job. Job says he is sorry for ever having any doubt of God's love:

Then Job replied to the Lord:
'I know that you can do all things;
no plan of yours can be thwarted.
You asked, "Who is this that obscures my counsel without knowledge?"
Surely I spoke of things I did not understand,
things too wonderful for me to know.
'You said, "Listen now, and I will speak;
I will question you,
and you shall answer me."
My ears had heard of you
but now my eyes have seen you.
Therefore I despise myself
and repent in dust and ashes.'

After Job had prayed for his friends, the Lord made him prosperous again and gave him twice as much as he had before. All his brothers and sisters and everyone who had known him before came and ate with him in his house. They comforted and consoled him over all the trouble the Lord had brought upon him, and each one gave him a piece of silver and a gold ring.

The Lord blessed the latter part of Job's life more than the first. He had fourteen thousand sheep, six thousand camels, a thousand yoke of oxen and a thousand donkeys. And he also had seven sons and three daughters. The first daughter he named Jemimah, the second Keziah and the third Keren-Happuch. Nowhere in all the land were there found women as beautiful as Job's daughters, and their father granted them an inheritance along with their brothers.

After this, Job lived a hundred and forty years; he saw his children and their children to the fourth generation. And so he died, old and full of years. (Job 42:1–6, 10–17)

However, there are still questions about why God allows evil and suffering to take place in the world. One of the arguments put forward to explain the existence of pain and suffering is that Adam and Eve disobeyed God in the Garden of Eden. Yet why did God allow them to disobey and choose evil if they had been created perfect?

Some theologians such as Irenaeus (130–202) said that people needed to suffer and needed to be made to choose between good and evil otherwise they would be like obedient automatons or robots and God wants people to choose to worship him. This may sound convincing as an argument, but how does it apply to the suffering of babies who have done nothing wrong themselves and cannot possibly learn from the experience?

Another theologian, St Augustine (354–430), believed that evil was a lack of good. Evil happens when people do not choose good and live according to the standards which God has set for human beings. This means that evil is not a thing in itself, but simply what is left when there is no good present.

▲ *Job Accepting Charity* by William Blake, 1825.

Exam tip
Remember that the story of Job is found in the Old Testament.

▲ Is it right that some newborn babies suffer from terrible diseases?

Exam practice

Explain why the existence of evil might lead people to say that God does not exist. *(6 marks)*

In your answer you should say that there are two kinds of evil, natural and moral. You might say that these different types of evil could produce different responses or that they both show that God is not intervening to help people and stop suffering. You might say that if God allows evil to exist then either he cannot or will not help people.

Coping with suffering

This topic will help you answer questions on:

● Understanding ways of coping with suffering

One way of dealing with problems of evil and suffering is just to say that they are part of what God does which simply cannot be explained.

> God moves in a mysterious way
> His wonders to perform;
> He plants His footsteps in the sea
> And rides upon the storm...
> Judge not the Lord by feeble sense,
> But trust Him for His grace;
> Behind a frowning providence
> He hides a smiling face.
> His purposes will ripen fast,
> Unfolding every hour;
> The bud may have a bitter taste,
> But sweet will be the flower.
> Blind unbelief is sure to err
> And scan His work in vain;
> God is His own interpreter,
> And He will make it plain.   (William Cowper)

Activity

Read the verses opposite from a hymn by William Cowper (1731–1800). Cowper suffered from periods of very serious depression and found comfort in religion. What does his hymn suggest about the way in which God rules the world?

Christianity teaches that God took human form and came to earth as Jesus of Nazareth. Jesus taught people how they should live according to God's wishes and then gave his life by dying on the cross. Because he was innocent of any sin and chose to die for others, the sins of humans were forgiven and so Christians believe that God shared in human suffering.

When they are suffering many Christians pray to God to help them or to give them the strength to cope with what is happening. Christians accept that God does not always answer prayers in the way they would like him to, but they believe that, whatever happens, God chooses the best for them.

Exam tip

When you are writing about Jesus as the Son of God remember to say that he was God in human form and part of the Trinity.

▲ *Christ at the Pool of Bethesda* by Bartolomé Esteban Murillo, 1667–70.

At the time of the New Testament many people believed that illness and suffering were punishments for sins that people had committed. An example is found in this miracle of Jesus:

Jesus stepped into a boat, crossed over and came to his own town. Some men brought to him a paralytic, lying on a mat. When Jesus saw their faith, he said to the paralytic, 'Take heart, son; your sins are forgiven.'

At this, some of the teachers of the law said to themselves, 'This fellow is blaspheming!'

Knowing their thoughts, Jesus said, 'Why do you entertain evil thoughts in your hearts? Which is easier: to say, "Your sins are forgiven," or to say, "Get up and walk"? But so that you may know that the Son of Man has authority on earth to forgive sins … .' Then he said to the paralytic, 'Get up, take your mat and go home.' And the man got up and went home. When the crowd saw this, they were filled with awe; and they praised God, who had given such authority to men.   (Matthew 9:1–8)

Exam practice

'Prayer is the best way to deal with suffering.'
Do you agree?   *(12 marks)*

In your answer you need to consider why Christians might believe that prayer is the best way of coping and suggest how it might help them, for example they feel that they can speak to God and that God loves them so this might make it more bearable.

From another point of view you might argue that people should try to find other ways of coping, talking to friends or finding an activity which helps them. You might say that people who do not believe in God would not pray and would have to find other ways of dealing with their problems.

Sources and reasons for moral behaviour

Activity

Read the Ten Commandments. Which of them do you think are the most difficult for people to keep today? Explain your answers.

This topic will help you answer questions on:

● Sources and reasons for moral behaviour:
  – the Bible
  – faith in Christ
  – conscience

Christians try to live according to God's wishes as found in the Bible and, in particular, in the teachings of Jesus. If God is perfectly good then that is what Christians should aim for themselves because they were made 'in the image of God' (Genesis 1:27).

The Ten Commandments (Exodus 20:1–17) show how God wants people to behave but there are many other passages where God's teachings about human behaviour are found; there are also examples where people are punished for not obeying God's rules.

Most of Jesus' teachings about what God wants of people are found in the Sermon on the Mount (Matthew 5–7), but there is also the passage know as the 'two great commandments' or the 'Dominical commandments' where Jesus summarises these teachings:

One of the teachers of the law came and heard them debating. Noticing that Jesus had given them a good answer, he asked him, 'Of all the commandments, which is the most important?'

'The most important one,' answered Jesus, 'is this: "Hear, O Israel, the Lord our God, the Lord is one. Love the Lord your God with all your heart and with all your soul and with all your mind and with all your strength." The second is this: "Love your neighbour as yourself." There is no commandment greater than these.'   (Mark 12:28–31)

When Jesus is asked 'who is my neighbour?':

In reply Jesus said: 'A man was going down from Jerusalem to Jericho, when he fell into the hands of robbers. They stripped him of his clothes, beat him and went away, leaving him half dead. A priest happened to be going down the same road, and when he saw the man, he passed by on the other side. So too, a Levite, when he came to the place and saw him, passed by on the other side. But a Samaritan, as he travelled, came where the man was; and when he saw him, he took pity on him. He went to him and bandaged his wounds, pouring on oil and wine. Then he put the man on his own donkey, took him to an inn and took care of him. The next day he took out two silver coins and gave them to the innkeeper. "Look after him," he said, "and when I return, I will reimburse you for any extra expense you may have." '

'Which of these three do you think was a neighbour to the man who fell into the hands of robbers?'

The expert in the law replied, 'The one who had mercy on him.'

Jesus told him, 'Go and do likewise.'   (Luke 10:30–37)

The Bible

When Christians want to know how God wants them to live, one of the obvious places to look is in the teachings of the Bible. The Bible is not always easy to apply to everyday situations however and although some teachings may be the same for all time:

So in everything, do to others what you would have them do to you, for this sums up the Law and the Prophets.   (Matthew 7:12)

Others, such as the teachings about the role of women in some of the New Testament epistles, would be unacceptable to many people in the twenty-first century:

… women should remain silent in the churches. They are not allowed to speak, but must be in submission, as the Law says. If they want to enquire about something, they should ask their own husbands at home; for it is disgraceful for a woman to speak in the church.   (1 Corinthians 14:34–35)

I do not permit a woman to teach or to have authority over a man; she must be silent. For Adam was formed first, then Eve. And Adam was not the one deceived; it was the woman who was deceived and became a sinner. (1 Timothy 2:12–14)

For man did not come from woman, but woman from man; neither was man created for woman, but woman for man.   (1 Corinthians 11:8–9)

> **Research task**
>
> Find out about Levites and Samaritans and why they are important examples in this parable.

> **Activity**
>
> People often say that the attitude towards women in the Epistles is different from the way in which Jesus treated women. Find an example from the gospels to support this view.

Faith in Christ

One way in which Christians might decide how God wants them to behave is by following the example of Jesus' life and teachings as found in the New Testament. Because Christians have faith in Jesus as their saviour and the Son of God the example of his life must be a good model for Christians to follow.

Before Jesus' resurrection teachings about what happened after death were very unclear. As Christianity teaches that Jesus' death cleansed the world of sin, they believe that they now have the chance to go to heaven.

Jesus was accused of blasphemy by the priests of the Jerusalem Temple and was crucified by the Roman authorities who ruled the country at the time.

Jesus on Trial Before the Sanhedrin by William Hole, nineteenth century. ▶

The accounts in the gospels say that Jesus refused to deny the charges which had been brought against him and so was found guilty. He was whipped by the Roman soldiers and a crown made of sharp thorns was placed on his head. Then he was made to carry his cross from the prison to Calvary (or Golgotha) which was one of the places in Jerusalem where criminals were executed.

Jesus was nailed to the cross through his hands and feet and then left to die. Jesus then asked God, his father, to forgive the soldiers:

'Father, forgive them, for they do not know what they are doing.'
(Luke 23:34a)

After three hours Jesus died. His body was taken down from the cross and, at the request of Joseph of Arimathea, one of his followers, it was placed in a nearby tomb. Usually the bodies were simply thrown into a pit when the prisoners were dead. This happened on a Friday and because it was almost the beginning of the Jewish Sabbath when no work can be done, he was buried very quickly and a stone was rolled across the entrance of the tomb. On the following Sunday morning he was seen again by the women who came to anoint the body and he was alive. Jesus stayed on earth teaching his disciples for a further 40 days before he finally ascended into heaven.

Fact box

Modern research says that, in fact, Jesus only carried the crossbar of the cross as the upright poles were permanent fixtures at these places of execution.

Christianity teaches that because Jesus gave up his life willingly and was innocent of any sin, his death atoned for all the sins of humanity so that all those who have followed his teachings and accepted him as the Son of God now have the opportunity to reach heaven when they die.

For this reason Jesus is sometimes referred to in the New Testament as the second Adam. Just as eating the fruit in the Garden of Eden brought sin into the world, so Jesus' death on the cross freed people from the burden of that sin:

Consequently, just as the result of one trespass [sin] was condemnation for all men, so also the result of one act of righteousness was justification that brings life for all men. For just as through the disobedience of the one man the many were made sinners, so also through the obedience of the one man the many will be made righteous.   (Romans 5:18–19)

The occasion on the night before Jesus died, when he ate the Last Supper with his disciples, is remembered by Christians at the eucharist.

On the night before he was put to death, Jesus had celebrated the Last Supper with his disciples. At this meal he shared bread and wine with them.

While they were eating, Jesus took bread, gave thanks and broke it, and gave it to his disciples, saying, 'Take it; this is my body.'

Then he took the cup, gave thanks and offered it to them, and they all drank from it.

'This is my blood of the covenant, which is poured out for many,' he said to them. 'I tell you the truth, I will not drink again of the fruit of the vine until that day when I drink it anew in the kingdom of God.'   (Mark 14:22–25)

▲ The paten and chalice used at the eucharist service link with the bread and wine Jesus shared at the Last Supper.

Christians believe that by celebrating the eucharist they are bringing Jesus into their lives again and remembering his act of atonement. When Christians take Jesus' life as an example of how they should live they look at his teachings in the gospels and, in particular, in the Sermon on the Mount, and also the way in which he treated people. Jesus was particularly concerned about the treatment of people who were regarded as outcasts by society. There are several examples of this, particularly in Luke's gospel:

They sailed to the region of the Gerasenes, which is across the lake from Galilee. When Jesus stepped ashore, he was met by a demon-possessed man from the town. For a long time this man had not worn clothes or lived in a house, but had lived in the tombs. When he saw Jesus, he cried out and fell at his feet, shouting at the top of his voice, 'What do you want with me, Jesus, Son of the Most High God? I beg you, don't torture me!' For Jesus had commanded the evil spirit to come out of the man. Many times it had seized him, and though he was chained hand and foot and kept under guard, he had broken his chains and had been driven by the demon into solitary places.

Jesus asked him, 'What is your name?'

'Legion,' he replied, because many demons had gone into him. And they begged him repeatedly not to order them to go into the Abyss.

A large herd of pigs was feeding there on the hillside. The demons begged Jesus to let them go into them, and he gave them permission. When the demons came out of the man, they went into the pigs, and the herd rushed down the steep bank into the lake and was drowned.   (Luke 8:26–32)

In pairs, make a list of the ways in which you make moral decisions. Try to be as honest as you can.

Conscience

People often say that they 'know' what to do because they are following their conscience. Sometimes people may feel that they cannot do something because their conscience will not allow it. It is difficult to say what this 'conscience' is. Is it simply people working through a question for themselves and deciding the right course of action based on their upbringing or is it, as some Christians would say, the 'voice of God' telling them what to do?

Most of the ways in which Christians find teachings and help in deciding about moral behaviour are not relevant to non-believers. Therefore they may use different sources in order to form their ideas of how to behave morally in the world. This statement is from the British Humanist Association:

Humanism is the belief that we can live good lives without religious or superstitious beliefs. Humanists make sense of the world using reason, experience and shared human values. We seek to make the best of the one life we have by creating meaning and purpose for ourselves. We take responsibility for our actions and work with others for the common good.

Humanism is an approach to life based on humanity and reason – humanists recognise that moral values are properly founded on human nature and experience alone. Our decisions are based on the available evidence and our assessment of the outcomes of our actions, not on any dogma or sacred text.

Humanists believe in individual rights and freedoms – but believe that individual responsibility, social cooperation and mutual respect are just as important.

However, many Humanists do believe in a conscience but they do not think that this comes from God.

Exam practice

'The Bible is a very old book which has nothing to teach people in the twenty-first century.'
Do you agree with this statement? *(6 marks)*

You might explain that, for Christians, the Bible is the living Word of God and that this means that it is what God wants to say to humanity for all time. Therefore it is still as relevant today as it was when it was first written.

On the other hand you could say that many people disagree over what is in the Bible and do not believe that it should be taken literally. You might also say that for many of the moral and social issues which people face today there is nothing in the Bible to help them.

Good and evil: Looking at Exam Questions

Each question has **five** parts (a–e), and you need to answer all the parts.
You will only answer **one** question on each topic. There is a total of
24 marks for each question.

(a) What is meant by evil? *(1 mark)*

You might describe evil in various ways but you could say that it is something which is immoral or wrong.

(b) Give two examples of human suffering.
(2 marks)

There are many different examples which you could give but you might include physical suffering such as illness, mental suffering which might include things like loneliness, or financial suffering such as poverty.

(c) What is the difference between natural and moral evil? *(3 marks)*

You need to make sure that you describe both natural and moral evil. You might say that natural evil is seen in events such as volcanoes, earthquakes and the 2004 Boxing Day tsunami. Moral evil is when people act badly towards others; here you could use the example of something such as the twentieth-century Holocaust. You might also use droughts and famines as examples of natural evil but if they are caused by the acts of human beings such as abuse of the environment and global warming then they are really moral evils.

(d) How might Christians explain the problem of evil in the world? *(6 marks)*

In answering this question there are several things you could say. You might explain the Christian understanding of the concepts of good and evil and the roles of God and the Devil (Satan); you might explain the theological ideas you have studied such as the Fall, original sin and redemption. You might also say that some people believe that the existence of evil is the result of God giving people free will. You might also explain that the existence of evil is necessary so that people can choose good.

(e) 'It is God who makes people suffer.'
Discuss this statement. You should include different, supported points of view and a personal viewpoint. You must refer to Christianity in your answer. *(12 marks)*

In your answer you might say that some people believe that suffering strengthens people and may help them to become more understanding and better Christians.

You might say that, for religious people, suffering is part of belief and a matter of acceptance. You could also say that if God does make people suffer then, for Christians, because God is all-loving, there has to be a good reason for this suffering.

On the other hand you could argue that suffering is the responsibility of the human beings who cause it and have the power to prevent it.

5 Religion, reason and revelation

This chapter will help you answer questions on:

- What Christians believe about revelation
- How Christians believe God reveals himself through the world
- How Christians believe God reveals himself through mystical and religious experiences
- How Christians believe God reveals himself through Jesus
- The authority of the Bible and reasons for it
- The significance and importance of the Bible

Form and nature of revelation

This topic will help you answer questions on:

- What Christians believe about revelation
- How Christians believe God reveals himself through the world
- How Christians believe God reveals himself through mystical and religious experiences
- How Christians believe God reveals himself through Jesus

▲ God reveals himself through the world.

How does anybody get to know God? If you want to get to know someone you might arrange to meet up, talk to them on the phone, make contact through a social networking site – but you cannot exactly do this with God.

Christianity claims to be a revealed religion. What does this mean and what is **revelation**? We are finite (alive only for a certain amount of time) so how can we ever know an infinite God? It seems impossible, but Christianity says it is possible because God takes the initiative. This is called revelation. It means 'unveiling' – something which was previously hidden becomes known.

If you look at this at a human level we can never really know each other, we can never really know what we are thinking about. However, people can know us and what we are thinking if we tell them. Christians believe that it is exactly the same with God.

There are two types of revelation:

- general or natural revelation
- special revelation.

General or natural revelation

This is called general because it is made available to everyone, and is natural because it comes to us through nature. Here are two Bible passages which explain what this means:

The heavens declare the glory of God;
the skies proclaim the work of his hands.
Day after day they pour forth speech;
night after night they display knowledge.
There is no speech or language
where their voice is not heard.
Their voice goes out into all the earth,
their words to the ends of the world.   (Psalm 19:1–4)

Since what may be known about God is plain to them, because God has made it plain to them. For since the creation of the world God's invisible qualities – his eternal power and divine nature – have been clearly seen, being understood from what has been made, so that men are without excuse.   (Romans 1:19–20)

Just as artists reveal themselves in their art, people believe that God has revealed himself in the creation. This is beautifully illustrated in a poem by Gerard Manley Hopkins (1844–89):

The world is charged with the grandeur of God ('God's Grandeur').

Most Christians do agree that God reveals himself through nature, but only for those who are looking:

Earth's crammed with heaven,
And every common bush afire with God;
And only he who sees, takes off his shoes –
The rest sit round it and pluck blackberries.
(Elizabeth Barrett-Browning)

Philosophers have also seen God revealed in the natural world. William Paley (1743–1805) saw the design of the natural world as evidence for God as a designer (see page 11). This also links in with human nature, that people have an inbuilt sense of 'the divine', that there is 'someone out there'. Christians also ask: where does our sense of right and wrong come from if there is no moral lawgiver? Human consciences are also seen as evidence of God revealing himself to us. However, we can only take this so far. People may believe deep down that there is a greater being than us and that he is powerful, creative and good. On the other hand, some of the signals we may receive are mixed and confusing. For all the order in the world, there is also disorder: earthquakes, flood, hurricanes and a multitude of other natural disasters. For all the good things, there are also the bad things: war, murder, rape.

Activities

1 Find more examples of Christian religious poetry and compare the way in which they describe God's creation.

2 Make a collage showing good and bad aspects of life and the world. Then consider which of the examples you have chosen may show the presence of God.

Exam tip

Remember that general revelation is indirect and available to everyone. It says that God shows himself through:

- the natural world
- reason
- a moral sense
- conscience.

Special revelation

God has taken the initiative to give this. For Christians, the Bible is the most obvious place for revelation, and starting with the Old Testament there are accounts of God acting in special ways and through special people speaking and gradually making his character and plans known. Christians believe that all of this is preparing us for, and pointing us to, the time when God would make himself known to us fully and finally in Jesus:

> In the past God spoke to our forefathers through the prophets at many times and in various ways, but in these last days he has spoken to us by his Son, whom he appointed heir of all things, and through whom he made the universe. The Son is the radiance of God's glory and the exact representation of his being, sustaining all things by his powerful word. After he had provided purification for sins, he sat down at the right hand of the Majesty in heaven. (Hebrews 1:1–3)

> The Word became flesh and made his dwelling among us. We have seen his glory, the glory of the One and Only, who came from the Father, full of grace and truth. … No one has ever seen God, but God the One and Only, he who is at the Father's side, has made him known. (John 1:14, 18)

Some Christians would say that the Bible is the Word of God and that it is all that they need. As the Bible is inspired by God, it tells people exactly what God is like:

> All Scripture is God-breathed and is useful for teaching, rebuking, correcting and training in righteousness. (2 Timothy 3:16)

Others would also add that God continues to reveal himself through the Church Teachings, and through the lives of great Christians who can be an inspiration to others. Others find God in Christian Worship, in the service of the Word (see page 26), the eucharist (see page 26), and in the inspiration of the Holy Spirit in the silence of Quaker worship (see page 29) and the joyfulness of charismatic worship. Christians feel that in worship they are in the presence of God.

Christians also believe that God can reveal himself directly to them. Many Christians have had personal experience of God when they feel he speaks directly to them. This may be through prayer, when on a pilgrimage, when meditating on a passage from the Bible, or when they simply feel awe in the presence of God or feel loved by God.

Revelation of God through mystical and religious experience

How does religious experience help a Christian to know God and receive guidance from him?

Conversion

Conversion for Christians means becoming a believer. There are many examples of this in the Bible, but one of the most important is the conversion of St Paul:

> Meanwhile, Saul was still breathing out murderous threats against the Lord's disciples. He went to the high priest and asked him for letters to the

▲ *Christ in Glory*, a modern Greek Orthodox fresco.

Research task

Research some of the people who claim that they have had a life-changing religious experience.

Exam tip

Remember that special revelation is when God reveals himself directly to an individual or a group.
This can be through:
- the Bible
- the person of Jesus
- Church teachings
- the lives of great Christians
- Christian worship
- personal experience.

Activity

1 Make a chart with examples showing the two different types of revelation.

synagogues in Damascus, so that if he found any there who belonged to the Way, whether men or women, he might take them as prisoners to Jerusalem. As he neared Damascus on his journey, suddenly a light from heaven flashed around him. He fell to the ground and heard a voice say to him, 'Saul, Saul, why do you persecute me?'

'Who are you, Lord?' Saul asked.

'I am Jesus, whom you are persecuting,' he replied. 'Now get up and go into the city, and you will be told what you must do.'

The men travelling with Saul stood there speechless; they heard the sound but did not see anyone. Saul got up from the ground, but when he opened his eyes he could see nothing. So they led him by the hand into Damascus. For three days he was blind, and did not eat or drink anything.

In Damascus there was a disciple named Ananias. The Lord called to him in a vision, 'Ananias!' 'Yes, Lord,' he answered.

The Lord told him, 'Go to the house of Judas on Straight Street and ask for a man from Tarsus named Saul, for he is praying. In a vision he has seen a man named Ananias come and place his hands on him to restore his sight.'

'Lord,' Ananias answered, 'I have heard many reports about this man and all the harm he has done to your saints in Jerusalem. And he has come here with authority from the chief priests to arrest all who call on your name.'

But the Lord said to Ananias, 'Go! This man is my chosen instrument to carry my name before the Gentiles and their kings and before the people of Israel. I will show him how much he must suffer for my name.'

Then Ananias went to the house and entered it. Placing his hands on Saul, he said, 'Brother Saul, the Lord – Jesus, who appeared to you on the road as you were coming here – has sent me so that you may see again and be filled with the Holy Spirit.' Immediately, something like scales fell from Saul's eyes, and he could see again. He got up and was baptised, and after taking some food, he regained his strength.   (Acts 9:1–19a)

▲ St Paul's conversion on the road to Damascus, by an unknown artist, twentieth century.

Today Evangelical Christians see conversion as the beginning of faith – it is for them almost more important than baptism. A person has to admit their sins to God and ask for his forgiveness. Evangelical Christians call this being 'born again' or 'saved'. Sometimes people have actual physical experiences like Saul when they are converted, and people who are sick may be healed. For some Christians conversion is the most important experience of their lives and changes them forever. They believe that God has revealed himself to them in a very particular way. Non-believers might think that these people are experiencing some sort of psychological experience rather than a direct revelation from God. However, conversion can happen in all Christian denominations through conversations with others, through Bible reading or through prayer.

Charismatic worship

Some Christians, after their conversion, have a later experience of 'baptism in the spirit' – the Holy Spirit (see page 28) is said to touch them in a particular way and they are given spiritual gifts such as speaking in tongues (glossolalia), prophesying, or having visions. Worshippers will feel very close to God and worship in an uninhibited way: singing, dancing, clapping and holding their hands in the air. These spiritual gifts started on the first day of Pentecost (see page 29).

Activities

2 Explain what a Christian would mean if they said they were 'born again'.

3 Explain what a non-believer might think about a claim that someone had received a conversion experience.

Research task

Research either:

- the event known as the 'Toronto Blessing'
- or: Evan Roberts and the Welsh Revival in 1904

and explain how it is an example of glossolalia.

From the very beginning of the Christian Church these gifts of the Spirit seem to cause some difficulty and Paul wrote about how to deal with them in the right way. He explains that people may receive different gifts but that they all come from the Spirit and should be used to help others:

Now to each one the manifestation of the Spirit is given for the common good. To one there is given through the Spirit the message of wisdom, to another the message of knowledge by means of the same Spirit, to another faith by the same Spirit, to another gifts of healing by that one Spirit, to another miraculous powers, to another prophecy, to another distinguishing between spirits, to another speaking in different kinds of tongues, and to still another the interpretation of tongues. All these are the work of one and the same Spirit, and he gives them to each one, just as he determines.
(1 Corinthians 12: 7–11)

This kind of worship always seems to have caused problems, but there have been times in the Church's history when it has been important. The Pentecostal Church came out of such a time. In the second half of the twentieth century the Charismatic Movement spread to mainstream churches. Many Christians believe that the spiritual gifts are a form of revelation by which God communicates directly with people.

Prayer and meditation

This is the way that most Christians believe that God reveals himself to them, and speaks directly to them. Meditation could be described as a peaceful focus on God. Meditation for a Christian is not emptying his or her mind but filling it with God's word. It may involve a single word or prayer such as the Jesus Prayer:

Jesus, Son of God have mercy on me.

Or meditation may involve concentrating on a Bible verse or passage.

Some Christians distance themselves from society in order to pray and be close to God. One example of this was St Julian of Norwich who lived at the end of the fourteenth and beginning of the fifteenth centuries (see page 7). When she was 30 years old, Julian suffered a severe illness from which she almost died. During that illness she had a number of visions of the Passion of Christ and the love of God. She then became an anchoress (a sort of hermit) at St Julian's church in Norwich, and spent the remainder of her life in prayer and meditation. She also offered comfort and advice to those who came to her window. Julian saw contemplative prayer or meditation as the highest form of prayer consisting in simply waiting on God.

Julian wrote a book, *The Revelations of Divine Love*, otherwise known as *Showing of Love*, containing insights into the nature of God and the human condition which were ahead of her time. The medieval church emphasised sin, punishment and purgatory, but Julian said that there is no anger in God. It is in God's nature, says Julian, to 'put away all our blame', and to 'regard us with pity and compassion as innocent and guiltless children'. Likewise, in contrast to the patriarchal language and concepts of the established church, she saw God not only as an all-powerful and mighty Father, but also as a tender loving Mother.

Activities

1 Compare the life of Julian of Norwich with either those of the Desert Fathers or the Celtic hermits.

2 Consider whether there has been any similar event in your life or that of someone you know. How would you explain these events?

▲ Nuns in prayer at the Basilica of the Holy Sepulchre, Jerusalem, Israel.

This sort of meditation or contemplative prayer has been part of Christianity from the beginning. Jesus spent whole nights alone in prayer. The Desert Fathers and the Celtic hermits sought places to be alone with God. For some centuries the Christian Churches neglected this most basic form of prayer; it became usual only in monastic communities. There was a revival in the 1960s and 1970s and people rediscovered some of the writings of Julian. As a result, interdenominational contemplative prayer groups called Julian Meetings were formed so that Christians could experience God in this way. Today there are over 400 such groups in the UK.

Contemplative prayer has been described as listening for God; opening ourselves to God; waiting silently upon God. Other descriptions are meditation, contemplation, or 'the prayer of quiet'. In contemplative prayer people seek to be aware of the presence of God and to remain silently and attentively in that presence, completely open to God, so that God can reveal himself to them. It is like the story of the old man who explained why he sat in church for hours: 'I look at Him, He looks at me.'

Revelation of God in the person of Jesus

He is the image of the invisible God, the firstborn over all creation. For by him all things were created: things in heaven and on earth, visible and invisible, whether thrones or powers or rulers or authorities; all things were created by him and for him. He is before all things, and in him all things hold together. And he is the head of the body, the church; he is the beginning and the firstborn from among the dead, so that in everything he might have the supremacy. For God was pleased to have all his fullness dwell in him, and through him to reconcile to himself all things, whether things on earth or things in heaven, by making peace through his blood, shed on the cross. (Colossians 1:15–20)

In this passage, Paul suggests that God reveals himself through Jesus, that people can know God through Jesus. How can people understand this when God is invisible and Jesus is dead?

Christians believe that Jesus reveals God to humanity because he enters into a relationship with people and creates a relationship between people. He was born as man – Christians believe that God became a human being in the person of Jesus – the incarnation. Jesus, it is believed, was fully human and fully God. 'Incarnation' means literally 'in flesh'.

Christians believe Jesus reveals God's nature through the Gospel stories of how he showed love and forgiveness, offering people a new start in life (see, for example, Zacchaeus the tax collector; the **penitent** thief). They believe he offers these same things to everyone.

The four gospel writers portray both Jesus' humanity and his divinity in the key events of his life (birth, teaching, healing, transfiguration, relationships with others, suffering, death, resurrection and ascension). They record Jesus' teaching about God and living according to God's way (for example, the Sermon on the Mount and parables of the Kingdom) (see page 63). Jesus reveals God to humanity because he reconciles humanity to God in person. He died on the cross.

Activities

1 Look up the following stories in the Bible and see how Jesus gave people a new start:

◆ Luke 7:36–50

◆ Luke 13:10–17

◆ Luke 19:1–10.

2 What have all these people got in common? Why were their lives changed? How did Jesus reveal God to them?

▲ Images representing the Bible stories about how Jesus gave people a new start: (from left) Luke 7:36–50, Luke 13:10–17 and Luke 19:1–10.

The Church and Bible teaching is that it was necessary for him to become a human so that he, on behalf of the human race, could make a full atonement for human sin, so that God's forgiveness might be made available to all people. Because Jesus, therefore, saves people from the consequences of their sin and wrong-doing, He is referred to as 'The Saviour' (see page 21). Jesus said: 'I am the way and the truth and the life. No one comes to the Father except through me' (John 14:6). So Christians believe that in Jesus Christ they have the fullest revelation of God in a human life. In Christ they see God and see that God is love.

Exam practice

Explain how religious experiences might make someone believe in God. *(6 marks)*

You could start by explaining conversion and how this changes people's lives so much that they believe in God. You could give the conversion of Paul as an example, or anyone else you have studied or know about.

You could also discuss how worship, especially charismatic worship might open the person to the Holy Spirit, so that they believe in God.

You could discuss how prayer, especially contemplative prayer or meditation, might then make this belief in God stronger.

The authority and importance of sacred texts

This topic will help you answer questions on:

● The authority of the Bible and reasons for it
● The significance and importance of the Bible

God reveals himself in the Bible

Christians believe the Bible reveals the truth about God; some say it is totally true, others interpret it differently. However, for all Christians it is a central source of authority and is used in public worship, private study, meditation and decision-making, and as an inspiration for writing prayers, modern songs and church liturgies.

The Bible was written over a long period and includes history, poetry, law, letters and prophecy. It has been preserved for centuries and is the most translated book in the world.

The Bible as the Word of God

Sacred texts are important for most religions. For Christians the Bible is the most sacred text and is a source of authority. The teachings in the Bible tell Christians what God wants of them and how he wants them to live. The Bible is in two parts: the Old Testament and the New Testament.

The Old Testament

The Old Testament contains the same books as the Jewish Scriptures (the Tenakh), but in a different order. The first five books are the writings of the Torah and tell the story of the early history of the Jews and their relationship with God, as well as the Laws which God wanted them to follow and the Covenants (promises) which were made between God and the Jews. There are 39 books in the Old Testament.

The other books of the Old Testament are a variety of different types of writings, including literature, law, prophecy, history, liturgy and poetry.

Most of the books in the Old Testament were originally written in Hebrew, but some later ones were written in Aramaic.

Jesus was a Jew and so were his first followers, so the Old Testament is still a very important part of the Bible for Christians. One of the most important ideas in the Old Testament is the relationship between God and humanity. The prophets wrote about the coming of a Messiah, who would bring peace to the earth. Isaiah also wrote that this Messiah or Servant of God would suffer for people's sins. Christians believe that this servant was Jesus.

The New Testament

The New Testament contains the writings of the early Christians. It was written in Greek. There are 27 books in the New Testament. The four Gospels, Matthew, Mark, Luke and John, tell of the life and teaching of Jesus. These are followed by the Acts of the Apostles that gives an account of the Early Church. There are 21 Epistles (letters) which are written to various early Christian communities. The final book is the book of Revelation which contains a vision or dream of an early Christian written in mystical language which seems to describe the Day of Judgement. It is difficult to understand but it is important because it shows the struggle between good and evil, with evil triumphing for a time, but God's followers being triumphant in the end. It is likely that it was written to give Christians hope at a time when they were being persecuted.

The **canon** or group of books which are now in the New Testament was not agreed by the Church until 367CE, and at that time many gospels and epistles were left out of the Bible because Christians were not convinced that they were genuinely inspired by God.

Christians believe that the Bible is the Word of God and therefore contains the true message of God. However, Christians have different ideas about how it is true:

* Some Christians will say that every word of the Bible is absolutely true and there are no errors or mistakes in it. These Christians are often called **fundamentalists** and they think that everything in the Bible happened exactly as it is written. They believe that if scientists or historians have different understandings of the world, it is the Bible that is right and the people who are wrong.

▲ Christians regard the Bible as the Word of God.

Research tasks

1 Research the order of the books in the Jewish Scriptures and compare it with the order in the New Testament. Look at the ending of the last book in each of these two collections and try to find out why the order is different.

2 Many books were left out of the canon of the Bible. Find out which books were omitted and why.

Activity

Explain why Christians value the Old Testament as well as the New Testament.

Discussion point

Discuss how, if Christians believe that the Bible is the actual Word of God, some Christians can then think that some of what it says is true while other parts are not.

- Other more **liberal** Christians say that although the writing is inspired by God, it is written by people and so may have mistakes in it, and may need to be interpreted for the age in which it is used. They are not saying that the Bible is unimportant, but that Christians should read it very carefully in order to understand the meaning, especially when even the scholars are unsure of what some of the words originally meant in Hebrew, Aramaic or Greek.

- Other Christians say that the stories in the Bible are symbolic or mythical; they contain truths but not literal ones. They may think that the Bible is true in some parts, but not in others. They may believe that the Bible sometimes shows a view of the world that is outdated now. For example, they might think the Bible's attitude to women is not appropriate for the modern world, or that scientists have a better understanding than the biblical writers of the origins of the world. These Christians might have difficulties in knowing which parts of the Bible are actually true and which are not.

The authority of the Bible

There are several different ways of looking at this and these will be considered below.

The Catholic view

The view held by Roman Catholics, Orthodox Christians and some Anglicans is that the Holy Spirit, God's gift to the Church, inspired both the people who wrote the books, which are part of the canon, and those who decided which books had been intended by God to be part of the New Testament. In other words, there is a balance between two sources of authority. The books were chosen by the Church *because* their content demonstrated to the Church that they had been inspired by God, unlike other gospels and epistles which were not considered authoritative in the same way. On the other hand, it was the Church that passed judgement on the content of the books, and not the books on the Church.

So the authority of the Church is seen to be above that of the Bible in the sense that the Church has the authority to define what Christians should believe *about* the words of the Bible. The classic example would be the doctrine of the Trinity, believed by all who call themselves Christian, defined by Councils of the Church such as that held at Nicaea in 325CE, but not specifically taught anywhere in the Old or New Testament. This view is that scripture is inspired by God but written by humans. Its words are not always self-evident in their meaning, and the Church as a whole has the authority to define and interpret its words.

The advantages of this way of looking at the authority of the Bible include:

- The Bible is understood as a complex series of books, which require understanding and interpretation. Some parts can be seen as allegorical, symbolic, poetic and mythic as well as historical.

- Experience and reason can be brought to bear on interpreting its words, which do not need to be accepted literally, so, for example, not every Christian needs to follow the command of Jesus to 'Go,

▲ The Council of Nicaea 325CE is believed to have been the first ecumenical council of the Christian Church.

sell everything you have and give to the poor, and you will have treasure in heaven ...' (Mark 10:21b).

- There is room for discussion and agreement as to the meaning of certain passages, their context and application.
- The inspiration of the Bible does not depend on it being historically accurate, but on the agreement of the Church. This means that people who take this view can neatly avoid arguments about who came first, Adam or the dinosaurs.

The disadvantages include:

- Christian groups have sometimes upset others by choosing to add to or disregard instructions given in the Bible.
- A 'pick and choose' attitude to some less easy biblical teachings is possible. For example, the Virgin Birth or the Resurrection are not seen as literal, physical events, and some Christians do not like the idea of seeing them as 'spiritual' rather than physical truths. This can lead to radical differences in belief, which can be interpreted as inconsistency.
- Scholars can be hampered in their examination of difficult issues or passages of scripture by fears that they will get into trouble from Church leaders. Hans Küng, a leading Roman Catholic theologian, had his licence to teach revoked by the *magisterium* of the Church after disagreeing with Catholic teaching on the nature of the Church. More recently, Lavinia Byrne, a well-known Roman Catholic broadcaster and writer, left her order of nuns after 25 years because when her book *Women at the Altar,* discussing the role of women in the Church, was published in 1994, the Archbishop of St Paul and Minneapolis, with the support of Rome, demanded its withdrawal, as it was not in line with Catholic teaching.

▲ Literalist Christians find difficulty with the claims of science that fossil evidence, such as this *Velociraptor* fossil, appears to cast doubt on the truth of the biblical stories of creation.

The literalist view

Many Protestant Churches and charismatic Christians hold this view. Contrary to some people's belief, seeing the Bible as literally accurate is not an ancient method of viewing the authority of the Bible. Neither Martin Luther nor St Augustine would have recognised it. It came about as a reaction to the Age of Enlightenment and the rise of modern science in the eighteenth and nineteenth centuries. As people began to question religion and saw that scientific discoveries sometimes disagreed with religious teachings, some people began to question the absolute authority of the Bible. The growth of a literalist view was a reaction to this.

Christians who follow this view say that the Bible has **verbal inerrancy**: that means that every word was inspired by God's guidance of the writers through the Holy Spirit. There is no error and even though they accept that there is poetry and allegory in the Bible, it is mostly an accurate account of history – so Adam and Eve, Noah and even Jonah in the belly of the whale were real people who existed at an actual point in history.

However, the world has changed dramatically since the Bible was written and literalists have to decide whether to reinterpret certain statements, such as those about women or lending money on interest, in the light of today's society.

▲ St Augustine (354–430CE) (left) was one of the early fathers of the Church. Martin Luther (1483–1546CE) (right) was one of the great Protestant reformers. Neither of these would have claimed that the Bible was literally true.

▲ This is Mount Ararat where the Bible says Noah's ark first came to rest after the flood. There is geological evidence of a succession of massive floods in the Mediterranean.

Activity

Read the following biblical references and discuss how a literalist view might explain them:

◆ Exodus 22:25

◆ Titus 2:3–5

◆ Titus 2:9–10

◆ Corinthians 11:3–10.

This has led to radical differences in practice. Some literalist Christian groups, for example, refuse to adopt modern culture at all, including modern technology, preferring to create a society mirroring 'New Testament' times, which usually means the time in which the community was founded. The Amish in the USA and the Bruderhof community in Robertsbridge, East Sussex, are examples. Some maintain very traditional views on the relationships between men and women or what women can and cannot do in church. Others have decided to try to find 'biblical principles' to apply to present-day situations, rather than trying to recreate first century conditions in their churches, so that, for example women are often encouraged to contribute to worship, leadership and ministry, albeit under the auspices of male leadership.

The advantages of this way of looking at the authority of the Bible include:

- It is clear, and to some extent, consistent. Verbal inspiration is verbal inspiration, and no part of the Bible can be arbitrarily disregarded.
- It provides clear straightforward guidance on how to live a good Christian life.
- It is a good starting point for explaining the faith to others. If you have confidence in the text, then that confidence can be transmitted to others.
- It takes the Bible seriously as a historical record.

The disadvantages include:

- It is difficult to maintain; most people can point out inconsistencies and errors in the Bible, and so it makes the Christians who follow this view very defensive. An example is the Cleansing of the Temple which is at the beginning of Jesus' ministry in John's gospel and at the end in Mark's gospel. Many literalists say that this means he cleansed it twice.
- It is becoming ever more difficult to support certain aspects of literalism, for example creationism, when scientific evidence shows that the world was not created in seven days.
- The Bible, in literalist hands, has too often been used as a weapon, both defensively, to prove that people's personal opinions and prejudices are actually God's, and as an offensive weapon to deny the opinions and experiences of other people who do not share the same interpretation of 'God's Word'.
- It can lead to prejudice against women, homosexuals and black people, see for example the attitude of the Dutch Reformed Church in South Africa in the twentieth century who used the Bible (Genesis 9:18–25) to support **apartheid**. It is also prejudiced against people from other faiths.

The liberal view of the authority of the Bible

The liberal view of the Bible is that it records the experiences of people seriously seeking after God in their own lives, situations and cultures. The words are therefore a product of people trying to understand God. They do not believe that the scriptures are inspired and authoritative in themselves and there are mistakes in them.

Therefore, it is the duty of *individuals* to weigh what is found in the Bible and apply it, if appropriate, to their own lives as they seek in their path after God. The essential difference between this view and the last two views, is that there is no perceived need for a *total community response* to all parts of the Bible. The assumption is that the individual response is what counts although this can lead to problems.

The advantages of this way of looking at the authority of the Bible include:

- Scripture can be made more personal and relevant to the believer.
- Errors or inconsistencies of theology, fact or history are no major problem for literalists, as they recognise that the Bible may include human error and inconsistency.
- Advances in science do not harm the application of the words of the Bible significantly, as they are not considered to be 'God given' in themselves.
- It is possible to disagree over interpretations of, and even the value of certain passages of the Bible.

The disadvantages include:

- The Bible will no longer be an effective instrument for teaching, as it is the believer who decides the value of individual passages. People can easily agree with the passages that fit in with the way they see the world and disagree with those that do not. They do not allow their religious beliefs to challenge their lifestyle or change the way they live.
- The 'inspiration and authority' of the Bible are thereby reduced to a personal response to each part of it.

The 'conservative' approach to biblical authority

This view is held by many Christians in the evangelical Protestant tradition across a broad range of denominations. They would agree that the authors of the books of the Bible wrote under God's inspiration. People holding this view would accept that the authority of the Bible comes directly from God, and not through the Church. They would claim that when pronouncing on issues of morality and doctrine, Church leaders should test their pronouncements against the authority of the Bible.

They accept that there can be human error in the Bible, and they recognise that it is the product of the culture of its time, so some things considered acceptable in biblical writings can be judged as wrong today, for example, an acceptance of slavery.

Nevertheless, 'conservatives' would take a 'conservative' position on the authority and reliability of biblical texts, particularly when they claim to be transmitting history. They would see the Gospels as giving an accurate account of what Jesus said and taught, but many conservatives would be happy to regard the stories about Adam and Eve and Noah as being myths rather than history.

Activity

To what extent do you think it is possible for Christians today to live their lives exactly as the Bible says?

Research task

Choose one of the groups who have refused to accept modern culture such as the Amish, Hutterites, Mennonites or the Bruderhof and explore their lifestyle and why they have chosen it.

Discussion point

How would a literalist and a liberal view each other's approach to the Bible?

The advantages of this way of looking at the authority of the Bible include:

- It takes seriously the historical claims of the Bible.
- The belief in divine inspiration will stop the believer from ignoring certain parts or passages in the Bible simply because they do not like them.

The disadvantages include:

- There are no clear guidelines about what is 'binding' and what is not.
- The believer still uses much personal judgement in deciding what is relevant and what is not.
- Seeing the Bible as inspired may stop some 'conservative' believers from taking a critical approach to it.

The secular view of the authority of the Bible

Many atheists and humanists would find much biblical moral teaching valuable, but would interpret it as being the product of human wisdom and experience, rather than divine revelation. They may see Jesus as an inspirational human being, but not as the Son of God.

Atheists, in particular, would reject the divine inspiration of the Bible, as they see no need of God for the universe to exist. They would also argue that religions, while they may have had their place in the past, are now destructive to human progress and happiness. They believe religion limits the 'spirit of enquiry' and quest for knowledge, and that it forces individuals and societies to conform to a set of outdated rules.

The supernatural elements of the Bible are seen as stories or, at best, myths to be rejected in the light of modern science. They only show how religion encourages people to be gullible and look for help to a non-existent deity rather than relying on themselves to solve problems and increase human happiness.

The significance and importance of the Bible for Christians

The Bible is the most important and holy book for Christians. They try to understand the message of the Bible and live their lives according to its teachings. In every church service there are readings from the Bible and usually the sermon explores and explains the teachings in the passage that has been read. During the eucharist there are usually three readings: one from the Old Testament, one from an Epistle or from the book of Revelation and one from the Gospels. A psalm is often read or sung as well.

The Bible usually has a special place of importance in a church. It is often kept on a special stand called a lectern (see page 35).

Some Christians read the Bible at home every day, and use it to pray. They may do this alone or as a family. Other Christians might

Activity

Create a table showing the similarities and differences between the different views of the authority of the Bible on pages 79–80.

Discussion point

The *Harry Potter* books have been hugely popular in dozens of languages all over the world. Should the author, J.K. Rowling, receive the credit for this, or do you think her translators also had a creative role? What might this mean for translations of the Bible and other sacred texts?

meet together in Bible study groups to read and study passages from the Bible together (see page 32).

Christians believe that the Bible contains the teachings they need to understand God and follow Jesus.

Different translations of the Bible

The Old Testament was written mostly in Hebrew, with some books in Aramaic, and the New Testament was written in Greek. The earliest translations of parts of the Bible were in Coptic, Syriac and Gothic and then in the fifth century St Jerome translated it into Latin. The first translations into English were in the seventh century. So, from very early in the Church's history the Bible was translated, but most of the translations used the Latin version. The Bible in its original languages was not translated until the sixteenth century by William Tyndale (1494–1536). He felt it was important that ordinary people could read the Bible for themselves and in spite of opposition from Church leaders (who had Tyndale strangled and then burnt at the stake), translations continued. Finally when James VI of Scotland became James I of England he authorised a new translation called the King James Bible which has become the basis of many translations since then.

Today, Christians feel it is vital that everyone should be able to read the Bible in their own language, and some languages have even been written down for the first time so that translators could write the Bible in them. Christians feel that it is a good thing that the Bible is translated into many languages, but that it is important that these versions are faithful to the original Hebrew and Greek so that the original meaning is not lost.

▲ William Tyndale, translator of the Bible into English in the sixteenth century, was arrested in Antwerp (now in Belgium), strangled then burnt in 1536.

God reveals himself in the teachings of the Church

Most Christians do accept the Bible as a source of authority, but some would also include the teachings and traditions of the Church. This is especially useful, some would say, when considering ethical issues, as many of these issues (for example abortion, **euthanasia** and test-tube conception) were not addressed in the Bible. This means that general principles from the Bible need to be used and applied to the issues in order to get some guidance. As we have seen in some traditions it is down to the individual to work out what the Bible would teach, but in others, especially the Catholic Church, the cardinals, bishops and the Pope decide the teachings. So Catholics would follow the decisions made by the leaders and the Church Councils as a source of authority and a way in which God reveals himself to the Church.

One of the most important events in which the Catholic Church made these decisions was in the 1960s when the leaders met to reconsider the teachings of the Church in light of the changes in the modern world. This meeting was called **Vatican II** (the second Vatican Council) and many hundreds of Church leaders from all over the world met in Rome. This meeting was called by Pope John XXIII and the conservatives and liberals within the Church worshipped and

▲ Pope John XXIII being carried to the second Vatican Council in Rome in 1962.

Activity

At Vatican II, Pope John XXIII said: 'It is our duty not only to guard this precious treasure, as if interested only in antiquity, but also to devote ourselves readily and fearlessly to the work our age requires.'

1 What do you think he meant by 'this precious treasure'?

2 What viewpoint do you think he was criticising when he talked of those 'interested only in antiquity'?

3 Explain what this quote suggests about the significance of the Bible to Roman Catholics.

prayed together before discussing the documents which were drafted and redrafted over four years.

The topics discussed included the use of Latin or local languages for worship, the study of the Bible, marriage, racism and many different social teachings. The Church has continued to update the teachings as the world continues to change and new issues such as genetically modified crops and the use of **stem cells** arise.

Exam practice

Explain why believing that the Bible is the actual Word of God is more important to some Christians than to others. *(6 marks)*

You could write that belief in the divine inspiration of the Bible might mean that some Christians would try to live completely in accordance with its teachings and so lead more prayerful and holy lives.

You may say that in doing so they may make constant reference to the Bible and its teachings in order to ensure that they are doing God's will. You could also write about how Christians may make moral decisions by making reference to Bible teachings.

You should also include detail about how the Bible is seen as the Word of God slightly differently by different groups of Christians.

Exam practice

Explain how believing that the Bible is the Word of God might affect the lives of Christians. *(6 marks)*

Your answer might include the suggestion that:
- *Christians might read the Bible regularly*
- *Christians might read and study the Bible together in groups*
- *Christians would look to the Bible for help in times of difficulty; you might give an example such as bereavement. (Look back at Chapter 4, page 61 for more on this)*
- *Christians would see the Bible as a source of encouragement and hope*
- *the Bible would help Christians make ethical decisions: again you might give an example such as abortion and the sanctity of life*
- *the Bible would be treated with respect and as a higher source of authority than other books.*

You might also consider the effects of believing the Bible literally, and the difficulties this might cause.

Religion, reason and revelation: Looking at Exam Questions

Each question has **five** parts (a–e), and you need to answer all the parts. You will only answer **one** question on each topic. There is a total of **24** marks for each question.

(a) What does the word 'revelation' mean?
(1 mark)

You could simply say that it is information which is given to people and which may be surprising or valuable.

(b) What is meant by scriptures or sacred texts?
(2 marks)

Again you only need a simple answer, such as that scriptures or sacred texts are religious writings which are revealed by God. Or you could say that they are writings that are believed to be the Word of God.

(c) What do Christians mean by revelation?
(3 marks)

You could start by explaining the difference between general and special revelation. You may describe the Bible as being the revealed Word of God, and what this means for Christians. You might also say that Christians accept the Bible as truth because it was revealed. Or you might talk about the different types of revelation through mystical and religious experience, perhaps using Julian of Norwich as an example. You may explain the idea of God's revelation through the world. Or you may choose to explain how God reveals himself in the person of Jesus, and how Christians see the life, teachings, death and resurrection of Jesus as a direct revelation of God.

(d) Explain the importance for Christians of their sacred texts.
(6 marks)

You might explain that Christians would read the Bible often and regularly and that they would use it in times of difficulty to give them encouragement and hope; or that it could also be used to provide guidance especially over ethical issues. You could include an example here, perhaps one you have looked at in one of your ethical topics.

You could explain how the Bible is used in Christian worship by the different Christian denominations. You could say that the Bible would be treated with respect and as a more important source of authority than other books. You might also consider the effects of believing the Bible literally, and the difficulties this might cause.

(e) 'Sacred texts are too old to be useful.'

Discuss this statement. You should include different, supported points of view and a personal viewpoint. You must refer to Christianity in your answer. *(12 marks)*

You might consider what 'useful' means, and for whom they are useful. You may conclude that they are too old as many of the situations in which people find themselves today are not addressed by the Bible.

On the other hand you may argue that because the Bible is sacred for Christians and that they believe it is the Word of God, that its writings and teachings will always be useful as they tell the Christian about God and how he wants people to live.

You could argue that even for an atheist or agnostic many of the teachings are very general and just help people lead a good life whatever their situation or beliefs.

6 Religion and science

This chapter will help you answer questions on:

◆ Scientific theories about the origins of the world and humanity
◆ What some Christians believe about the origins of the world and humanity
◆ The relationship between scientific and Christian understandings of the origins of the world and humanity
◆ What Christians believe about the relationship between humanity and animals
◆ Attitudes to animals and their treatment
◆ What Christians believe about stewardship and environmental issues

Introduction

It is a shared belief among most of the world's religions that God or the gods created the world and the life on it. A number of religions include these stories in their sacred writings and others in their oral traditions. However, few religions, if any, claim that there were any humans present at the time of creation and therefore these cannot be first-hand human accounts of the events. There are many similarities between some of the creation stories which might suggest a common heritage or origin, but there are also some very significant differences.

How life and the world came into existence is one of the big questions that has always concerned religious believers. It is one of the questions to which religions try to provide an answer and, for Christians, this lies in the first three chapters of the book of Genesis.

Research task

Briefly research creation stories from three religions other than Christianity. What do they have in common? What is different between them?

The cosmic turtle. In the Hindu creation story the universe was supported by a giant turtle. ▶

Scientific theories about the origins of the world and humanity

This topic will help you answer questions on:

- Scientific theories about the origins of the world and humanity
- What some Christians believe about the origins of the world and humanity
- The relationship between scientific and Christian understandings of the origins of the world and humanity

Cosmology and evolution are the two sciences that have proposed theories of these origins and which have also been seen as a threat to religious belief by some.

Cosmology is concerned with the origins of the universe. It is based on science not religious belief and so is not concerned with ideas about God creating the universe but with theories such as the Big Bang. The Big Bang theory suggests that there was a massive explosion about 18 billion years ago and that this led to the creation of the whole universe. As the gases and matter released by the explosion began to cool, the individual stars and planets of the galaxies were formed. Evidence that appears to confirm this theory is being found by the use of the most modern high-powered telescopes. Of course, the Big Bang theory does not tell us whether there is anything unique about the earth itself or whether life exists on any other planet in the universe.

The origins of life and of humanity are considered by the theory of evolution. In 1740 a Swiss naturalist called Charles Bonnet (1720–93) completed and published a scientific paper about aphids (small plant-eating insects). He argued that aphids carried future generations inside themselves. This process he called 'preformationism'. There were other thinkers who had also set out theories of how animals might evolve to be better suited to their environment: how giraffes stretched to reach high leaves until they had long necks for example. However, the founder of evolutionary theory is generally considered to be Charles Darwin (1809–82) because he presented a theory backed by a huge weight of evidence. In 1830 Darwin left England on a two-year expedition to chart the South American coast aboard a ship called the *Beagle*. He was not to return home until September 1835 having travelled around the world. In 1859 he published *On the Origin of Species by Means of Natural Selection or the Preservation of Favoured Races in the Struggle for Life*, based on the observations which he had made on this journey.

In this work Darwin suggested that life began with a simple single cell and evolved and developed into the variety of plant and animal life which is now on the earth. His theory was that animals and plants survived through a process of natural selection. Those which were best suited to the demands of their environment survived to reproduce more while those which were weaker did not. Darwin

Activity

Why do you think people were so angry about what Darwin wrote?

▲ A cartoon by André Gill, showing Charles Darwin (with beard) and the French positivist philosopher Émile Littré depicted as performing monkeys breaking through gullibility, superstitions, errors and ignorance, c.1867.

Exam tip
Remember that although most scientists would probably not support ideas of creationism or intelligent design, this does not mean that they do not have religious beliefs and many scientists are practising Christians.

believed that humans had evolved in the same process and that this meant they were not a special creation of God on the final day of creation. This theory also challenged the view that the earth exists for the benefit of humanity.

Understandably this theory shocked many people who could not accept that humans were evolved from apes. The simplest way in which to challenge Darwin's theory was by arguing that it was untrue because it disagreed with the creation stories in the Bible. People came up with extraordinary arguments to oppose his theory and a famous geologist, Edmund Gosse, argued that Darwin was wrong and that the reason that fossils of supposedly extinct creatures were found in rocks was because God had put them there to test the faith of Christians.

Science and religion were in conflict with the development of these theories. There are still many people who believe very literally in the stories of creation found in Genesis (even though the word translated into English as 'days' really means 'periods of time': created in six periods of time rather than in six days). These people are generally called 'Creationists'. Another problem is that Christianity has taught that the universe exists for the benefit of humanity, while scientists would claim that humanity evolved to suit the conditions of the universe.

A relatively new theory is called intelligent design. This says that God must have created the universe and all living things as there are particular features of these which can only be explained by an intelligent designer and not by evolution. However, there is so far no scientific evidence to support this idea.

Being a scientist does not mean that a person is an atheist. There are many scientists who are Christian. Many would argue that not accepting the creation stories does not mean that you cannot believe in God. They believe that God did create everything but that science has now explained how that happened in a way which is obviously more sophisticated than the creation accounts.

Christian teachings about the origins of the world and humanity

The book of Genesis contains two different accounts of the creation of the world and of humanity. Many scholars believe that the second account printed in the Bible is older than the first account. It is the first of these accounts that people usually quote:

In the beginning God created the heavens and the earth. Now the earth was formless and empty, darkness was over the surface of the deep, and the Spirit of God was hovering over the waters. And God said, 'Let there be light,' and there was light.   (Genesis 1:1–3)

These opening verses of the Bible are very important because they raise one of the key issues found in Chapter 4: good and evil.

According to the teachings of the Roman Catholic Church, this passage means that the world was created out of nothing – *ex nihilo*. God started the entire process of creation with a blank canvas and no materials. However, some other Christians believe that the raw materials of the world were already there when God began the creation. The text says that the earth was formless (had no shape) and was empty,

◄ Detail of mosaics from the Basilica of San Marco, Rome, showing the creation of animals from the Genesis accounts.

but it is not clear what this means. If there was nothing there at all then would the Bible say that the earth was formless? This may seem a very small matter to argue about but the importance of it is:

- if God created the world out of nothing at all and because people believe that God is good, then everything he created would also be good
- on the other hand, if God created the world from matter which was already there, then if there was evil present in that matter God is not responsible for it. Therefore, this might mean that God is not responsible for the existence of evil in the world.

The first account of creation shows God making the world in six days:

- day 1: light and dark – day and night
- day 2: land and water
- day 3: plants
- day 4: sun, moon and stars
- day 5: fish and birds
- day 6: animals and humans.

The importance of this passage is not how long a day lasted – the Hebrew word 'ayin' simply means a 'period of time'. Nor is it important whether it matches up to scientific studies about the order of creation, but that it shows that God planned creation and put everything in place, in order:

And God said, 'Let the land produce living creatures according to their kinds: livestock, creatures that move along the ground, and wild animals, each according to its kind.' And it was so. God made the wild animals according to their kinds, the livestock according to their kinds, and all the creatures that move along the ground according to their kinds. And God saw that it was good. (Genesis 1:24–25)

On the sixth day God creates human beings and places them in charge of the whole of creation:

Then God said, 'Let us make man in our image, in our likeness, and let them rule over the fish of the sea and the birds of the air, over the livestock, over all the earth, and over all the creatures that move along the ground.' So God created man in his own image, in the image of God he created him; male and female he created them. God blessed them and said to them, 'Be fruitful and increase in number; fill the earth and subdue it. Rule over the fish of the sea

Exam tip

When writing about the creation stories in Genesis remember not to use the phrase 'Christians believe these are true'. You can say that some Christians believe they are literally true but that many others think that they are myths.

Activity

Work out the similarities and differences between these two biblical accounts of creation. You could also compare the similarities and differences between the biblical and the scientific accounts of the origins of life on earth.

Discussion point

Look at the sentence opposite: 'Some people say that this viewpoint means that only one source can be right, either the Bible or science, but not both.' Do you think this statement is true? Give reasons to support your answer.

and the birds of the air and over every living creature that moves on the ground.' Then God said, 'I give you every seed-bearing plant on the face of the whole earth and every tree that has fruit with seed in it. They will be yours for food. And to all the beasts of the earth and all the birds of the air and all the creatures that move on the ground – everything that has the breath of life in it – I give every green plant for food.' And it was so. God saw all that he had made, and it was very good. And there was evening, and there was morning – the sixth day.   (Genesis 1:26–31)

In the second account of creation, humans are made before the plants and animals. This is the account of the heavens and the earth when they were created:

When the Lord God made the earth and the heavens – and no shrub of the field had yet appeared on the earth and no plant of the field had yet sprung up, for the Lord God had not sent rain on the earth and there was no man to work the ground, but streams came up from the earth and watered the whole surface of the ground – the Lord God formed the man from the dust of the ground and breathed into his nostrils the breath of life, and the man became a living being … .

The Lord God took the man and put him in the Garden of Eden to work it and take care of it … .

The Lord God said, 'It is not good for the man to be alone. I will make a helper suitable for him.'

Now the Lord God had formed out of the ground all the beasts of the field and all the birds of the air. He brought them to the man to see what he would name them; and whatever the man called each living creature, that was its name. So the man gave names to all the livestock, the birds of the air and all the beasts of the field.

But for Adam no suitable helper was found. So the Lord God caused the man to fall into a deep sleep; and while he was sleeping, he took one of the man's ribs and closed up the place with flesh. Then the Lord God made a woman from the rib he had taken out of the man, and he brought her to the man.   (Genesis 2:4–7, 15, 18–22)

This passage is, perhaps, more important than it at first seems. When God first makes the man, the being he creates is neither male nor female in the Hebrew text. The being does not become 'male' until the woman is created. Therefore neither of the creation accounts say that God created men first.

The relationship between scientific and Christian understandings of the origins of the world and humanity

The problems between scientific and religious accounts of creation are particularly significant for those Christians who believe that the Bible is the exact Word of God and that everything in it is literally true. Some people say that this viewpoint means that only one source can be right, either the Bible or science, but not both.

James Ussher, a seventeenth century English bishop, calculated the actual time of creation by working through all the dates and times given in the Bible. He eventually worked out that it took place at 9a.m. on 26 October 4004BCE, many billions of years after the date given by science.

Many Christians have resolved this conflict for themselves because they consider the creation accounts to be myths. This means that they contain important truths: God is ultimately responsible for the creation of the world and humanity, but they are not supposed to be factual accounts of what happened. A phrase often used to support this view is that:

> Science explains how and religion explains why.

Another argument which is often used to suggest that, however the world was created there was a guiding hand behind it, is found in the teleological argument and the story of the divine watchmaker (see Chapter 1, page 11). In fact the majority of people now appear to accept the Big Bang theory of creation even if they also believe that God was present and may have caused the Big Bang.

In the fourth century St Augustine said that this type of argument did not present a problem to Christianity because God must have invented time when he made the rest of creation. This means that time was relative to God and did not work in the way we understand it today where one period of time simply moves on to the next. So it would not really matter if the Bible chronology was at odds with the geological record: God's creation would have happened outside of time as we understand it.

Darwin's theory of evolution has also caused a problem for many Christians. It was not finally accepted by the Roman Catholic Church until 1996 and there are parts of the USA where it is still illegal to teach evolutionary theory in schools as, in some people's opinion, it goes against biblical teaching. These people find it totally unacceptable to believe that humans are evolved from the great apes.

Again it was St Augustine who, more than 1600 years ago, seems to have anticipated this problem:

> In the beginning were created only germs or causes of the forms of life which were afterwards to be developed in gradual course.

St Augustine's is a theory of gradual evolution and it is possible to put this in line with much of the biblical creation accounts as showing the gradual development of more complex species.

> **Exam tip**
> Remember many Christians do accept the Big Bang theory so do not say that it is a scientific theory which is opposed by Christianity.

> **Research task**
> Find out what happened at the Scopes (monkey) trial.

Exam practice

'If science is right then religion must be wrong.' Do you agree?
(12 marks)

In answering this question you need to explain that this is not a simple statement with two opposite views. You can say that some people do believe that science is right about creation and evolution and that therefore religion must be wrong. You might also say that for some Christians who believe that every word of the Bible is literally true, then they believe that science does not hold the truth. However, you should also explain that for many Christians who believe that the Bible is the Word of God but not to be taken as literally true, science does not present any problems as the creation stories were intended to be read as myths. You might also use the teachings of St Augustine to support this view.

People and animals

This topic will help you answer questions on:

● What Christians believe about the relationship between humanity and animals

● Attitudes to animals and their treatment

The place of humanity in relation to animals

In the first account of creation, the animals are made first and humans are created last and are told:

Rule over the fish of the sea and the birds of the air and over every living creature that moves on the ground.   (Genesis 1:28b)

In the second account it says:

Now the Lord God had formed out of the ground all the beasts of the field and all the birds of the air. He brought them to the man to see what he would name them; and whatever the man called each living creature, that was its name. So the man gave names to all the livestock, the birds of the air and all the beasts of the field.   (Genesis 2:19–20)

Here the human is given power over all the creatures by giving them their names. Animals are shown as clearly different from human beings. God allowed people to have free choice in the way they treat the world and may choose to worship and obey God. Animals were created in the same way as the plants but humans were different:

So God created man in his own image,
in the image of God he created him;
male and female he created them.   (Genesis 1:27)

They were created in God's image – *in imago dei*. This difference is also found in the second account where:

the Lord God formed the man from the dust of the ground and breathed into his nostrils the breath of life, and the man became a living being. (Genesis 2:7)

This passage is often interpreted as God giving a soul to humanity which again makes humans different from animals.

Attitudes to animals and their treatment

All over the world the majority of people are horrified by cruelty to animals. For many people this has nothing to do with religious belief. Non-believers, as well as religious people, feel that humans have a responsibility to care for animals and to treat them with respect. It is important to remember that animals can be useful to humans and are not just part of life as pets.

Many people are shocked when animals are used for sport such as with hunting. There are also protests over the wearing of fur coats with 100 million animals killed for this every year. However, it is important to remember that in some countries animals are shot for food and their coats are used to enable people to keep warm.

Activities

1 Are humans always more important than animals?

2 Could humans survive without animals? Could animals survive without humans?

▲ The French actress Brigitte Bardot is an animal-rights activist who has led a campaign to stop baby seals being killed for their fur.

Many people choose to be vegetarian because they do not want to eat meat and feel that it is wrong to kill animals for this purpose. Others would say that while some animals eat plants for food, some eat other animals. Being a carnivore or a vegetarian or vegan (someone who does not eat fish, meat or dairy products) does not necessarily have anything to do with whether a person is religious or not.

Many non-believers do feel that as humans are, in some ways, the most advanced species, they have a duty of stewardship for the earth and its life forms. There is disagreement among Christians about their attitude towards animals, particularly in relation to their use in scientific research. Many people believe that it may be permissible to use animals in medical research which may help to save human lives. However, most Christians believe that animals were part of God's creation of the world, even if they are seen as a lesser creation than human beings. Therefore, it is wrong to hurt or harm animals unnecessarily and this would include research on items such as cosmetics.

Activity

3 What arguments do people use to support hunting? How convincing do you think these arguments are?

Exam tip
Animals and their treatment is one area where people often feel very strongly about the issues involved. Remember that although it is right to give your own opinion and to support it you must also give other opinions and explain the reasons for them.

◄ A mouse used in an experiment to help research muscular dystrophy in humans.

Many people are also opposed to the use of animas for sport: in the UK over 13 million birds are shot in sporting activities every year. In recent years bans have been imposed on some forms of fox and stag hunting even though there are opinions that these are necessary activities to prevent other aspects of the countryside being harmed.

Many animals are slaughtered for food. However, raising animals to slaughter for food is seen by some people as wrong while others point out that much more human food could be grown from the land on which the animals are kept. Livestock also contribute to global warming through their emissions of methane gas (mostly through belching).

In Genesis, God gives different instructions about human food. The first is:

Then God said, 'I give you every seed-bearing plant on the face of the whole earth and every tree that has fruit with seed in it. They will be yours for food.' (Genesis 1:29)

After the flood this changes to:

Everything that lives and moves will be food for you. Just as I gave you the green plants, I now give you everything.   (Genesis 9:3)

Research task

Go to the website of the Research Defence Society (www.rds-online.org.uk) and find out about its aims and its justification for these. Now find out about the work of the British Union for the Abolition of Vivisection (www.buav.org) and compare the approaches of the two organisations.

So it seems that originally humans were to be vegetarians.

When it comes to medical research, animals are usually used for experiments which would be too dangerous or costly to carry out directly on human beings. In 2006 there were more than three million experiments conducted on animals worldwide and an estimated 50 million animals were used for these. These include a growing number of genetic engineering and cloning experiments which are taking place on animals. You can find out more about this topic in Chapter 8 (see pages 136–8).

One Christian saint who spoke out about animals and their treatment was St Francis of Assisi (1181–1226). There is a famous sermon which he is said preached to some birds (see page 42) and there are also other stories associated with St Francis. When he was given a large fish by a fisherman he put it back into the water and thanked God for its life. When he released a hare from a trap the hare ran up to him and he held it in his arms.

Many Christian Churches have also spoken out against the treatment of animals:

- Church of England: 'developments in science, medicine and technology' should be monitored 'in the light of Christian ethical principles'.
- **Methodist Church**: 'The universe as a whole is a product of God's creative and imaginative will. Men and women are to be stewards and curators not exploiters of its resources, material, animal and spiritual.'
- Religious Society of Friends (Quakers): 'believe that the air, sea, earth, forests, animals and ourselves are all intimately connected, and the way in which we treat all of those things reflects on ourselves and consequently on God.'

In 1986, at the World Wide Fund for Nature (WWF), Father Lanfranco Serrini, the Christian representative, said:

Every human act of irresponsibility towards creatures is an abomination. According to its gravity, it is an offence against that divine wisdom which sustains and gives purpose to the interdependent harmony of the universe.

Activity

Look at the statements from the Church of England, the Methodist Church, the Religious Society of Friends and the World Wildlife Fund opposite. Which ones do you think a non-believer would agree with and why?

Exam practice

'Humans were given authority over all life so they can do what they like with it.' Do you agree? *(12 marks)*

In your answer you need to consider the arguments that in the Bible humans are given power over all other forms of life in the Garden of Eden. You then need to explain what this authority means. You might explain how different Christians might interpret these teachings in different ways. From another point of view you might say that the fact that humans were given authority over all forms of life means that they have been given responsibility and are supposed to care for and protect this life.

Environmental issues

This topic will help you answer questions on:

● What Christians believe about stewardship and environmental issues

Exam tip
Stewardship is a very popular topic in exam questions so make sure that you understand it fully and can explain what it means both for Christians and non-believers.

According to Christianity, at the time of creation people were intended to act as 'stewards' (someone who looks after something for someone else):

Be fruitful and increase in number; fill the earth and subdue it. Rule over the fish of the sea and the birds of the air and over every living creature that moves on the ground.   (Genesis 1:28b)

This view is repeated in the Book of Psalms where it is made clear that everything in and on the earth belongs to God:

The earth is the Lord's, and all that is in it, the world, and those who live in it. (Psalm 24:1)

The Bible teaches that all life was created by God and Christians see this as making it sacred. Jesus did not say, as is commonly thought, that all life is sacred. For many centuries there have been discussions among Christians as to whether animals have souls. It appears that when God breathed into Adam he gave humanity something different from the animals; however this is not clear and Christians will try to show respect for all forms of life. In the New Testament Jesus taught:

Look at the birds of the air; they do not sow or reap or store away in barns, and yet your heavenly Father feeds them.   (Matthew 6:26)

Are not two sparrows sold for a penny? Yet not one of them will fall to the ground apart from the will of your Father.   (Matthew 10:29)

It is clear from Jesus' words that God cares about animals as well as people. St Francis also appears to have believed that animals did have souls. There are also other, early, teachings about Christians and animals and one of these is found in the New Testament Apocrypha (see page 56 for more on the Apocrypha). The *Acts of Paul* was probably written about 160–80CE. It tells the story of a young woman called Thecla who listened to Paul's preaching and wanted to follow Jesus' teachings. She was persecuted for this:

▲ The Bible shows that God cares for animals, but do they have souls?

> Then Thecla was taken out of the hand of Trifina, stripped naked, had an encircling cloth put on, and was thrown into the place appointed for fighting with the beasts. Then the lions and the bears were let loose upon her. But a she-lion, which was of all the most fierce, ran to Thecla and fell down at her feet. At that, the multitude of women shouted aloud. Then a she-bear ran fiercely toward her; but the she-lion met the bear and tore it to pieces. Again, a he-lion who had been accustomed to devour men, and which belonged to Alexander, ran toward her; but the she-lion encountered the he-lion, and they killed each other.
>
>   Then the women had a greater concern because the she-lion that had helped Thecla was dead. Afterwards they brought out many other wild beasts, but Thecla stood with her hands stretched towards heaven and prayed. When she finished praying, she turned about and saw a pit of water and said, Now is a proper time for me to be baptised.   (Acts of Paul, chapter 8)

Activity

Consider the story of Thecla and explain what reasons a Christian might give for the lioness defending her. Write a paragraph about what this account says about the sacredness of all life.

Religion and human relationships

Activity

In pairs make two lists showing what you think are the traditional roles of men and women. Then make two more lists showing what you think should be the roles of men and women. Compare the lists – what has changed? What do you think should change?

This chapter will help you answer questions on:

◆ Roles of men and women in a Christian family
◆ Roles of men and women in the Church family
◆ Marriage ceremonies and the ways in which the ceremonies reflect and emphasise Christian teaching about marriage
◆ Christian responses to civil partnerships
◆ Beliefs about the ethics of divorce
◆ Beliefs about the ethics of remarriage
◆ Beliefs about sexual relationships
◆ Beliefs about contraception

Roles of men and women in a Christian family and in the Church

This topic will help you answer questions on:

● What Christians believe about the roles of men and women in the family and in the Church

Roles of men and women in a Christian family

Even in the twenty-first century there are still many arguments and discussions about the roles of men and women both in religion and also in society in general. This can be over particular religious issues such as whether women can be ordained in the Church or other

A Staffordshire University student campaigns for equal pay for women, commenting that 'it is shocking to think that in 2009 women are still fighting for equality'. The Fawcett Society is committed to ensuring that this issue is not forgotten. ▶

non-religious issues such as men and women receiving equal pay for equal work or men opening doors for women or standing up to give them a seat on the bus or the train.

The majority of people, particularly in the Western world, would probably say that men and women are equal. However, some of these people would still argue that men and women are intended to have different roles in life and that they were created for different purposes. Some Christians might use the Genesis creation stories to argue that women have a lesser, or at least different, role to men.

In the first creation story, which is found in Genesis 1, it says that men and women were created at the same time:

Then God said, 'Let us make man in our image, in our likeness, and let them rule over the fish of the sea and the birds of the air, over the livestock, over all the earth, and over all the creatures that move along the ground.'

So God created man in his own image, in the image of God he created him; male and female he created them.   (Genesis 1:26–27)

What is meant by *imago dei* – in the image of God – is not clear. Some people believe this is a literal use of the word, meaning people look like God, whereas others suggest it means that humans are spiritually like God or that they have a conscience.

The second account in Genesis 2 and 3 is different. Scholars believe this second account was actually written before the one found in Genesis 1:

The Lord God took the man and put him in the Garden of Eden to work it and take care of it.

The Lord God said, 'It is not good for the man to be alone. I will make a helper suitable for him.'

Now the Lord God had formed out of the ground all the beasts of the field and all the birds of the air. He brought them to the man to see what he would name them; and whatever the man called each living creature, that was its name. So the man gave names to all the livestock, the birds of the air and all the beasts of the field.

But for Adam no suitable helper was found. So the Lord God caused the man to fall into a deep sleep; and while he was sleeping, he took one of the man's ribs and closed up the place with flesh. Then the Lord God made a woman from the rib he had taken out of the man, and he brought her to the man.

The man said, 'This is now bone of my bones and flesh of my flesh; she shall be called "woman", for she was taken out of man.'

For this reason a man will leave his father and mother and be united to his wife, and they will become one flesh.   (Genesis 2:15, 18–24)

For many centuries people have used this account in order to suggest that the reason the woman was created was so that she could be a companion and helpmate for the man. Obviously, this can be seen as putting women into a secondary role in society.

However, this view is based on translations of the Bible and does not take account of the original Hebrew of Genesis. According to the Hebrew, the first person created was neither male nor female and God then tried to find a companion from the other animals for this person. It is because he cannot find a companion for the person that he splits the person and creates the first man and first woman.

▲ A sinful woman (possibly Mary Magdelene) anointing the feet of Jesus.

Teach the older men to be temperate, worthy of respect, self-controlled, and sound in faith, in love and in endurance.

Likewise, teach the older women to be reverent in the way they live, not to be slanderers or addicted to much wine, but to teach what is good. Then they can train the younger women to love their husbands and children, to be self-controlled and pure, to be busy at home, to be kind, and to be subject to their husbands, so that no one will malign [speak evil of] the word of God. (Titus 2:2–5)

There are still Christians, and Christian denominations who believe that these teachings are correct today and that a woman should stay at home and care for the children and her husband. However, most people would probably take the view in Paul's Epistle to the Galatians that all Christians are equal whether male or female:

There is neither Jew nor Greek, slave nor free, male nor female, for you are all one in Christ Jesus. If you belong to Christ, then you are Abraham's seed, and heirs according to the promise.   (Galatians 3:28–29)

It seems that the New Testament is not consistent in its view of the role and position of women and that even individual authors, such as Paul, express different ideas in their writings.

Roles of men and women in the Church family

It seems clear from the New Testament that Jesus' disciples were all men even though some of the accounts of his followers suggest that there were many women among them. There are some books in the New Testament Apocrypha (see page 56) which suggest that Jesus did have women disciples and that Mary Magdalene was one of them.

In the canon of the New Testament there are also examples of women such as Priscilla and Lydia who appear to be in positions of authority within the early Church:

Meanwhile a Jew named Apollos, a native of Alexandria, came to Ephesus. He was a learned man, with a thorough knowledge of the Scriptures. He had been instructed in the way of the Lord, and he spoke with great fervour and taught about Jesus accurately, though he knew only the baptism of John. He began to speak boldly in the synagogue. When Priscilla and Aquila heard him, they invited him to their home and explained to him the way of God more adequately. (Acts 18:24–26)

The churches in the province of Asia send you greetings. Aquila and Priscilla greet you warmly in the Lord, and so does the church that meets at their house.   (1 Corinthians 16:19)

One of those listening was a woman named Lydia, a dealer in purple cloth from the city of Thyatira, who was a worshipper of God. The Lord opened her heart to respond to Paul's message. When she and the members of her household were baptised, she invited us to her home. 'If you consider me a believer in the Lord,' she said, 'come and stay at my house.' And she persuaded us.   (Acts 16:14–15)

After Paul and Silas came out of the prison, they went to Lydia's house, where they met with the brothers and encouraged them. Then they left. (Acts 16:40)

Activity

Explain Christian attitudes to the role of men and women in the family.

Exam tip

Remember films such as *The Da Vinci Code* are fiction. Do not use arguments from films like this to support your answers.

Some of the **Free Churches** have had women ministers for many years: Baptists since 1918 and Methodists since 1880, for example. The Anglican Church ordained its first women priests in 1974 in the USA and 1994 in Britain. However, there is a still a debate within the Anglican Church as to whether women should be allowed to be ordained as bishops.

The first woman bishop was the Reverend Barbara C. Harris who was consecrated as a bishop in the Episcopal Church in Boston, USA in 1989.

Neither the Roman Catholic nor Orthodox Churches allow women to be ordained ministers. There are many reasons given for this. It is argued that Jesus chose only men to be his disciples and therefore women cannot be priests. It is also said that, at the eucharist, the priest represents Jesus and that therefore a woman cannot perform this ceremony.

Until recently women were not allowed into the sanctuary of a church, the area beyond the communion rail where the altar is traditionally placed. The only exceptions to this rule were 'crowned heads', for example the Queen, and nuns. Part of the argument against women being allowed near the altar is based on the idea that menstruation and childbirth can make women 'unclean'.

Discussion point

Consider the arguments for and against women priests. What do you think is the answer?

◀ Bishop Barbara C. Harris (second from left) blesses the crowd after becoming the first woman bishop of the Episcopal Church in Boston, Massachusetts, USA in 1989.

Exam practice

'Everyone is equal.' Consider different Christian responses to this statement and also give your own opinion. *(12 marks)*

In your answer you need to give examples of Christian responses. You might say that because God created everything, that means that everyone is equal and is in imago dei *(the image of God). On the other hand you could say that not everyone is equal and you could give different reasons in support of this, such as are very good and very evil people equal or are disabled people equal, should they be treated in a particular way to help them to overcome their disability. You must also give your own opinion and support it.*

Marriage and marriage ceremonies

This topic will help you answer questions on:

- Marriage ceremonies and the ways in which the ceremonies reflect and emphasise Christian teaching about marriage
- Christian responses to civil partnerships

The family is at the centre of much Christian religious teaching and therefore the marriage ceremony is of great importance. This was stressed by Jesus in the gospels:

But at the beginning of creation God 'made them male and female.' 'For this reason a man will leave his father and mother and be united to his wife, and the two will become one flesh.' So they are no longer two, but one. Therefore what God has joined together, let man not separate. (Mark 10:6–9)

The marriage service of the Church of England as it appeared in the Book of Common Prayer (1662) stated that one of the purposes of marriage was:

a remedy against sin, and to avoid fornication [sex outside of marriage]; that such persons as have not the gift of continency [self-restraint] might marry.

The Christian Church believes that it is a sin for people to have sexual relations with each other unless they are married. This passage also suggests that marriage should only take place when people cannot manage to live **celibate** lives (not have sexual relations).

The marriage ceremony

The preface

In the presence of God, Father, Son and Holy Spirit, we have come together to witness the marriage of N [man's name] and N [woman's name], to pray for God's blessing on them, to share their joy and to celebrate their love.

Marriage is a gift of God in creation through which husband and wife may know the grace of God. It is given that as man and woman grow together in love and trust, they shall be united with one another in heart, body and mind, as Christ is united with his bride, the Church.

Marriage is a way of life made holy by God. Marriage is a sign of unity and loyalty which all should uphold and honour. It enriches society and strengthens community. No one should enter into it lightly or selfishly but reverently and responsibly in the sight of almighty God.

The priest then explains the importance of marriage: because Jesus attended the marriage at Cana and performed his first miracle there:

On the third day a wedding took place at Cana in Galilee. Jesus' mother was there, and Jesus and his disciples had also been invited to the wedding. When the wine was gone, Jesus' mother said to him, 'They have no more wine.'

'Dear woman, why do you involve me?' Jesus replied. 'My time has not yet come.'

Activity

Read the preface to the marriage ceremony and list the key points showing what Christian teachings believe about marriage, for example that it is a 'gift from God'.

▲ *The Marriage at Cana* by Andrea Boscoli, c.1580–5.

His mother said to the servants, 'Do whatever he tells you.'

Nearby stood six stone water jars, the kind used by the Jews for ceremonial washing, each holding from twenty to thirty gallons.

Jesus said to the servants, 'Fill the jars with water'; so they filled them to the brim.

Then he told them, 'Now draw some out and take it to the master of the banquet.'

They did so, and the master of the banquet tasted the water that had been turned into wine. He did not realise where it had come from, though the servants who had drawn the water knew. Then he called the bridegroom aside and said, 'Everyone brings out the choice wine first and then the cheaper wine after the guests have had too much to drink; but you have saved the best until now.' This, the first of his miraculous signs, Jesus performed at Cana in Galilee. He thus revealed his glory, and his disciples put their faith in him.   (John 2:1–11)

The other reasons for the importance of marriage are:

- Marriage is a gift from God because he intended men and women to live together.
- Men and women should help and support one another and be faithful.
- Marriage is for bringing up children.

These three statements show the particular importance of Christian marriage in that it was how God intended men and women to live and also they stress the important role of the relationship in upbringing of children in a stable family environment.

Activity

Compare the teachings of the marriage vows with what Paul says about women (see page 104) and then answer the following question: 'Women should always obey their husbands.' Do you agree? Remember to support your opinion with examples.

The vows

The vows you are about to take are to be made in the presence of God, who is judge of all and knows all the secrets of our hearts;
therefore if either of you knows a reason why you may not lawfully marry, you must declare it now.
The minister says
N, will you take N to be your wife/husband?
Will you love her/him, comfort her/him, honour and protect her/him, and, forsaking all others,
be faithful to her/him as long as you both shall live?

These vows are now the same for men and women, but in the past the woman made a different vow to her husband in which she was asked to promise to: 'obey him, and serve him, love, honour, and keep him in sickness and in health; and, forsaking all other, keep thee only unto him, so long as ye both shall live'.

The declarations

I, N, take you, N,
to be my wife/husband,
to have and to hold
from this day forward;
for better, for worse,
for richer, for poorer,
in sickness and in health,
to love and to cherish,
till death us do part;
according to God's holy law.
In the presence of God I make this vow.

▲ A wedding ceremony.

The giving of rings

N, I give you this ring
as a sign of our marriage.
With my body I honour you,
all that I am I give to you,
and all that I have I share with you,
within the love of God,
Father, Son and Holy Spirit.   (Common Worship)

One of the most important aspects of a Christian marriage is that, for Roman Catholics and the Orthodox Church, it is regarded as a sacrament. Although the Anglican Church says that the marriage is made in the sight of God and that the promises are made 'with' God it does not consider marriage to be a sacrament (see page 27).

The Roman Catholic and Orthodox Churches teach that there are seven sacraments: baptism, confirmation, marriage, ordination, reconciliation, anointing of the sick and the eucharist. It is because marriage is a sacrament that divorce is seen as such an important issue in these Churches.

In a Roman Catholic marriage the service is followed by a special eucharist called a nuptial mass. The fact that the couple are freely choosing to marry each other is stressed in the questions which they are asked at the beginning of the service in a Roman Catholic church. If one or other of the parties did not wish to marry this would make the marriage invalid and be grounds for an **annulment**:

And so, in the presence of the Church, I ask you to state you intentions:
   Are you ready freely and without reservation to give yourselves to each other in marriage?
   Are you ready to love and honour each other as man and wife for the rest of your lives?
   Are you ready to accept children lovingly from God, and bring them up according to the law of Christ and his Church?   (Missal)

> **Exam tip**
> Remember that the giving of a ring by the groom to the bride is an important part of the ceremony, as are the promises which he makes to her. The giving of a ring by the bride to the groom is not always part of the ceremony.

> **Exam tip**
> Remember you need to be clear which Churches regard marriage as a sacrament and which do not.

Activity

Consider the arguments for and against a religious marriage rather than a civil one.

◄ A nuptial mass in Seville, Spain.

Christian responses to civil partnerships

On 5 December 2005 civil partnerships became legal in the UK. These services, conducted by a **public registrar** in licensed premises, permit same-sex couples to have a formal ceremony in which they can make promises to each other and which gives them the same legal status as married heterosexual couples.

Civil partnership ceremonies, by law, do not have any religious content to them. However, the idea that homosexual couples are legally recognised by the State has caused problems for some Christians. Homosexuality is usually defined as emotional and sexual attraction to members of the same sex. Heterosexuality is attraction to members of the opposite sex. Some people believe that heterosexuals are 'normal' while homosexuals are 'abnormal'. Female homosexuals are generally referred to as lesbians but many homosexual men and women describe themselves as 'gay'.

Many Christians believe that the Bible is quite clear in saying that homosexuality or, at least, homosexual activity, is a sin. Some people believe that it was because of homosexual acts that God destroyed the cities of Sodom and Gomorrah in Genesis chapter 19:

But before they lay down, the men of the city, the men of Sodom, both young and old, all the people to the last man, surrounded the house; and they called to Lot, 'Where are the men who came to you tonight? Bring them out to us, so that we may know them.'   (Genesis 19:4–5) (NRSV)

The problem lies with the word in verse 5 which here is translated as 'know them'. Other translations of the Bible are different, for example the NIV says 'have sex with them'. Some scholars have argued that the passage only means that the people wanted to meet the guests, not to have sex with them.

In Leviticus it says: 'Do not lie with a man as one lies with a woman; that is detestable' (Leviticus 18:22). However, this is often seen as a reference to the practices of **idol** worship.

In the New Testament Paul appears to be very clear about homosexuality:

God gave them over to shameful lusts. Even their women exchanged natural relations for unnatural ones. In the same way the men also abandoned natural relations with women and were inflamed with lust for one another. Men committed indecent acts with other men, and received in themselves the due penalty for their perversion.   (Romans 1:26–27)

Do you not know that the wicked will not inherit the kingdom of God? Do not be deceived: neither the sexually immoral nor idolaters nor adulterers nor male prostitutes nor homosexual offenders nor thieves nor the greedy nor drunkards nor slanderers nor swindlers will inherit the kingdom of God. (1 Corinthians 6:9–10)

Again, some people have said that he was referring to homosexual prostitutes rather than homosexuals in general.

Over the years the attitude of the Christian Church has changed and many Christians would say that while homosexual feelings are acceptable because the person can do nothing about them, nevertheless they must live celibate lives because homosexual activity is always a sin. It is only the Religious Society of Friends (Quakers) who fully accept homosexual couples in their meetings. The Methodist Church has always been open to discussion of homosexuality but still states that it:

> does not consider that homosexual genital practice [homosexual sex] … is acceptable.

The Roman Catholic Church sees homosexual activity as essentially being masturbation, which it believes is always wrong:

Judah got a wife for Er, his firstborn, and her name was Tamar. But Er, Judah's firstborn, was wicked in the Lord's sight; so the Lord put him to death.

Then Judah said to Onan, 'Lie with your brother's wife and fulfil your duty to her as a brother-in-law to produce offspring for your brother.' But Onan knew that the offspring would not be his; so whenever he lay with his brother's wife, he spilled his semen on the ground to keep from producing offspring for his brother. What he did was wicked in the Lord's sight; so he put him to death also.   (Genesis 38:6–10)

This is the passage which the Church has used against masturbation. However, what Onan did was to refuse to marry the widow of his dead brother which was his duty according to Jewish law.

◄ Civil partnerships have been legal in Britain since 2005.

Discussion point

'Homosexuality is just as acceptable as heterosexuality.' Discuss.

Exam practice

'It would be better for everyone if people lived together for a time before they were married.' Do you agree with this statement? Give reasons to support different viewpoints.   *(12 marks)*

From a Christian view you might say that Christianity does not approve of sex outside of marriage and therefore people must not live together or, indeed, have sexual intercourse, until after they are married. From a secular view you might argue that people can decide for themselves what they want to do and that marriage is just a ceremony which gives a legal status to the relationship between the couple.

Christian beliefs about divorce and remarriage

This topic will help you answer questions on:

● Beliefs about the ethics of divorce
● Beliefs about the ethics of remarriage

In the Sermon on the Mount Jesus said that divorce was wrong and that the Old Testament rules about divorce were not strict enough:

It was also said, 'Whoever divorces his wife, let him give her a certificate of divorce.' But I say to you that anyone who divorces his wife, except on the ground of unchastity, causes her to commit adultery; and whoever marries a divorced woman commits adultery.   (Matthew 5:31–32)

This text is also used to argue that if people are divorced then they should not be remarried. In most Christian Churches divorce is permitted although Christians believe that they should do everything they can to try to help the couple stay together.

In 1981 the Church of England decided that although a person had been divorced this should not prevent them from marrying someone else in a church ceremony. This view is accepted by most Protestant Churches.

The Orthodox Church is generally opposed to divorce but does allow divorced people to marry a second or third time. The Church says that these marriages are performed by 'economy' – out of concern for the spiritual well-being of the people involved. However, the ceremonies for these second or third marriages are different and have a penitential nature, which means they include an element of being sorry for past mistakes.

The Roman Catholic Church has very strict views on divorce and remarriage. It accepts that people may get a divorce, which is a civil matter and takes place in a court, but this does not change their status according to the Church and they are still seen as married. This means that they can continue attending church and receiving communion. However, if they have a sexual relationship with another person or get married again in a civil ceremony they are not allowed to receive communion as what they are doing is seen as a sin.

In certain circumstances the Church may grant an annulment to the couple who wish to divorce. In order to be granted an annulment, which comes from the Pope, they have to obtain a civil divorce and then apply to their local bishop. An annulment says that the original marriage was flawed and therefore did not actually take place. In order for an annulment to be granted the couple need to prove that, for example: the marriage was not consummated (the couple did not have sex); that one or both of them was married already; that one or both was mentally incapable of knowing what they were doing; that one or both was unable to have sexual intercourse; that one or both

▲ The former Danish Princess Alexandra was married to her new husband Martin Jørgensen at the Øster Egede Church in Fakse, Sjælland, Denmark on 3 March 2007 after her divorce from Prince Joachim in 2004.

of them was forced to marry. However, if the couple have children, an annulment does not make those children illegitimate. Once an annulment has been granted the couple are free to marry again in church.

Exam practice

Explain why some Christians think that divorced people should not be allowed to remarry in church. *(6 marks)*

Here you need to explain that Christians have different attitudes towards the remarriage of divorced people. Some Christian denominations believe that the people should be given a second chance and may argue that Jesus taught forgiveness so therefore people should be allowed to move on with their lives and marry again. On the other hand there are many Christians who believe that, because marriage is a sacrament, the vows cannot be broken and so once people are married it is for the rest of their lives.

Beliefs about sexual relationships

This topic will help you answer questions on:

- Beliefs about sexual relationships
- Beliefs about contraception

Even though many people now choose to live together in relationships without being married this is not welcomed by the Christian Church. Some Protestant Churches receive cohabiting people (those living together without being married) to their congregations but still see this as not being what God wants.

The Roman Catholic Church is completely opposed to **cohabitation**:

> The sexual act must take place exclusively within marriage. Outside marriage it always constitutes a grave sin and excludes one from sacramental communion. Some today claim a right to trial marriage where there is an intention of getting married later. However firm the purpose of those who engage in premature sexual relations may be, the fact is that such liaisons can scarcely ensure mutual sincerity and fidelity [faithfulness] in a relationship between a man and a woman.
> (Catechism of the Catholic Church)

As well as stressing the priority of looking after any children in a relationship whether the parents are married or not, Christianity is also concerned that people should respect their own bodies:

Flee from sexual immorality. All other sins a man commits are outside his body, but he who sins sexually sins against his own body. Do you not know that your body is a temple of the Holy Spirit, who is in you, whom you have received from God? You are not your own; you were bought at a price. Therefore honour God with your body. (1 Corinthians 6:18–19)

†NBCW *Consultative Body to*
NATIONAL BOARD OF *the Bishops' Conference*
CATHOLIC WOMEN *of England & Wales*

National Board of Catholic Women

A Guide to the Annulment Process

(3rd Edition)

▲ The National Board of Catholic Women which advises the Bishops of England and Wales has published a guide to the annulment process in order to explain the procedure.

Christianity also considers the Ten Commandments in relation to sexual relationships. The seventh commandment, 'You shall not commit adultery' is often interpreted as it being wrong to have a sexual relationship with anyone to whom you are not married. Jesus expanded this further in the Sermon on the Mount:

You have heard that it was said, 'Do not commit adultery.' But I tell you that anyone who looks at a woman lustfully has already committed adultery with her in his heart.   (Matthew 5:27–28)

It is clear from these teachings that Christians believe that any sexual relations outside of marriage are wrong as God intended people to marry but not to cohabit.

St Paul remained unmarried and appears to have thought that the ideal was for everyone to be celibate:

Now for the matters you wrote about: it is good for a man not to marry. But since there is so much immorality, each man should have his own wife, and each woman her own husband. The husband should fulfil his marital duty to his wife, and likewise the wife to her husband. The wife's body does not belong to her alone but also to her husband. In the same way, the husband's body does not belong to him alone but also to his wife. Do not deprive each other except by mutual consent and for a time, so that you may devote yourselves to prayer. Then come together again so that Satan will not tempt you because of your lack of self-control. I say this as a concession, not as a command. I wish that all men were as I am. But each man has his own gift from God; one has this gift, another has that. Now to the unmarried and the widows I say: it is good for them to stay unmarried, as I am. But if they cannot control themselves, they should marry, for it is better to marry than to burn with passion.   (1 Corinthians 7:1–9)

Here Paul seems to consider that sexual activity is a very strong and dangerous thing and that people should protect themselves from it. However, some scholars have suggested that Paul thought that Jesus' return – the second coming or Parousia – would happen very soon and that people should stay celibate and wait for this.

In the Roman Catholic Church priests are required to take a vow of celibacy. The Church believes that if a priest was married he would be distracted from loving and serving God. While some people see this as a sacrifice which people make to show their love for God, others think that leading a celibate life can be unhealthy and could mean that priests are less able to understand the problems of their congregation.

The love which a priest should show to his congregation is called agape: this is a non-sexual love which is completely selfless and spiritual. Agape – often called Christian love – is shown in the teachings of the New Testament. A particular explanation is found in the first epistle of John:

Dear friends, let us love one another, for love comes from God. Everyone who loves has been born of God and knows God. Whoever does not love does not know God, because God is love. This is how God showed his love among us: He sent his one and only Son into the world that we might live through him. This is love: not that we loved God, but that he loved us and sent his Son as an atoning sacrifice for our sins. Dear friends, since God so

Exam tip
Make sure you can explain cohabitation and celibacy accurately.

▲ A Catholic priest from Africa.

Research task

Find out more about Christian beliefs about the Parousia. (You can find more information on page 21.) If Paul was expecting the Parousia to happen very soon, does that alter how we should view his statement on marriage and celibacy?

loved us, we also ought to love one another. No-one has ever seen God; but if we love one another, God lives in us and his love is made complete in us. (1 John 4:7–12)

Beliefs about contraception

Then God said, 'Let us make man in our image, in our likeness, and let them rule over the fish of the sea and the birds of the air, over the livestock, over all the earth, and over all the creatures that move along the ground.' So God created man in his own image, in the image of God he created him; male and female he created them.   (Genesis 1:26–27)

This passage from the first creation account shows the importance attached to human beings in creation. From teachings such as these Christians believe that life is a gift from God and sacred. Because of this belief many Christians feel that **contraception** (or birth control) is preventing a new life which God wishes to be born and is therefore a sin. Many others believe that the Bible should be interpreted for the age in which Christians live.

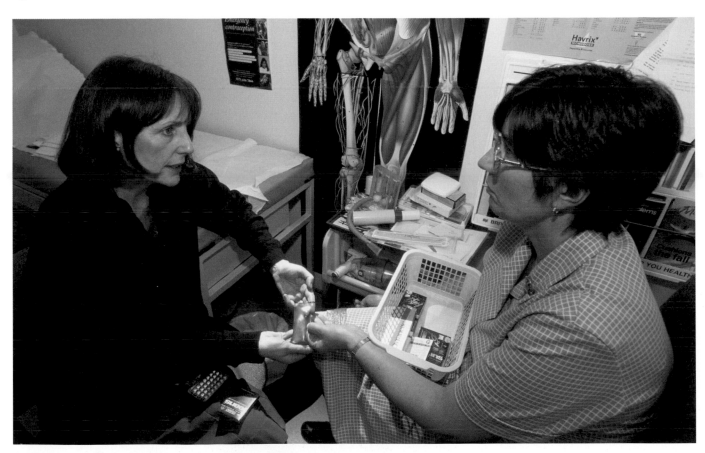

▲ Learning about family planning in a GP's practice.

The Roman Catholic Church considers that conception is a natural outcome of sexual intercourse and believes that anything which prevents this happening is wrong. It says that humans have an obligation to 'Be fruitful and increase in number' (from Genesis 1:28). This means that the Roman Catholic Church does not approve of any artificial form of contraception such as the pill, coil, condoms, diaphragm, anti-spermicide creams or pessaries. In particular, it is opposed to the so-called 'morning-after pill' (levonorgestrel) which it is believed works by preventing the fertilised egg from attaching itself to the wall of the womb. This is called an **abortifacient** because it may kill the fertilised egg. The Church views the morning-after pill as a form of abortion not contraception.

The only form of contraception which is permitted for Roman Catholics is the 'rhythm method'. Using this technique couples only have sex during the times of the month when the woman is known to be least fertile. This means that the method uses the natural cycles of the body and is not seen to be artificial.

The Anglican Church ruled that decisions about the number of children in a family and when they were born was a matter for the parents' conscience which is influenced by God. Therefore people should decide for themselves 'in such ways as are acceptable to man and wife'.

The Orthodox Churches do not have a single view about contraception except that abortifacients such as the morning-after pill are not permitted. Some Orthodox priests believe that sex is for procreation – for the purpose of making babies – and that even natural family planning is prohibited. Others say that natural family planning is acceptable, because it simply involves abstinence from sex during times when fertility is likely (abstinence from sex means deciding not to have sex). Others think that contraception is acceptable if it is used with the blessing of the priest, and if it is not used simply to avoid having children for purely selfish reasons.

The Methodist Church welcomes contraception as a means of spacing a family and providing fulfilment in marriage.

Discussion point

'Christian views on sex and marriage are no longer relevant and the Churches should recognise the relationships of people who have long-term relationships but are not married.' Do you agree?

Exam tip

Make sure you can distinguish clearly between different types of contraception: natural, artificial and abortifacient.

Exam practice

Explain Christian attitudes to the use of contraception. *(6 marks)*

In answering this question make sure that you do not confuse contraception with abortion.

You need to explain that many Christians, particularly Catholics, see one of the main purposes of marriage as the procreation of children and that contraception prevents this happening. You might then continue to say that some Christians believe that it is more responsible for them to plan their family and to make sure that they can properly support any children which they have.

'People should not have any kind of sexual relationships outside of marriage.' Do you agree with this statement? *(12 marks)*

Part of your answer can be that many Christians would agree with this statement entirely because of biblical teachings. You might then say that some Christians do not object to so-called 'trial marriages' provided that the people concerned are serious in their intention to marry if possible. You could also say that some Christians do accept homosexual couples and their relationships. From a secular viewpoint you might say that people would argue that provided no one else is harmed by the relationship it is up to the individuals concerned.

Religion and human relationships: Looking at Exam Questions

Each question has **five** parts (a–e), and you need to answer all the parts.
You will only answer **one** question on each topic. There is a total of
24 marks for each question.

(a) What is meant by 'marriage'? *(1 mark)*

In your answer you might say that marriage is a legally recognised relationship established by a civil or religious ceremony between two people who intend to live together as man and wife.

(b) Give two purposes of a Christian marriage? *(2 marks)*

In your answer there are several things which you could say; the most obvious are:

- *mutual support of the husband and wife*
- *procreation of children.*

(c) Name three key elements which might form part of a Christian wedding. *(3 marks)*

Here you can list any three elements from the wedding ceremony, for example:

- *vows made before God and the congregation*
- *exchange of rings*
- *blessings*
- *nuptial mass.*

(d) How may a Christian marriage ceremony reflect belief? *(6 marks)*

In your answer you might explain some of the following and how they reflect belief:

- *the importance of the vows*
- *the fact that the vows are made before God as well as the congregation*
- *the ceremony stresses faithfulness, and having children.*

(e) 'Divorce is wrong.'

Discuss this statement. You should include different, supported points of view and a personal viewpoint. You must refer to Christianity in your answer. *(12 marks)*

In your answer you might say that it is wrong because the married couple made promises to God in the ceremony and said that they would always stay together. You might also say that according to the Bible marriage is forever and the vows cannot be broken except in very particular circumstances. For another point of view you could write that Christianity teaches love and forgiveness and that marriages do not always work and that mistakes should be forgiven and divorce may be necessary rather than people being forced to be unhappy. You may also choose to write about annulment. Remember that you also need to give your own opinion and support it.

8 Religion and medical ethics

This chapter will help you answer questions on:

◆ Different Christian attitudes towards abortion

◆ The different reasons for these attitudes

◆ How Christians respond to issues raised by fertility treatment and cloning

◆ Different attitudes towards euthanasia

◆ Different attitudes towards suicide

◆ Why Christians have different attitudes towards euthanasia and suicide

◆ Beliefs about the use of animals in medical research

Introduction: the 'sanctity of life'

Christians often say that they believe in the '**sanctity of life**'. They mean that they believe there is something special and holy about life. For Christians, human life is different from other kinds of life, because people share something of the nature of God. The book of Genesis describes how God made Adam, and then 'breathed into his nostrils the breath of life'. Christians regard this as the giving of the soul (Genesis 2:7). In this creation story, this only happened with humans. Genesis also says that people are made 'in the image of God':

So God created man in his own image,
in the image of God he created him;
male and female he created them.   (Genesis 1:27)

Christians usually believe that this means that people are in some way reflections of God, and that in human life something can be seen of God himself. This can be seen in the example of people who choose to devote their lives to God's work in order to help others, such as the Grey Nuns and the Hospitalières.

Christians believe that each person has a 'soul', which does not die when the body and the mind die, but lives on after death. It is the soul that is judged by God, and which can join God in heaven for ever. They say that, because people have souls, they have to be treated as different from other species of animal. The Bible also teaches that God plans each human life.

For you created my inmost being; you knit me together in my mother's womb.
I praise you because I am fearfully and wonderfully made;
your works are wonderful, I know that full well.
My frame was not hidden from you when I was made in the secret place.
When I was woven together in the depths of the earth,
your eyes saw my unformed body.

All the days ordained for me were written in your book
Before one of them came to be.   (Psalm 139:13–16)

In the Bible there is the command not to take life; the biblical writers saw this as part of the covenant with God and his people:

You shall not murder.   (Exodus 20:13)

The belief that human life is special, sacred and holy, affects Christians in many ways:

- Christians believe that God makes each person, so everyone has value, whether they are newly born or elderly, healthy or ill, useful members of society or in need of care. This means that Christians should treat all human life with respect. Some Christians choose to become doctors or nurses because of their faith: they want to put into practice their beliefs about the value of human life.
- Because Christians believe that God has given their lives to them, they think that they have a responsibility to take care of themselves. They should do something useful with their lives, and should take care of their own health as well as the health of other people. For some, this means that unhealthy activities such as smoking and overeating are wrong, because they show ungratefulness for God's gift of life. In 1 Corinthians, a New Testament letter to one of the earliest Christian Churches, the Apostle Paul, one of the most important of the early Christian **missionaries**, writes:

Don't you know that you yourselves are God's temple and that God's Spirit lives in you? If anyone destroys God's temple, God will destroy him; for God's temple is sacred, and you are that temple.   (1 Corinthians 3:16–17)

Attitudes to abortion

This topic will help you answer questions on:

- Different Christian attitudes towards abortion
- The different reasons for these attitudes

An abortion is when a foetus is expelled from its mother's uterus before the pregnancy reaches 'full term' (usually 40 weeks). Sometimes this happens naturally and is called a 'miscarriage', or a 'spontaneous abortion'. However, 'abortion' usually means 'procured abortion', when the foetus is removed deliberately.

Procured abortions usually happen in the very early stages of pregnancy, within the first three or four months. In rare cases, abortions are carried out later; sometimes because the woman is young and too frightened to tell other people that she is pregnant; sometimes because, as the foetus grows, serious health problems for the woman or the foetus are discovered. Procured abortion is against the law once the foetus has been developing for 24 weeks (except in certain medical circumstances) because, after this time, if it is born it could survive.

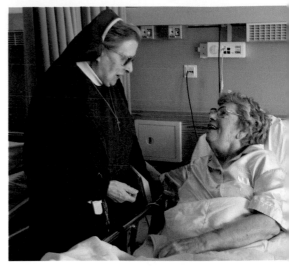

▲ Many nuns belong to nursing orders such as the Sisters of Charity. Sister Jozefta worked for 29 years at the hospital of St John of God, later the Medical Centre in The Hague, The Netherlands.

Exam tip

For the exam you need to know the meaning of the teaching of the sanctity of life. You will need to know how Christians might apply it to different moral issues.

Activity

Mind map all the ideas about the sanctity of life. Include in your mind map some of the difficult questions:

- Is the life of a foetus sacred?
- Is the life of someone who is severely brain-damaged sacred?
- When does life start/stop being sacred?
- Are some lives more sacred than others?
- Is animal life sacred?
- Is the life of a murderer sacred?

Add some more of your own. You will not find answers to these questions, but in this topic you will be able to consider some of the different Christian responses to these questions.

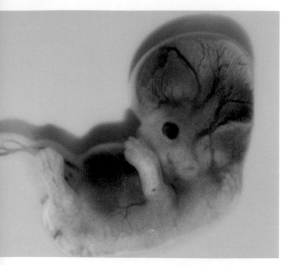

▲ A human foetus at the eighth week of development.

Abortion has been legal in Britain since 1968. The law was amended in 1990.

The law

The abortion must be carried out on registered premises.

Two doctors have to agree that it is necessary for one of the following reasons:

A: The life of the pregnant woman is at risk
B: The physical or mental health of the pregnant woman is at risk
C: The continuance of the pregnancy would involve risk, greater than if the pregnancy were terminated, of injury to the physical or mental health of the pregnant woman
D: The family and existing children will suffer if the pregnancy continues
E: There is a substantial risk that if the child were born it would suffer from such physical or mental abnormalities as to be seriously handicapped;
or: in emergency, certified by the operating practitioner as immediately necessary:
F: To save the life of the pregnant woman, or:
G: To prevent grave permanent injury to the physical or mental health of the pregnant woman

The law says that, in relation to C and D, the doctor can take account of the environment of the pregnant woman. From 1990 the time limit for abortions has been 24 weeks but A, B, E, F and G do not have a time limit. The Abortion Act allows for medical staff not to provide abortions if they have a moral objection to the procedure.

Different Christian attitudes towards abortion

Christians are divided about abortion. Roman Catholics are opposed to any abortion while some Protestant Churches may argue that it is acceptable under certain circumstances. The morality of an abortion must rest with the pregnant woman. Whatever she decides she must live with the consequences of her decision. Christians believe it is vital to offer support to all who face hard choices, regardless of what they decide. Christians should be concerned with enhancing life and relieving suffering.

Is the foetus a person?

Christian responses to abortion depend on whether a foetus is considered a person or not. Christians who think that abortion is murder believe that the foetus is a person, with the same rights and the same value to God as a child who has already been born. However, others believe that the foetus is not yet a person, only a 'potential person', and so its life is not sacred. Sometimes, people say that it is like an acorn and an oak tree; the acorn is a potential oak tree, but it is not one yet: it would be wrong to kill a living child but it is not as wrong to end the life of a foetus which is only a potential child.

Roman Catholics believe that life begins from the moment of conception, on the very first day of pregnancy. It does not matter if the life only consists of a group of cells, it is still a life. Many

Activity

There are many reasons why a woman might want an abortion, for example:

◆ the baby might be severely handicapped
◆ the pregnant woman might be still at school
◆ the pregnant woman might have split from her partner
◆ the woman might have become pregnant as a result of rape
◆ the pregnancy might not fit in with the woman's career plans.

Think of as many reasons as you can, and discuss whether an abortion is justified. Give your reasons in each case. After you have read the section on abortion come back to this activity and consider how Christians might react to these conditions.

Christians from different Churches agree with this. However, others believe that the foetus cannot really be described as a person until later in the pregnancy, when it becomes more recognisably human. Some believe that it becomes a person when it is capable of surviving on its own, at about 22 weeks.

Biblical teaching on abortion

In the Bible, there is not much teaching that is directly related to abortion, because it was not the common occurrence that it is today, although at the time of Jesus it was permitted under Roman law. The Bible does not use the word 'abortion' or deal with the issues directly, but many Christians use the Bible to support their views. They might point out that the Bible stresses the sanctity of human life (see page 118), where humanity is made 'in the image of God' (Genesis 1:26) and people are commanded not to murder (Exodus 20:13). This commandment is often taken to mean that it is wrong to kill except in cases of capital punishment or war.

Christians might refer to the book of Jeremiah when discussing abortion. God tells Jeremiah:

Before I formed you in the womb I knew you, before you were born I set you apart; I appointed you as a prophet to the nations.   (Jeremiah 1:5)

This could be used to argue that the Bible teaches that God knows and plans every person even before they are born. To prevent a baby from being born would go against God's plan. God is considered to have power over life and death:

Naked I came from my mother's womb, and naked I will depart. The Lord gave and the Lord has taken away; may the name of the Lord be praised. (Job 1:21)

This passage deals with miscarriage:

If men who are fighting hit a pregnant woman and she gives birth prematurely but there is no serious injury, the offender must be fined whatever the woman's husband demands and the court allows. But if there is serious injury, you are to take life for life, eye for eye, tooth for tooth, hand for hand, foot for foot, burn for burn, wound for wound, bruise for bruise.   (Exodus 21:22–25)

So the foetus is considered to have the protection of the law, but causing the death of an unborn child is not as serious as other forms of killing. The punishment suggested is a fine.

> **Exam tip**
> The commandment does not say 'do not kill'; it says 'do not murder'.

Church teaching about abortion

Some early Christians taught that abortion was allowable up to 40 days after conception for a male and 90 days for a female. It was believed that this was the time when the unborn child received its soul ('ensoulment'). This is not generally accepted now. Another early theory was 'quickening': the time when the baby starts to move in the womb. This is supported by the experience of John the Baptist's mother, Elizabeth:

When Elizabeth heard Mary's greeting, the baby leaped in her womb, and Elizabeth was filled with the Holy Spirit.   (Luke 1:41)

▲ Samaritans sign with phone number at the notorious Beachy Head suicide spot near Eastbourne.

Activity

Why might a Christian decide to apply to work for the Samaritans?

Discussion point

What do you think a 'good death' is? If you had to make a decision between sanctity of life and quality of life, which would you choose and why?

In the Bible, after Judas betrayed Jesus and had taken the 30 pieces of silver that he had been promised, he hanged himself. The Bible does not say whether Judas was right or wrong to do this.

Paul compared the body to the temple (see page 119). Christians might use this passage to show that the body should be treated as a place where God lives, and should be respected. It is clear from the Bible that human beings are not to choose when they die:

There is a time for everything,
and a season for every activity under heaven:
a time to be born and a time to die,
a time to plant and a time to uproot,
a time to kill and a time to heal ...   (Ecclesiastes 3:1–3a)

Most Christians believe that the right response to suicide is to be loving and forgiving. People who attempt suicide should be helped, not condemned. Christians responding to someone contemplating suicide may advise the person to go to the **Samaritans**.

The Samaritans is an organisation that was started in 1953 by Reverend Chad Varah who was working as a Church of England vicar in London. One of the first things he did was to conduct the funeral of a 14-year-old girl. She had started her periods, and did not know what was happening to her; she thought she had a disease and, too embarrassed to talk to anyone about it, she committed suicide. Chad Varah decided there was a need for an organisation where people could talk about their problems in confidence, not even giving their names unless they wanted to. This organisation had to be available day and night, whenever people needed help, including over Christmas when there is the biggest demand for their services.

Although Chad Varah was a Christian, the Samaritans is available to anyone, of any religion or none. The volunteers, who can come from any background or religious belief, do not give advice or tell the caller what to do about their problems, but they listen, and help people to work out their own answers.

There are many branches of the Samaritans in the UK and overseas. It is estimated that if all the volunteers were paid for their work it would cost more than £10 million a year.

Christians might also talk to people about their problems and read passages from the Bible about life being God's gift. They may quote Genesis 1 which says people are made in the image of God. They may quote Paul who said God had a plan for him as he did for all people. They should be compassionate towards them, as Jesus said people should help the sick and those in need:

I was thirsty and you gave me something to drink ... I was sick and you looked after me ... .   (Matthew 25:35b–36a)

Euthanasia

The word euthanasia comes from two Greek words: 'eu', meaning good, and 'thanatos', meaning death. Literally, it means 'a good death'. When people talk about euthanasia, they mean making the choice about when death occurs. Euthanasia is related to suicide, because it is about people choosing when and how a life should end;

either their own life, or the life of someone who is unable to make the choice. The difference between euthanasia and suicide is that euthanasia involves more than one person. As well as the person who is dying, there is someone else who performs the killing, or provides the drugs or injection, or withholds life-saving treatment, because the dying person is unable to commit suicide alone. There are different types of euthanasia.

- **Voluntary euthanasia** is when someone asks for the end of his or her own life but is unable to commit suicide without help. This is often called **'assisted suicide'**.
- **Involuntary euthanasia** is when other people decide that it would be for the best if someone's life ends, because he or she is not able to make that decision independently. They might have been in a coma for a very long time or be only a few hours old.
- **Active euthanasia** is when action is taken to bring life to an end; for example, a lethal dose of drugs might be given. This is against the law.
- **Passive euthanasia** is when a decision is made to stop giving further treatment, even though death will be the result. This happens quite often. It is not always easy to say whether some of these circumstances 'count' as euthanasia or not.

Euthanasia is a complicated problem because there are so many medical treatments to keep people alive. If someone is so badly injured in an accident that they lose the ability to think or feel, and there is no chance of recovery, they can still be kept alive for a long time. If a baby is born with severe abnormalities, it can be kept alive artificially. Euthanasia is about deciding whether it is kinder and more sensible not to do everything possible to prolong life.

There are many different circumstances that might lead people to think about euthanasia. If someone is suffering from an incurable illness which is causing pain and a loss of independence, they might think about whether they want to carry on suffering or die quickly while they are still able to say goodbye to their families and friends before the pain becomes unbearable.

The **quality of life** of the patient is often one of the main issues. If someone is enjoying happy relationships with other people, can communicate and is not in unbearable pain, then most people would agree that euthanasia would be wrong; but if the patient cannot communicate or is suffering so much that they cannot enjoy life, then some would argue that euthanasia might be the best option.

Some people believe that euthanasia should be legal. They say that it is unreasonable that fit people can choose to commit suicide, but that people who are not well enough cannot make the same choice. It is cruel to force someone to endure long suffering unnecessarily. Most people would have their pets put down if they were suffering from an incurable illness, so why should this same kindness not be allowed for humans? The Voluntary Euthanasia Society works to change the law to allow for people to make 'advance directives'; these are statements which tell others what the patient's wishes are in case they reach a stage when they cannot speak for themselves but want to be allowed to die.

Research task

Research examples of different types of euthanasia: online newspaper archives will be useful for this.

▲ Dr Jack Kevorkian was imprisoned from 1999 to 2007 because he was found guilty of second degree murder for helping more than 130 patients to die.

▲ An animal rights protest in London in 1999.

Activity

Explain the differences between the Christian views on using animals for medical research and the view of the animal liberation movement.

So while many Christians would be happy to eat animals, and would be supportive of some form of animal testing for life-saving drugs, they still believe that animals are God's creation and should not be allowed to suffer. However, many Christians do not approve of using animals in medical research. They point out that in the Bible God made his covenant with animals as well as humans and that both humans and animals have the same origin in God.

I now establish my covenant with you and with your descendants after you and with every living creature that was with you – the birds, the livestock and all the wild animals, all those that came out of the ark with you – every living creature on earth. (Genesis 9:9–10)

St Francis of Assisi said that animals 'had the same source as [himself]'. These Christians would argue that inflicting pain on any living creature is incompatible with living in a Christ-like way. Animals are weak compared to humans and Christ tells his followers to be kind to the weak and helpless so they should show compassion to animals.

Many Christians would follow their individual consciences as far as using animals for medical research. This approach is illustrated by the Religious Society of Friends (Quakers) who are divided as to whether animal experimentation should be allowed for medical research:

… as by his breath the flame of life was kindled in all animal and sensitive creatures, to say we love God … and at the same time exercise cruelty toward the least creature … was a contradiction in itself. (John Woolman, 1720–72, *Journal*)

Exam practice

Explain Christian attitudes towards the use of animals in medical research. *(6 marks)*

The question asks for 'attitudes' as it is difficult to determine exact teachings which relate specifically to animals. However, you may use some teachings in your answer. These might be Church teachings on creation and stewardship, or the ideas of the Quakers or St Francis of Assisi.

Your answer will probably concentrate on whether Christians think it is right or wrong to use animals in this way. You may consider that humans were given dominion over the rest of creation and so can do as they wish with animals who have no soul anyway, or you might see this as a responsibility rather than an absolute power.

You could explain that Christians may think it is better to use animals because some drugs, which are likely to aid human suffering, cannot be tested on humans.

Religion and medical ethics: Looking at Exam Questions

Each question has **five** parts (a–e), and you need to answer all the parts.
You will only answer **one** question on each topic. There is a total of
24 marks for each question.

(a) What is fertility treatment? *(1 mark)*

You could simply say that it is a medical treatment to enable a woman to have a baby when she cannot conceive normally.

(b) What are Christian attitudes towards fertility treatment? *(2 marks)*

You could write that some Christians are in favour of fertility treatment which would enable a woman to have children and fulfil the command to 'Be fruitful and increase in number'.

You could then say that some Christians say it is wrong as it interferes with God's work, and they are concerned about the spare embryos and the way in which semen is collected which they say is against God's will.

(c) What does Christianity teach about abortion? *(3 marks)*

You would need to show the difference in opinion between Roman Catholics and some Protestants about this topic.

You would need to say that for Roman Catholics it is always wrong except in cases of double effect.

You would also need to show that Protestants do not think abortion is a good thing but would allow it in cases of rape or, for example, where the mother's life is in danger.

(d) Explain Christian attitudes to the use of animals in medical research. *(6 marks)*

You could explain the benefits to humans and the importance of limiting animal suffering. You could use the idea of humans being superior to animals, humans being made in the 'image of God', and humans having souls.

You could explain the ideas of stewardship.

You could explain how some Christians see animals as of equal worth as members of God's creation.

It would be a good idea to support your explanation with biblical and Church teachings.

(e) 'Every woman has the right to have a baby.' Discuss this statement. You should include different, supported points of view and a personal viewpoint. You must refer to Christianity in your answer. *(12 marks)*

You could discuss whether a child is a right or a gift. You could use the command 'Be fruitful and increase in number' and discuss whether it is the duty of every married woman to have a child.

You may even discuss the right of lesbian couples to have a child.

You could include in your answer the cost and use of medical resources to help an infertile woman.

You may include a secular viewpoint that infertility is a medical condition that needs treating just like any other.

You need to make sure that you support your answers with biblical or Church teaching and that you include a personal viewpoint with reasons why you hold such a view.

Religion, poverty and wealth

This chapter will help you answer questions on:

◆ **Christian views of wealth and of the causes of hunger, poverty and disease**
◆ **Responses to the needs of the starving, the poor and the sick**
◆ **Biblical teaching about caring for others**
◆ **Understandings of 'charity'**
◆ **Different ways charity is put into practice**
◆ **Teachings about the use of money (e.g. gambling, lending)**
◆ **Giving to charity**
◆ **The concept of moral and immoral**
◆ **Teachings about moral and immoral occupations**
◆ **The impact of teachings on believers**

Christian views on the causes of hunger, poverty and disease

This topic will help you answer questions on:

● Christian views of wealth and of the causes of hunger, poverty and disease
● Responses to the needs of the starving, the poor and the sick

Activities

1 Make a list of what you think are the causes of hunger, poverty and disease among people. Discuss your list with a partner. After you have reached the end of this chapter look at your lists again and see what you would change or add to them.

2 'God is good so no one should suffer.' Discuss this statement. Explain your personal view.

3 Using an outline map of the world, shade or colour the poor countries of the world. How closely do these match the north/south divide?

One of the central beliefs of Christianity is that God is good. This goodness is sometimes described as omnibenevolence. It is reasonable to think that a God who is good would want people to be safe, happy and healthy in their lives. As God wants his creation to be happy and content so Christians believe that they also have a duty to make the earth a better place for everyone to live in. The truth is, of course, that many people are not happy, healthy or safe and that millions live in poverty and squalor, have no health care or education and have barely enough food to survive on. Many of these people are Christians. Many other Christians, particularly in the Western world, have lives which are the opposite in every way.

The divide between rich and poor is clearly shown between the northern and southern hemispheres, with the poor countries of the developing world in the south and the richer countries of the developed world in the north. Even within these countries however, there can still be enormous differences between rich and poor.

There are many different reasons why some people are so poor and live such terrible lives. At the time of Jesus many people believed that illness was a punishment for sin or a lack of faith in God:

Some men came carrying a paralytic on a mat and tried to take him into the house to lay him before Jesus. When they could not find a way to do this because of the crowd, they went up on the roof and lowered him on his mat through the tiles into the middle of the crowd, right in front of Jesus.

When Jesus saw their faith, he said, 'Friend, your sins are forgiven.'

The Pharisees and the teachers of the law began thinking to themselves, 'Who is this fellow who speaks blasphemy? Who can forgive sins but God alone?'

Jesus knew what they were thinking and asked, 'Why are you thinking these things in your hearts? Which is easier: to say, "Your sins are forgiven," or to say, "Get up and walk"? But that you may know that the Son of Man has authority on earth to forgive sins ... .' He said to the paralysed man, 'I tell you, get up, take your mat and go home.' Immediately he stood up in front of them, took what he had been lying on and went home praising God. (Luke 5:18–25)

This sort of belief continued into the Middle Ages when sinfulness was blamed for the plague. There are probably few people who still believe this although it is worth remembering that some religious leaders and some prominent politicians across the world referred to HIV/AIDS as the 'gay plague' and said that it was God's righteous judgement on homosexuals. Many of the instances of the poverty in the developing world have been caused by the way in which these countries were exploited for their wealth and natural resources by the rich countries of the West. This may not happen to the same extent in the twenty-first century, but control of the wealth and resources of the world still remains largely in the northern hemisphere, especially as more and more companies now operate around the world, and frequent **media** reportage of exploited workers, particularly children, shows that the situation has not changed completely.

It may be possible then to see reasons for some of the very poor conditions in which people live, but it is not so straightforward for Christians to explain or understand the natural disasters of famine, drought, floods and hurricanes which bring so much death and misery and this often to the people who are least able to survive these disasters. In the past it was thought that natural disasters were the work of the Devil. People believed that the Devil brought disasters on to people to test their faith. If things went very badly wrong and the harvest was destroyed by a storm it was possible that people would stop believing in God who apparently was not taking care of them.

Another view was that God allowed the Devil to tempt people in this way in order to show how strong their faith was. An example of this can be found in the Book of Job in the Old Testament (see pages 59–60). Today Christians are unlikely to think that natural disasters are the work of the Devil. Many natural disasters can be explained by science. However, it can be argued that the way in which people have exploited the environment in the last 200 years has brought about climatic changes that could account for many recent disasters.

Christians believe that God intended humans to rule over the earth: 'fill the earth and subdue it' (from Genesis 1:28) but not to exploit and damage it. Christianity teaches a responsibility for others, 'love your neighbour as yourself' (Mark 12:31a) which implies caring stewardship not domination.

▲ Rio de Janeiro, Brazil, is a city of extreme contrasts between rich and poor.

▲ The Fairtrade movement is one attempt to ensure that workers in the developing world receive better remuneration for their products.

141

Exam tip

Remember 'ruling' and 'dominating' are different and make sure you can explain the difference:
- Ruling means to have authority or control over something.
- Domination is often used to mean exercising that power over a less powerful being.

In 1948, the General Assembly of the United Nations (UN) signed the Universal Declaration of Human Rights. This declaration clearly establishes the basic rights to which every human being is entitled and which the member countries of the UN would work to establish:

The preamble

Whereas recognition of the inherent dignity and of the equal and inalienable rights of all members of the human family is the foundation of freedom, justice and peace in the world,

Whereas disregard and contempt for human rights have resulted in barbarous acts which have outraged the conscience of mankind, and the advent of a world in which human beings shall enjoy freedom of speech and belief and freedom from fear and want has been proclaimed as the highest aspiration of the common people,

Whereas it is essential, if man is not to be compelled to have recourse, as a last resort, to rebellion against tyranny and oppression, that human rights should be protected by the rule of law,

Whereas it is essential to promote the development of friendly relations between nations,

Whereas the peoples of the United Nations have in the Charter reaffirmed their faith in fundamental human rights, in the dignity and worth of the human person and in the equal rights of men and women and have determined to promote social progress and better standards of life in larger freedom,

Whereas Member States have pledged themselves to achieve, in co-operation with the United Nations, the promotion of universal respect for and observance of human rights and fundamental freedoms,

Whereas a common understanding of these rights and freedoms is of the greatest importance for the full realisation of this pledge …

The First Article of the Declaration is particularly important:

All human beings are born free and equal in dignity and rights. They are endowed with reason and conscience and should act towards one another in a spirit of brotherhood.

Christians might find that something they want would mean that they would be behaving dishonestly or exploiting other people:

You shall not covet your neighbour's house. You shall not covet your neighbour's wife, or his manservant or maidservant, his ox or donkey, or anything that belongs to your neighbour.
(Exodus 20:17 – the tenth commandment)

Research task

Some countries voted against the Universal Declaration of Human Rights. Find out which countries these were and try to explain the different reasons why they might have been opposed to it.

Exam practice

Explain what is meant by stewardship and how Christians might try to put this into practice. *(6 marks)*

You may explain that, at the time of creation, Adam and Eve were placed in charge of the world and everything that lived on it. As stewards their job was to look after God's creation. You could also explain that although they had dominion over all of creation, this does not mean that they should dominate it. Christians who try to help the less fortunate, those who care for the environment and for animal welfare are all demonstrating this stewardship.

Biblical teaching about caring for others

This topic will help you answer questions on:

- Biblical teaching about caring for others
- Understandings of 'charity'
- Different ways charity is put into practice

Teachings about caring for the poor, the starving and the sick, the outcasts of society, are found in the Old Testament and are central to Christian belief:

If one of your countrymen becomes poor and is unable to support himself among you, help him as you would an alien or a temporary resident, so he can continue to live among you. Do not take interest of any kind from him, but fear your God, so that your countryman may continue to live among you. You must not lend him money at interest or sell him food at a profit. (Leviticus 25:35–37)

One of the teachers of the law came and heard them debating. Noticing that Jesus had given them a good answer, he asked him, 'Of all the commandments, which is the most important?'
   'The most important one,' answered Jesus, 'is this: "Hear, O Israel, the Lord our God, the Lord is one. Love the Lord your God with all your heart and with all your soul and with all your mind and with all your strength." The second is this: "Love your neighbour as yourself." There is no commandment greater than these.'   (Mark 12:28–31)

> **Exam tip**
> Remember Mark 12:28–31 contains the two great commandments but they are not part of the Ten Commandments which are in Exodus 20:1–17.

In Luke's gospel, Jesus explained his mission to help the poor:

The Spirit of the Lord is on me,
because he has anointed me
to preach good news to the poor.
He has sent me to proclaim freedom for the prisoners
and recovery of sight for the blind,
to release the oppressed,
to proclaim the year of the Lord's favour.   (Luke 4:18–19)

In the Sermon on the Plain he said:

"Blessed are you who are poor,
for yours is the kingdom of God.
Blessed are you who hunger now,
for you will be satisfied.   (Luke 6:20b–21)

Some people have pointed out that in the sermon Jesus appears to be talking to people about future happiness and not an improvement in their present lives. Some have therefore compared this view with that of the White Queen in Lewis Carroll's book *Through the Looking Glass and What Alice Found There* (1871), in which the White Queen offers Alice 'jam tomorrow':

'I'm sure I'll take you with pleasure!' the Queen said. 'Twopence a week, and jam every other day.'
   Alice couldn't help laughing, as she said, 'I don't want you to hire ME – and I don't care for jam.'
   'It's very good jam,' said the Queen.

▲ Alice adjusts the White Queen's shawl.

143

Activities

1 Explain the teachings from Exodus and Matthew about interest.

2 What jobs would you have a moral objection to doing? For each one, explain why.

3 Make a list of jobs which might be considered immoral or moral and link each job to a specific Christian teaching.

Exam practice

'It does not matter what job people do provided they can support their family.' Do you agree with this statement? Give reasons for your answers.

(12 marks)

In answering this question you need to consider the teachings on moral and immoral occupations. You might say that a Christian would not agree with this statement because there are some jobs which go against Christian teachings and it would be sinful to do them: these might include gambling, drug dealing, prostitution, being a mercenary or even working on a Sunday. On the other hand you could say that their family is a Christian's first responsibility and that if these sorts of jobs are the only ways in which they can be taken care of then the person would have to consider their conscience. Or you might say that a Christian would pray to God for help and guidance in such a situation.

The lending of money at interest also produces different responses from Christian groups. This may be due, in part, to different teachings found in the Bible:

If you lend money to one of my people among you who is needy, do not be like a moneylender; charge him no interest. (Exodus 22:25)

Again, it will be like a man going on a journey, who called his servants and entrusted his property to them. To one he gave five talents of money, to another two talents, and to another one talent, each according to his ability. Then he went on his journey. The man who had received the five talents went at once and put his money to work and gained five more. So also, the one with the two talents gained two more. But the man who had received the one talent went off, dug a hole in the ground and hid his master's money.

After a long time the master of those servants returned and settled accounts with them. The man who had received the five talents brought the other five. 'Master,' he said, 'you entrusted me with five talents. See, I have gained five more.'

His master replied, 'Well done, good and faithful servant! You have been faithful with a few things; I will put you in charge of many things. Come and share your master's happiness!'

The man with the two talents also came. 'Master,' he said, 'you entrusted me with two talents; see, I have gained two more.'

His master replied, 'Well done, good and faithful servant! You have been faithful with a few things; I will put you in charge of many things. Come and share your master's happiness!'

Then the man who had received the one talent came. 'Master,' he said, 'I knew that you are a hard man, harvesting where you have not sown and gathering where you have not scattered seed. So I was afraid and went out and hid your talent in the ground. See, here is what belongs to you.'

His master replied, 'You wicked, lazy servant! So you knew that I harvest where I have not sown and gather where I have not scattered seed? Well then, you should have put my money on deposit with the bankers, so that when I returned I would have received it back with interest.

'Take the talent from him and give it to the one who has the ten talents. For everyone who has will be given more, and he will have an abundance. Whoever does not have, even what he has will be taken from him. And throw that worthless servant outside, into the darkness, where there will be weeping and gnashing of teeth.' (Matthew 25:14–30)

These two extracts have been used to suggest that, whereas the Old Testament does not approve of lending money at interest, Jesus thought that it was acceptable.

Although there may be some examples here of what occupations are not acceptable for Christians, moral occupations may be easier to explain. Most Christians would believe that any job which helped others, such as working in medicine or caring for the less fortunate, was suitable. To these may be added jobs which help care for the environment so that Christians are acting as stewards for God and protecting creation for future generations.

Religion, poverty and wealth: Looking at Exam Questions

Each question has **five** parts (a–e), and you need to answer all the parts.
You will only answer **one** question on each topic. There is a total of
24 marks for each question.

(a) What is meant by an immoral occupation?
(1 mark)

In your answer you have to say what an
immoral occupation is, not just give an example
of one. You might write that it is any occupation
or job which goes against general moral or
religious teachings. You might say that it is
something which might cause harm to other
people.

(b) What occupations might Christians believe to be immoral?
(2 marks)

Here you are being asked for examples: you could
write gambling, selling illegal drugs and
prostitution.

(c) What do Christians teach about concern for the poor?
(3 marks)

In your answer you might say some of the
following: you cannot be a true believer if you do
nothing for the poor; Christian teaching about
concern for the poor is exemplified in the teaching
of Jesus and the behaviour of the disciples in the
New Testament.

(d) Why might Christians give money to charity?
(6 marks)

Here you might include an explanation of
Christian teaching about caring for the poor; the
fact that charity has always been part of
Christianity since the time of the Deacons in
Jerusalem and before; that tithing or church
collections are practical examples of helping those
less fortunate.

(e) 'People must look after their family before they worry about the poor.'
Discuss this statement. You should include
different, supported points of view and a
personal viewpoint. You must refer to
Christianity in your answer.   *(12 marks)*

One point of view might be that someone caring
for their family goes without saying as a first
principle of life, regardless of religion. On the
other hand you could say that, certainly from a
Christian point of view, concern for the poor is
such an important aspect of faith that it must
override all other considerations.

Remember that you must include your own
viewpoint and support it.

10 Religion, peace and justice

This chapter will help you answer questions on:

- ◆ Attitudes towards war
- ◆ What is meant by the 'just war' theory
- ◆ Christian attitudes towards the use of violence
- ◆ Christian attitudes towards pacifism
- ◆ Reasons for these attitudes
- ◆ The concept of justice
- ◆ The aims of punishment
- ◆ Beliefs about the treatment of criminals
- ◆ Responses to the treatment of criminals
- ◆ Attitudes towards capital punishment
- ◆ The concept of social justice and injustice
- ◆ Beliefs about social injustice
- ◆ Responses to social injustice

Attitudes towards war

This topic will help you answer questions on:

- ● Christian attitudes towards war
- ● What is meant by the 'just war' theory

Activity

From memory, how many different wars can you name? Compare your lists with other students in the class and see how many you have altogether.

War is defined as a period of hostile relations between countries, states or factions that leads to fighting between armed forces, especially in land, air or sea battles.

In the past 100 years there have been very few days when war was not being fought somewhere in the world. War inevitably brings physical suffering and often in its ultimate form: death. Despite the many ways in which war appears in the media – news reporting, films and computer games – there is nothing glamorous about war and one of the main consequences of war is always suffering.

All wars are the attempt of one power to defend itself against another or to take something from another group which may be as fundamental as people's freedom. Although most people would probably say that war is wrong, nevertheless religion has developed two theories which could be seen as ways of justifying war.

Holy war

Holy War is an argument that it can sometimes be necessary to use physical violence in order to defend a religion. From 1101 to 1271 there were nine crusades. These were largely based on the belief of Christian Europe that it should take back the Holy Land from the governing Muslims.

These battles were often unsuccessful and frequently the crusaders did not even reach the Holy Land. As well as the great numbers killed, they also produced opportunities for looting and many relics and valuables were brought back by the crusader knights which had little or nothing to do with their mission.

Not all crusades were against the Muslims. The Albigensian or Cathar Crusade (1209–29) was fought by the Roman Catholic Church against a Christian group it considered to be heretical (it did not hold traditional Christian beliefs).

'Just war'

The idea of a 'just war' which is fought according to particular conditions has developed from the ideas of Cicero (106–43BCE), Thomas Aquinas (1224–74) and Hugo Grotius (1583–1645). 'Just war' theory has the following criteria:

- *Jus ad bellum*, whether it is right to go to war.
- *Jus in bello*, correct conduct during a war.
- *Jus post bellum*, conduct after the war.

Jus ad bellum

- There must be a just cause for going to war.
- The injustices suffered by one group must clearly be greater than those of the other group.
- Only a legitimate authority can start the war.
- The war must be fought with the right intention – material gain is not a just purpose.
- There must be a reasonable chance of success.
- Force must be a last resort after all peaceful means and negotiations have failed.
- The hoped for benefits of the war must be greater than the probable evil and harm it will cause.

Jus in bello

- War must only be fought against enemy soldiers, and civilians must be protected.
- The force used should be proportional to the wrong that has been done and the possible good which may come from the war.
- Minimum force should be used to limit unnecessary death and destruction.

Jus post bellum

- There should be just cause to end the war: the wrong has been righted and the enemy is ready to negotiate surrender. Or a war may be ended if it is clear it cannot be won.
- There must be no revenge taken.
- Peace terms must be made and accepted by legitimate authorities.
- The victor must ensure that any punishment is limited to the people who were directly responsible for the conflict.
- Any terms of surrender must be proportional to the original reason for the war.

▲ Detail from *Taking of Jerusalem by the Crusaders, 15th July 1099* painted by Émile Signol in 1847.

Activities

1 Research a war which has taken place in the past 100 years. Work through the conditions of the 'just war' theory and see which were met or not met during this war. Discuss your findings with a partner. Was the example you chose a 'just war' and if not, why not?

2 Do you think that any war can be justified?

A wounded British prisoner of war is stretchered to an ambulance by German troops during the First World War. Many of these ambulances were driven by pacifists such as Quakers. ▶

The purposes of 'just war' theory are to prevent war happening and to limit the effects of any conflict.

Pacifism

Many people, whether they are religious or not, believe that all war and fighting is wrong regardless of the purpose or eventual outcome. These people would be considered pacifists. Usually pacifists will never approve of fighting although there are some who might say that this is justified in self-defence. One of the best-known groups of pacifists is the Religious Society of Friends (Quakers). Although they will drive ambulances and provide support services under fire in the front line of a war they will not fight under any conditions.

Choosing not to be involved in other people's wars can sometimes be difficult. This poem was written by a Christian minister living in Nazi Germany:

First they came for the Jews
and I did not speak out –
because I was not a Jew.
Then they came for the Communists
and I did not speak out –
because I was not a communist.
Then they came for the trade unionists
and I did not speak out –
because I was not a trade unionist.
Then they came for me –
And there was no one left
to speak out for me.   (Pastor Niemöller)

Christian attitudes towards war

As with many religions, Christianity teaches that people should work towards a peaceful world and that fighting is always essentially evil. While some may feel that there are occasions when a war is just, others such as Quakers become conscientious objectors.

Activity

Explain why a Christian might feel that they should help someone from another religion.

In general, pacifists would argue that all response to war or conflict must be non-violent and that negotiations and sanctions (refusing to trade with a country, for example) should be used instead. Christians might also use non-violent protest such as boycotts and demonstrations to try to persuade other people not to go to war. A boycott is when someone refuses to take part in something, for example someone might boycott a shop because they thought that the products sold there were made by slave labour.

Christian pacifists argue that the Christian principle of agape – selfless love – means that violence is never acceptable (see page 98 for more on agape):

Greater love has no one than this, that he lay down his life for his friends. (John 15:13)

Dear friends, let us love one another, for love comes from God. Everyone who loves has been born of God and knows God. (1 John 4:7)

> ## Exam practice
>
> **'People should never use violence.' Do you agree with this statement? Give reasons to support your answer.** *(12 marks)*
>
> *In your answer you might start by considering what is meant by violence. Is it possible to be verbally violent for example? You might say that many Christians, such as Quakers, will not use physical violence under any circumstances because they believe that Jesus taught a message of pacifism. On the other hand you might consider whether Christians would fight in a 'just war' and why. From a secular viewpoint you should discuss whether non-believers might be pacifists and why.*

> ### Exam tip
> Remember that although Gandhi did preach a message of *satyagraha* (non-violent protest) he was a Hindu and not a Christian.

▲ Gandhi leading the Salt March protest to Dandi, India, in 1930.

Violence and pacifism

This topic will help you answer questions on:

- Attitudes towards the use of violence
- Attitudes towards pacifism
- Reasons for these attitudes

There are many occasions in Jewish scriptures where God orders the Israelites to fight wars in order to protect their promised homeland:

Then Moses went out and spoke these words to all Israel: 'I am now a hundred and twenty years old and I am no longer able to lead you. The Lord has said to me, "You shall not cross the Jordan." The Lord your God himself will cross over ahead of you. He will destroy these nations before you, and you will take possession of their land. Joshua also will cross over ahead of you, as the Lord said. And the Lord will do to them what he did to Sihon and Og, the kings of the Amorites, whom he destroyed along with their land. The Lord will deliver them to you, and you must do to them all that I have commanded you. Be strong and courageous. Do not be afraid or terrified because of them, for the Lord your God goes with you; he will never leave you nor forsake you.' (Deuteronomy 31:1–6)

This teaching is also found in the writings later in the Old Testament:

Proclaim this among the nations:
Prepare for war!
Rouse the warriors!
Let all the fighting men draw near and attack.
Beat your plough shares into swords
and your pruning hooks into spears.
Let the weakling say,
'I am strong!'
Come quickly, all you nations from every side,
and assemble there.   (Joel 3:9–11)

Sometimes people say that in the Ten Commandments all killing is forbidden. However, an examination of the original Hebrew shows that the sixth commandment is:

You shall not commit murder.   (Exodus 20:13)

Murder and killing are different and this can be seen in the next chapter of Exodus which lists the punishments for crimes carried out against God's instructions:

Anyone who attacks his father or his mother must be put to death.
Anyone who kidnaps another and either sells him or still has him when he is caught must be put to death.
Anyone who curses his father or mother must be put to death.
(Exodus 21:15–17)

This does not mean that the writers of the Old Testament were not looking forward to a time of peace in the world. Compare the passage above from Joel with this one from Micah:

'Come, let us go up to the mountain of the Lord,
to the house of the God of Jacob.
He will teach us his ways,
so that we may walk in his paths.'
The law will go out from Zion,
the word of the Lord from Jerusalem.
He will judge between many peoples
and will settle disputes for strong nations far and wide.
They will beat their swords into ploughshares
and their spears into pruning hooks.
Nation will not take up sword against nation,
nor will they train for war anymore.
All the nations may walk
in the name of their gods;
we will walk in the name of the Lord
our God for ever and ever.   (Micah 4:2–3, 5)

In the New Testament Jesus does seeming to be stressing the need for peace even though, at the time he was speaking, Palestine was occupied by the Romans and there were frequent outbreaks of fighting.

Blessed are the peacemakers, for they will be called children of God. (Matthew 5:9)

You have heard that it was said, 'Love your neighbour and hate your enemy.' But I tell you: Love your enemies and pray for those who persecute you, that

Fact box

Killing: the act of causing the death of a person or animal.

Murder: the crime of killing another person deliberately and not in self-defence or with any other extenuating circumstance recognised by law

◄ *The Destruction of the Temple in Jerusalem by Titus*, Nicolas Poussin, c.1638–9. At the time of Jesus, Jerusalem was ruled by the Romans. They finally destroyed the Temple in 70CE.

you may be sons of your Father in heaven. He causes his sun to rise on the evil and the good, and sends rain on the righteous and the unrighteous. (Matthew 5:43–45)

Although there are several occasions on which Jesus teaches the need for peace:

Then the men stepped forward, seized Jesus and arrested him. With that, one of Jesus' companions reached for his sword, drew it out and struck the servant of the high priest, cutting off his ear. 'Put your sword back in its place,' Jesus said to him, 'for all who draw the sword will die by the sword.' (Matthew 26:51–52)

And he touched the man's ear and healed him.   (Luke 22:51b)

There are two incidents in his final week in Jerusalem when Jesus appears to be angry and takes direct action. The first is when he curses a fig tree which has no fruit, and shows the power of faith:

Early in the morning, as he was on his way back to the city, he was hungry. Seeing a fig tree by the road, he went up to it but found nothing on it except leaves. Then he said to it, 'May you never bear fruit again!' Immediately the tree withered.

When the disciples saw this, they were amazed. 'How did the fig tree wither so quickly?' they asked.

Jesus replied, 'I tell you the truth, if you have faith and do not doubt, not only can you do what was done to the fig tree, but also you can say to this mountain, "Go, throw yourself into the sea," and it will be done. If you believe, you will receive whatever you ask for in prayer.'   (Matthew 21:18–22)

Activity

1 Evaluate the two events in Jerusalem. What do you think Jesus was trying to teach by his actions?

The other occasion was when he threw the traders and money-changers out of the temple in Jerusalem:

Jesus entered the temple area and drove out all who were buying and selling there. He overturned the tables of the money-changers and the benches of those selling doves. 'It is written,' he said to them, ' "My house will be called a house of prayer," but you are making it a "den of robbers".'
(Matthew 21:12–13)

Some Christians might say that the incident in the temple was an example of 'righteous anger' – what was happening was so bad that Jesus was right to express himself as he did.

Many Christians, seeing Jesus' example as being one of pacifism, have refused to respond to provocation with violence. A black American Christian, Rustin Bayard (1912–87) worked for the non-denominational Fellowship of Reconciliation and later organised the Congress of Racial Equality. Although working against any form of racial segregation, he was committed to non-violent pacifist agitation. He was an adviser to Martin Luther King Jr and organised the 1963 March on Washington for Jobs and Freedom.

Research task

Find out more about the life and work of Rustin Bayard. Why do you think he was such an important figure?

Dietrich Bonhoeffer (1906–45) was a German Lutheran minister who was killed by the Nazis for helping Jews to escape from concentration camps, and also for his part in a plot to assassinate Adolf Hitler. Although Bonhoeffer was a Christian and a pacifist [he had visited India to study *satyagraha* (non-violent protest) with Gandhi], he believed the atrocities in Germany had to be stopped whatever the cost.

Bonhoeffer considered the Germans' treatment of the Jews as an abomination. He joined the Abwehr, a group which planned to assassinate Hitler. The plan failed and in 1945 he was hung for treason at Flossenbürg. Bonhoeffer was tortured and led naked into the execution yard. With piano wire around his neck he was hung from a meathook. He died about half an hour later.

Discussion point

Although he had planned to kill another human being, Bonhoeffer is still known as a pacifist. Do you think that is right?

Forgiveness is still an important aspect of Christian teaching, even in the case of war, and it therefore is always wrong to treat prisoners of war badly or to kill anyone unnecessarily. This is based on Jesus' instruction to Peter:

Then Peter came to Jesus and asked, 'Lord, how many times shall I forgive my brother when he sins against me? Up to seven times?' Jesus answered, 'I tell you, not seven times, but seventy times seven times.'
(Matthew 18:21–22)

Activities

2 American soldiers have been accused of treating Iraqi prisoners badly in the war in Iraq. Why were prisoners being mistreated and what was the reaction around the world to this?

3 Discuss with a partner why Jesus said 'seventy times seven times'. Why do you think he chose this number?

Exam practice

Explain Christian attitudes to war and peace. *(6 marks)*

Remember that the question is asking for an explanation of attitudes towards 'war' and 'peace'. You must deal with both of these in your answer and you must explain the attitudes rather than just describing them. You could start by talking about 'just war' theory and the extent to which Christians might regard this as an argument that wars may sometimes be necessary. You might also argue that many Christians are pacifists because they believe that this was Jesus' teaching and therefore any type of war is wrong.

Crime and punishment

This topic will help you answer questions on:

- The concept of justice
- The aims of punishment
- Beliefs about the treatment of criminals
- Responses to the treatment of criminals
- Attitudes towards capital punishment

The concept of justice

Justice is defined as the maintenance or administration of what is just by the impartial adjustment of conflicting claims or the assignment of merited rewards or punishments. This explanation might be simplified to 'fair treatment for all'. In Christian teaching it is one of the four 'cardinal virtues' (important good qualities): prudence, temperance, fortitude and justice. The concept of God's justice is found in both Testaments of the Bible:

Your eyes are open to all the ways of men; you reward everyone according to his conduct and as his deeds deserve.   (Jeremiah 32:19b)

Anyone who does wrong will be repaid for his wrong, and there is no favouritism.   (Colossians 3:25)

The aims of punishment

The punishment of criminals or people who break the law can be said to have four possible aims:

- Deterrence – this may be applied individually to deter the person from doing the same thing again, or generally to deter other people from doing the same thing.
- Protection – to protect society and innocent people from harm from others.
- Retribution – so that society and the victims of crime can see that the person has been punished.
- Reformation – to give the criminal the chance to reform and live a better life.

The specific aims may depend on the crime or the person being punished.

Activity

Explain which is the most important aim of punishment in your opinion.

Exam tip

Make sure that you know the four aims of punishment and can explain each one clearly.

Beliefs about the treatment of criminals

Jesus' message is often seen as one of preaching love and forgiveness for everyone. Does this mean therefore that criminals should not be punished? Actually, many Christians would say that Jesus was preaching a true justice so that people were not judged and punished by those who were themselves no better than the accused. This is seen in the following story:

Exam practice

'Capital punishment should never happen.' Give reasons for and against this statement.

In answering this question you need to ensure that you give a balanced answer, however strongly you may feel about the issues. You need to be able to explain that many Christians are opposed to the use of capital punishment because it is the taking of a life and they do not believe this can ever be justified. You might want to say that many non-Christians are also strongly opposed to capital punishment for the same reasons. On the other hand you can say that there are Christians who feel that, for some crimes, loss of the criminal's life is the right punishment because it also prevents them from ever repeating the crime.

Social injustice

This topic will help you answer questions on:

- The concept of social justice and injustice
- Beliefs about social injustice
- Responses to social injustice

Activity

1 In groups write a list of unfair treatment in the world and a list of fair treatment. Which list is the longest?

Exam tip

Make sure you can explain, with examples, what is meant by social injustice.

The phrase 'social injustice' is often used when some people are seen to be **discriminated** against in a society and have fewer rights or benefits than others. These rights may be denied by individuals, businesses or governments.

Christian teaching is that social injustice is wrong because all life was created by God and is therefore equally valuable to God and should be shown the same respect. The prophets of the Old Testament and, in particular, Amos told people that they must fight social injustice:

This is what the Lord says:
'For three sins of Israel,
even for four, I will not turn back my wrath.
They sell the righteous for silver,
and the needy for a pair of sandals.
They trample on the heads of the poor
as upon the dust of the ground
and deny justice to the oppressed.'   (Amos 2:6–7a)

People are also told to have respect for foreigners (aliens):

When an alien lives with you in your land, do not mistreat him. The alien living with you must be treated as one of your native-born. Love him as yourself, for you were aliens in Egypt. I am the Lord your God.   (Leviticus 19:33–34)

These teachings are repeated in the New Testament, particularly in the letter of James:

My brothers, as believers in our glorious Lord Jesus Christ, don't show favouritism. Suppose a man comes into your meeting wearing a gold ring and fine clothes, and a poor man in shabby clothes also comes in. If you show special attention to the man wearing fine clothes and say, 'Here's a good seat for you,' but say to the poor man, 'You stand there' or 'Sit on the floor by my feet,' have you not discriminated among yourselves and become judges with evil thoughts?

Listen, my dear brothers: Has not God chosen those who are poor in the eyes of the world to be rich in faith and to inherit the kingdom he promised those who love him? But you have insulted the poor. Is it not the rich who are exploiting [taking advantage of] you? Are they not the ones who are dragging you into court? Are they not the ones who are slandering [speaking badly of] the noble name of him to whom you belong?

If you really keep the royal law found in Scripture, 'Love your neighbour as yourself,' you are doing right. But if you show favouritism, you sin and are convicted by the law as lawbreakers.   (James 2:1–9)

Many Christians take positive action against social injustice by joining organisations designed to fight for social equality. These might include: Anti-slavery International, the Howard League, Amnesty International or organisations working to help disadvantaged people such as Mencap.

Liberation theology

Liberation theology is a modern development in the Christian Church which is particularly concerned with issues of equality for all. It maintains that people who follow the teachings of Jesus have an obligation to take positive action to oppose social injustice and governmental abuse of power. Liberation theology has supporters in both the Protestant and Roman Catholic Churches. The work of liberation theologians is seen most clearly in Latin America and in some parts of Asia and Africa.

If the law of a country acts against the ordinary people in a way which can be seen as un-Christian then it must be opposed and, if necessary, broken:

The Spirit of the Lord is on me, because he has anointed me to preach good news to the poor. He has sent me to proclaim freedom for the prisoners and recovery of sight for the blind, to release the oppressed.   (Luke 4:18)

The leaders of the movement in Latin America believed that people were being exploited by the government and forced into poverty. They believed that this treatment of the poor challenged Christian teachings about love and concern and also showed that Christianity was being used as a means of pacifying the people rather than help them improve their condition. They decided that often the only way in which this could be challenged was by direct action against the governments and people concerned. This sometimes meant that priests were leading armed guerrilla attacks.

Two of the most famous priests of this movement in the twentieth century were Father Camillo Torres and Archbishop Óscar Romero.

Camillo Torres was from Columbia. He took part in armed uprisings and said that any Catholic who was not a revolutionary was living in mortal sin by not fighting for justice for the poor. Torres left the Ministry of the Church because it did not support him and he became a guerrilla fighter. He was shot dead in 1966 and buried in an unmarked grave.

Activity

2 What does 'love your neighbour as yourself' mean for the way Christians should lead their lives? How does it relate to discrimination and injustice?

Exam tip
Remember that liberation theology is not just limited to Latin America.

Activities

3 Are there any circumstances when it is right to use violence? Give examples to explain what you mean.
4 Building on the answer you gave above, do you think encouraging other people to fight for justice is the same as fighting yourself, or different?

11 Religion and equality

This chapter will help you answer questions on:

◆ Biblical teaching about equality
◆ Different views about prejudice and equality in relation to race
◆ Practices in relation to racism
◆ Different views about prejudice and equality in relation to gender
◆ The role of women in Christian society
◆ Attitudes towards other religions with reference to missionary work, evangelism, ecumenism
◆ Beliefs about forgiveness and reconciliation
◆ The impact of beliefs about forgiveness and reconciliation on believers

Activities

1 People are always saying 'it's not fair'; they do not say 'it's fair' quite so frequently. With a partner make a list in two columns: things you think are fair and things which you think are unfair. These should be things that affect many people, not simply that someone's parents would not let them stay out after midnight.

2 You have been allowed to ban just one type of discrimination. Which would you choose and why?

Introduction: the principle of equality

'Fair' is defined as something which is free from bias, fraud or injustice. From this meaning it could be said that 'fair' really means 'reasonable'. Two of the words commonly used when talking about whether something important is fair are prejudice and **discrimination**:

• Prejudice is an idea or feeling which one person holds and which affects another person.
• Discrimination is when they act on this prejudice and treat the other person accordingly.

The first two articles of the United Nations Universal Declaration of Human Rights (see page 142) state:

Article 1. All human beings are born free and equal in dignity and rights. They are endowed with reason and conscience and should act towards one another in a spirit of brotherhood.

Article 2. Everyone is entitled to all the rights and freedoms set forth in this Declaration, without distinction of any kind, such as race, colour, sex, language, religion, political or other opinion, national or social origin, property, birth or other status.

This statement says that everyone should have exactly the same rights and freedoms whoever, whatever and wherever they are. However, as we know from the media and quite possibly from our own lives, thousands of people suffer from discrimination and prejudice. This may be because of race, sex, religion, colour, sexuality, age, disability, language, social class, or simply living in the wrong place or wearing the wrong clothes.

Discrimination against these people can take place whenever someone with power exercises that power over people who do not have power:

discrimination = prejudice + power

Most people probably feel that at some point they have been discriminated against. This does not necessarily mean that our lives have been threatened; to some people the event may seem trivial, but it nevertheless hurts when someone is excluded from something or made to feel different in some way.

People often say that young children can be the cruellest people in the way they treat others because they 'don't know any better', but this defence cannot be used for adults. It might be said that adults who consider themselves civilised should not only make an attempt not to be prejudiced or to discriminate but should also oppose prejudice and discrimination whenever they see it. It is important to remember that although laws can be made against discrimination, it is impossible to legislate against what people think; only education may eventually change that.

▲ Children can be very cruel to each other and many suffer from bullying.

Christian beliefs about equality

This topic will help you answer questions on:

● Biblical teaching about equality

According to Christian teaching God created everything and therefore no one is superior or inferior in God's eyes other than by their own actions. Therefore, it seems that, for a Christian, it should make no difference whether people are male or female, black or white, rich or poor because they should all be shown the same love. Jesus taught that people must love others, and that in this way humanity would eventually be saved from war and suffering:

A new command I give you: Love one another. As I have loved you, so you must love one another.   (John 13:34)

This teaching is also in the Acts of the Apostles:

Then Peter began to speak: 'I now realise how true it is that God does not show favouritism but accepts men from every nation who fear him and do what is right.'   (Acts 10:34–35)

For a Christian to make someone feel inferior or suffer is breaking one of the two great commandments:

Love your neighbour as yourself.   (Matthew 22:39b)

▲ Blessed Mother Teresa (1910–97), the founder of the Missionaries of Charity.

The fight against prejudice and discrimination has been taken up by people such as Blessed Mother Teresa:

> We all long for Heaven where God is, but we have it in our power to be in Heaven with Him at this very moment. But being happy with Him now means:
> Loving as He loves,
> Helping as He helps,
> Giving as He gives,
> Serving as He serves,
> Rescuing as He rescues,
> Being with Him twenty-four hours,
> Touching him in his distressing disguise.
> (Prayer from Blessed Mother Teresa)

Mother Teresa and her followers lived by the teachings of the Parable of the Sheep and the Goats (see page 145). In the New Testament teaching on equality is found in Acts:

> From one man he made every nation of men, that they should inhabit the whole earth; and he determined the times set for them and the exact places where they should live.   (Acts 17:26)

And also in Paul:

> There is neither Jew nor Greek, slave nor free, male nor female, for you are all one in Christ Jesus.   (Galatians 3:28)

Activity

Look carefully at the quotation from Galatians on the right. What exactly is it saying about equality? Give reasons to support your conclusions.

Exam practice

'Everyone must be treated equally.' Do you agree with this statement? Give reasons to support your answer.   *(12 marks)*

Here you need to consider what is meant by 'equally' in the statement. You might say that Christians believe that God created all life and that therefore they believe that all life is sacred and equal. You then might say that non-believers also believe that everyone should be treated equally. You could say that some Christians in the past have not treated people equally, for example, Christians from different denominations. You could also say that people with disabilities, for example, need to be treated differently in order to help them and demonstrate Christian love.

Christian attitudes towards racism

This topic will help you answer questions on:

● Different views about prejudice and equality in relation to race
● Practices in relation to racism

Possibly the most famous example of biblical teaching about racism and equality is found in the Parable of the Good Samaritan:

One day Jesus was asked by someone how they could ensure that they inherited eternal life:

'What is written in the Law?' he replied. 'How do you read it?'

He answered: 'Love the Lord your God with all your heart and with all your soul and with all your strength and with all your mind'; and, 'Love your neighbour as yourself.'

'You have answered correctly,' Jesus replied. 'Do this and you will live.'

But he wanted to justify himself, so he asked Jesus, 'And who is my neighbour?'

In reply Jesus said: 'A man was going down from Jerusalem to Jericho, when he fell into the hands of robbers. They stripped him of his clothes, beat him and went away, leaving him half dead. A priest happened to be going down the same road, and when he saw the man, he passed by on the other side. So too, a Levite, when he came to the place and saw him, passed by on the other side. But a Samaritan, as he travelled, came where the man was; and when he saw him, he took pity on him. He went to him and bandaged his wounds, pouring on oil and wine. Then he put the man on his own donkey, took him to an inn and took care of him. The next day he took out two silver coins and gave them to the innkeeper. "Look after him," he said, "and when I return, I will reimburse you for any extra expense you may have."

'Which of these three do you think was a neighbour to the man who fell into the hands of robbers?'

The expert in the law replied, 'The one who had mercy on him.'

Jesus told him, 'Go and do likewise.' (Luke 10:26–37)

This parable demonstrated Jesus' teaching that everyone should be treated with love. In answering the question '… who is my neighbour?' Jesus is explaining that people should treat everyone well and that the priest and the Levite did not do this.

Jesus' parable reflects the teaching found in the Old Testament:

When an alien lives with you in your land, do not ill-treat him. The alien living with you must be treated as one of your native-born. Love him as yourself, for you were aliens in Egypt. I am the Lord your God. (Leviticus 19:33–34)

Although the Christian Church should represent the principles of Christian teaching and always put them into action, there have been many occasions over the centuries when it has rightly been accused of racism and intolerance. For example:

- In the crusades (see pages 152–3) thousands of people were killed in the name of Christianity.
- When the Spanish navy invaded South America tens of thousands of the local people were massacred in attempts to force them to become Christians, while the Spaniards also stole their wealth.
- In 1948 the South African Prime Minister, Daniel François Malan, a Dutch Reformed minister, introduced the apartheid legislation into South Africa which segregated black, coloured and white people. This was supported by the Dutch Reformed Church.

In the early 1980s the World Alliance of Reformed Churches declared apartheid to be a heresy and expelled the Dutch Reformed Church from the Alliance. In 1986 all congregations in the Church were desegregated and in 1994 apartheid was finally abolished in South Africa. The Church has now expressed repentance for the sin of supporting apartheid.

> **Research task**
>
> What made it significant that the man who helped was a Samaritan?

> **Exam tip**
> Remember this is the Parable of the Good Samaritan; the people who run phone lines for people who are suffering or considering suicide are called the Samaritans.

The religious support for the teaching of apartheid came from a text in Genesis:

The sons of Noah who came out of the ark were Shem, Ham and Japheth [Ham was the father of Canaan]. These were the three sons of Noah, and from them came the people who were scattered over the earth.

Noah, a man of the soil, proceeded to plant a vineyard. When he drank some of its wine, he became drunk and lay uncovered inside his tent. Ham, the father of Canaan, saw his father's nakedness and told his two brothers outside. But Shem and Japheth took a garment and laid it across their shoulders; then they walked in backward and covered their father's nakedness. Their faces were turned the other way so that they would not see their father's nakedness.

When Noah awoke from his wine and found out what his youngest son had done to him, he said,
'Cursed be Canaan!
The lowest of slaves
will he be to his brothers.'
He also said,
'Blessed be the Lord, the God of Shem!
May Canaan be the slave of Shem.
May God extend the territory of Japheth;
may Japheth live in the tents of Shem,
and may Canaan be his slave.'   (Genesis 9:18–27)

The story says that Noah was drunk and was sleeping naked in his tent. One of his sons, Ham, came in to see him and saw him naked. Because of this Noah cursed Ham's son, Canaan, and ordered that he should be a slave to Ham's brothers, Shem and Japheth. This might not seem a particularly pleasant story but when an old tradition that Canaan was black is added to this story it can be seen how it was used to justify the apartheid system to some people.

In what is now the USA, many Christians became very rich slave owners in the 'Deep South'. Slaves were almost always black people. Many other people in both North America and Europe opposed slavery very strongly: Christians were also very active in the campaigns to end slavery, as it caused terrible suffering and was directly against biblical teachings. Slavery was officially abolished after the end of the US Civil War in 1865. The southern states were forced to accept the thirteenth amendment to the US constitution:

Neither slavery nor involuntary servitude, except as a punishment for crime whereof the party shall have been duly convicted, shall exist within the United States, or any place subject to their jurisdiction.

However, many southern landowners, furious at losing their unpaid labour, introduced new legislation which separated blacks and whites in the same way as apartheid was to do in South Africa. These were called the 'Jim Crow Laws' and were not finally abolished until the 1960s.

One of the most famous Americans of all time and the leader of the protests against racial discrimination was Martin Luther King Jr (1929–68). He was a black Baptist minister and his father was also a Baptist minister. As a life-long victim of racism and segregation he

> **Exam tip**
> Remember the US Civil Rights campaigner was Martin Luther King Jr. Martin Luther King was his father. Martin Luther was somebody completely different.

▲ Martin Luther King Jr (1929–68).

spent most of his life trying to get the law in the USA changed. As an admirer of Ghandi he aimed to do this through peaceful protest.

Martin Luther King Jr's most famous speech was made on 28 August 1963 on the steps of the Lincoln Memorial in Washington, DC:

> I have a dream that one day every valley shall be exalted, every hill and mountain shall be made low, the rough places will be made plain, and the crooked places will be made straight, and the glory of the Lord shall be revealed, and all flesh shall see it together.
>
> This will be the day when all of God's children will be able to sing with a new meaning, 'My country, 'tis of thee, sweet land of liberty, of thee I sing. Land where my fathers died, land of the pilgrim's pride, from every mountainside, let freedom ring.'
>
> And when this happens, When we allow freedom to ring, when we let it ring from every village and every hamlet, from every state and every city, we will be able to speed up that day when all of God's children, black men and white men, Jews and Gentiles, Protestants and Catholics, will be able to join hands and sing in the words of the old Negro spiritual, 'Free at last! free at last! thank God Almighty, we are free at last!'

After the March on Washington, Martin Luther King Jr continued his campaign but on 4 April 1968 he was assassinated by an escaped white convict, James Earl Ray, in Memphis, Tennessee where he had made a speech the night before.

◄ Barack Obama (left) takes the oath of office as president of the USA with his wife, Michelle, by his side at the US Capitol building in Washington, DC, on 20 January 2009. The Obamas were joined by their daughters Sasha and Malia.

Activity

America elected its first black President in 2008. What effect do you think the election of President Obama will have on attitudes towards racism in (a) the USA and (b) the rest of the world?

Exam practice

Explain Christian attitudes to racism. *(6 marks)*

The question asks for attitudes rather than teachings or beliefs. You need to explain what Christians think about racism and how they may respond to instances of racism. You can use the example of people such as Martin Luther King Jr. In explaining this you can then refer to teachings and beliefs as the reason for these attitudes.

Christian attitudes towards gender

This topic will help you answer questions on:

● Different views about prejudice and equality in relation to gender
● The role of women in Christian society

The Christian Church has often been accused of **sexism**. The language of the Church has always been in favour of men and God is almost always referred to as male. For some Christians who take the Bible very literally, passages such as 'God made Man in his own image' are often used against those who demand greater equality in the Church and society. In the New Testament, Paul in particular seems to indicate that women are in a subservient role:

Women should remain silent in the churches. They are not allowed to speak, but must be in submission, as the Law says. If they want to enquire about something, they should ask their own husbands at home; for it is disgraceful for a woman to speak in the church.   (1 Corinthians 14:34–35)

Now I want you to realise that the head of every man is Christ, and the head of the woman is man, and the head of Christ is God. Every man who prays or prophesies with his head covered dishonours his head. And every woman who prays or prophesies with her head uncovered dishonours her head – it is just as though her head were shaved. If a woman does not cover her head, she should have her hair cut off; and if it is a disgrace for a woman to have her hair cut or shaved off, she should cover her head. A man ought not to cover his head, since he is the image and glory of God; but the woman is the glory of man.   (1 Corinthians 11:3–7)

On the other hand, Jesus appears to show great respect towards women:

While Jesus was in Bethany in the home of a man known as Simon the Leper, a woman came to him with an alabaster jar of very expensive perfume, which she poured on his head as he was reclining at the table. When the disciples saw this, they were indignant. 'Why this waste?' they asked. 'This perfume could have been sold at a high price and the money given to the poor.' Aware of this, Jesus said to them, 'Why are you bothering this woman? She has done a beautiful thing to me. The poor you will always have with you, but you will not always have me. When she poured this perfume on my body, she did it to prepare me for burial. I tell you the truth, wherever this gospel is preached throughout the world, what she has done will also be told, in memory of her.'   (Matthew 26:6–13)

However, some people feel that Jesus was unnecessarily critical of his mother, Mary, at the wedding at Cana:

When the wine was gone, Jesus' mother said to him, 'They have no more wine.' 'Dear woman, why do you involve me?' Jesus replied.
(John 2:3–4a)

On the other hand, according, to Mark's gospel, it was a woman to whom Jesus first appeared after his resurrection:

When Jesus rose early on the first day of the week, he appeared first to Mary Magdalene, out of whom he had driven seven demons. She went and told those who had been with him and who were mourning and weeping. When they heard that Jesus was alive and that she had seen him, they did not believe it.   (Mark 16:9–11)

There are still Christians who feel that there should be a clear distinction between the roles of men and women. This is a traditional view that women should look after the home and the children while men go out to work and ultimately make all the decisions for the family. This is dcfcndcd by the argument that men are physically stronger than women. However, particularly in modern society, there are many Christians who believe that men and women were created equal and should be treated equally (see Chapter 7).

The Christian Church is slow to change its position in relation to women and many old prejudices still exist. However, in recent years an increasing number of Christians feel that women should have an equal role in worship and the priesthood not only on grounds of equality but also because of what happened in the early Church:

Then they returned to Jerusalem from the hill called the Mount of Olives, a Sabbath day's walk from the city. When they arrived, they went upstairs to the room where they were staying. Those present were Peter, John, James and Andrew; Philip and Thomas, Bartholomew and Matthew; James son of Alphaeus and Simon the Zealot, and Judas son of James. They all joined together constantly in prayer, along with the women and Mary the mother of Jesus, and with his brothers.   (Acts 1:12–14)

It also seems from the writings of Paul that women had greater importancc in thc carly Church:

I commend to you our sister Phoebe, a servant of the church in Cenchrea. I ask you to receive her in the Lord in a way worthy of the saints and to give her any help she may need from you, for she has been a great help to many people, including me.
    Greet Priscilla and Aquila, my fellow workers in Christ Jesus. They risked their lives for me. Not only I but all the churches of the Gentiles are grateful to them.
    Greet also the church that meets at their house.   (Romans 16:1–5)

These passages from the Acts of the Apostles and Paul's letter to the Christians in Rome appear to suggest that women had greater importance in the early years of the Church than they had later. The first passage shows that there were other women present in the upper room on the day of Pentecost as well as Jesus' mother and they were all praying together. Phoebe and Priscilla helped Paul on his missionary journeys and he asks people to show them great respect. However, there is no real evidence that women were allowed to be deacons or priests in the early Church (see Chapter 7).

It is only in the last 100 years that women have been allowed to be priests or ministers and this is still not permitted in the Roman Catholic and Orthodox Churches.

▲ A female employee working on the production line at a Renault car factory in Brazil. The twentieth century saw dramatic changes in the role of women, particularly in the workplace.

Discussion point

'Women cannot be priests.' Do you agree?

Exam practice

'Men and women should always be treated equally.' Do you agree with this statement? Give reasons to support your answer. *(12 marks)*

This question gives a great deal of scope for your answer. You could consider whether Christianity treats men and women equally and also whether it teaches that they should be treated equally. Are they 'equal but different'? You should also consider whether, from a secular view, men and women are treated equally, or should be.

Attitudes to religion

This topic will help you answer questions on:

● Attitudes towards other religions with reference to:
  – missionary work
  – evangelism
  – ecumenism

It is probable that the majority of the world's population would say that they belong to a particular religion. For most of these people they would also say that they believe that their religion is true and that it is the 'right' religion. However, some religions such as Hinduism and Judaism do not encourage converts because they believe that often a person is serving God even though they are a member of a different religion. However, some other religions, in particular Islam and Christianity are **proselytising** religions. They believe that it is their duty as members of their religion to go out and convert people.

Although Christians believe that everyone should have the right to practise their own religion, they also believe that only Christianity has the complete truth about God:

> Jesus answered, 'I am the way and the truth and the life. No one comes to the Father except through me.'   (John 14:6)

It appears from the New Testament that it is only Jesus' followers who can go to heaven when they die. Christians might argue that God's sacrifice in dying as Jesus on the cross atoned for the sins of the whole world and that his resurrection proves that he is the only way in which people can reach God.

> **Exam tip**
> Remember not every religion teaches that it is the only way to reach God.

Missionary work

For centuries many Christians travelled abroad as missionaries. They believed that it was their Christian duty and obligation to convert as many people to Christianity as possible. There are still missionaries and missionary societies today, but although they still believe that they must spread the message of Jesus wherever they go, many of them are now most concerned with helping people in developing countries rather than trying to convert them: it could be said that they serve their mission by showing the example of Jesus in their lives. Nevertheless, Christianity remains a religion which sees itself as having an obligation to lead other people towards Christianity:

> The Church still has the obligation and also the sacred right to evangelise all men.
> (Catechism of the Roman Catholic Church, section 848)

Evangelism

Evangelism is the spreading of the teachings of Jesus from the gospels or 'good news'. Many Christian groups have a strong tradition of evangelism and believe that it is a very important part of their Christian life and duty. The Salvation Army is an example of a

▲ A European Christian missionary with two Tahitian converts in the nineteenth century.

Christian group who believe it is their mission to spread Jesus' teachings as well as to carry out essential work to help the poor and disadvantaged. The Mission for Seafarers (part of the Anglican Church) is another organisation which works to help and support sailors of whatever faith as well as providing teaching about Christianity.

Today, some Christians believe that evangelising is a misunderstanding of Jesus and that people should follow their own religion and their own God. Arguments are that someone's religion may depend on where they were born in the world and that a Christian God would not be willing to punish someone who is a devoted follower of a non-Christian religion.

Since the twentieth century interfaith dialogue has increased and many services are held where people from different religions and religious traditions take part.

Exam tip
Not all Christians believe that they have a duty to convert people but many do.

Ecumenism

There are many thousands of denominations within the Christian Church. Although Christians would agree that they should respect the differing beliefs, practices and emphases of denominations other than their own, many of these groups are now working together with joint services and community work. This shows then that although there may be major differences between some groups, they still share the same essential beliefs.

Taizé, a Christian community in a small village in France, was founded in 1940, during the Second World War, by Brother Roger Schutz. The original purpose of Taizé was to offer hospitality to refugees, in particular Jews who were escaping from Nazi Germany. There are now more than 100 brothers, mainly Protestants, working at Taizé and since the late 1960s the community has worked towards improving relationships between Protestants and Catholics.

◄ Thousands of worshippers pray in Geneva at the opening day of the thirtieth annual meeting of the Taizé community. During the five-day gathering, which unites the Catholic and Protestant denominations, the young people will pray, sing, read the bible, contemplate and meet other people.

Research task

Research Taizé or another Christian ecumenical community (for example, Iona) and find out how it tries to put Christian teachings into practice.

12 Religion and the media

Activity

Before you start reading this chapter make a list of as many different types of media as you can. Now sort the list into those types of media that you think might concern religion and those which do not. When you have finished studying this topic go back to the list and see if you have changed your mind about any of them.

This chapter will help you answer questions on:

◆ The different forms of media
◆ The influence of the media
◆ The portrayal of Christianity in the media
◆ The portrayal of important religious figures
◆ Responses and attitudes towards films, books and comics which focus on religious/philosophical messages
◆ Using the media to represent Christianity and to educate both Christians and non-Christians
◆ The concept of censorship and freedom of speech
◆ Beliefs and attitudes towards the portrayal of violence and sex
◆ Attitudes and responses to issues raised by freedom of speech

Christianity and the media

This topic will help you answer questions on:

● The different forms of media
● The influence of the media

The different forms of media

Media can be television, radio, videos, DVDs, CDs, newspapers, magazines, books, posters, advertisements, computers and the internet, art, music, dance and drama. It is anything which is a medium for communicating with other people.

From the beginning of human history people have given each other information, demonstrated new methods of doing things, passed on ideas, communicated their feelings, hopes and fears, made each other laugh and shared their opinions and beliefs. At the same time as some people have taken on new ideas, there have always been those who resist change because of the threat which they think it brings to established ways of life and beliefs. In all religions and in all cultures there are some people who say that the media is a bad influence on life today and that young people especially are misled by the media and by modern forms of entertainment.

There are some religious people who welcome new inventions in the media and communication. They feel that modern technology will improve the quality of life for everyone and they see mass media as providing a wonderful opportunity to spread their beliefs. There are, however, many religious people who have mixed feelings about the media and entertainment.

▲ The media takes many forms.

When looking at specific issues concerning the media and entertainment, not all Christians share exactly the same opinion. Christian ethics are based on two general positive principles that Jesus gave his followers. They are 'love God' and 'love your neighbour'. Jesus told the story in Luke 10:25–37 of the Good Samaritan and at the end he said, 'Go and do likewise.' When Christians are trying to decide what to think and do about an issue, they may turn to various sources of authority to find help:

- they read the Bible
- they take the advice of the Church and of their Christian friends
- they use their conscience and pray to God and ask to be guided by the Holy Spirit.

The influence of the media

Influence on family life

Many Christian families are concerned about the influences that television has on family life. Some see the television as being like a one-eyed idol in the corner of the living room, demanding attention and time. They feel that it has a bad effect on family life, especially if families sit in front of the television eating instead of making mealtimes an occasion where everyone comes together.

Many people spend a lot of their leisure time watching television and they could have been using this time to talk to each other or to do something more useful than simply sitting and staring. For this reason, a few Christians refuse to own a television. Most Christians in the UK do use the media, but they believe that they need to choose carefully what to watch and read. They may limit the time they spend and try not to neglect church attendance, for example, on Sundays.

Christian parents are likely to try to make sure that their children only watch programmes or read magazines that are suitable for their age group and which do not promote the wrong values. Most parents would share this concern and try to monitor what their children watch, listen and read. They are likely also to want to supervise their children when they use the internet.

> **Exam tip**
> Remember that not everyone from a particular religious tradition will agree about whether the media is a good or bad influence.

Activities

1 Look at the following list of types of media. For each one, list the dangers that some parents would associate with them:

  ◆ internet
  ◆ video games
  ◆ song lyrics
  ◆ comics
  ◆ graphic novels
  ◆ books.

2 Do you think that these worries are justified or really exaggerated?

◀ Many families now eat meals in front of a television rather than at a table.

Activity

1 Look back at the passage from 1 Corinthians 6:19 on page 113. How might this teaching influence a Christian's view of soap-opera lifestyles?

Research task

Why did the Methodist Church and the Salvation Army adopt teetotalism?

Exam tip

Remember that Christians as a whole are not opposed to alcohol and that it was an accepted part of life for Jesus and his followers.

▲ There is no biblical teaching against the use of alcohol. Here, people from all over the world celebrate the Oktoberfest beer festival in Munich, Germany.

Influence on lifestyle

Wasting money and time is not the only media issue that might concern Christians. To some extent, popular culture is both created and reflected by the media. Some of the media present a view of the world that does not fit with Christian views about the priorities in life and the values people should live by. Lifestyles portrayed in the media and advertising may have a bad effect particularly on impressionable young people or older people who are less well educated. In many drama series, for example, the main characters are married and divorced several times, have affairs and commit crimes. Even soap operas, supposedly about everyday life, can have stories about people burying bodies under the patio. The stories are interesting and entertaining, but they give the impression that this is normal and acceptable behaviour.

Alcohol

The regular use of alcohol is another feature of many television dramas. Christians belonging to some Protestant evangelical denominations are **teetotal**; they never drink alcohol. There are individual Christians in other traditions whose conscience may lead them also to abstain from it. Abstinence is not usually because these Christians are against pleasure. Mostly, it is because they have seen the harm that the consumption of excess alcohol can cause. They feel that the safest approach for themselves and the clearest way to show a good example to society is the total abstention from drinking alcohol.

Other Christians believe that, for themselves, moderation is the key to living in the modern material world. They try to behave responsibly.

Many Christian denominations and individual believers feel they have to rethink how best to apply their principles as times change and society evolves. Methodism, for example, was associated with teetotalism from its beginnings but in 1987 the Methodist Conference made this statement:

All Methodists [should] consider seriously the claims of total abstinence, and make a personal commitment either to total abstinence or to responsible drinking.

The Christian Church uses biblical teaching about alcohol to apply to the use and abuse of all drugs. Christianity is not against pleasure but it is against selfishness. Selfish enjoyment is false pleasure according to the Christian viewpoint. Addicts become increasingly selfish and self-centred until they do not care whom they hurt. They can bring great sorrow even to the people they say that they love. Also, Christianity is against all forms of addiction because addicts have placed something other than God at the centre of their lives and lifestyles.

You shall have no other gods before me.

You shall not make for yourself an idol in the form of anything in heaven above or on the earth beneath or in the waters below. You shall not bow down to them or worship them … . (Exodus 20:3–5a)

Role models

Another way in which the media influences lifestyles is by creating **role models**. In the West, we live in a consumer society. People buy things to fit the lifestyle they want. The media shows us what is desirable and fashionable for the sort of person we would like to be. Advertisers pay celebrities to sponsor their products, but also in the media there are reports of all the material accessories of the lifestyles of the famous. Fame is big business. Film stars, pop stars and sports celebrities fill the media in the Western world and it is very difficult, in particular for young people, to ignore the role models of popular culture.

Christians feel that the media tends to make idols of people. For some, this is a breaking of the second commandment that tells them not to make idols nor worship false images. Some Christians are simply concerned that celebrities may be a bad influence on the behaviour of fans, especially children. Other Christians accept that having heroes and heroines is a natural part of a young person's life and they rely on education, church and family values to help their children to have a sensible attitude to role models. The New Testament attitude to fame is expressed in this verse:

What good will it be for a man if he gains the whole world, yet forfeits his soul? Or what can a man give in exchange for his soul?   (Matthew 16:26)

Many celebrities are very aware that they have enormous influence and try to behave responsibly, but the very fact that people can become rich and famous by being involved in the media affects the hopes and dreams of many young people. As larger numbers of television and radio channels compete to fill their schedules with cheaper and cheaper material, the 'reality TV' programmes, live talk shows and talent-spotting contests flood the networks. Magazines and newspapers add to the hype. The message is that anybody can become a star. The word 'wannabee' is now included in some dictionaries.

People sometimes criticise programmes because they are considered to be in poor taste, crude, coarse or vulgar. This is just a matter of taste. The word 'vulgar' comes from the Latin for 'the common people'. Christianity set out to be a religion for the common people. Some light entertainment programmes may be brash in style but they can be helpful to viewers in coping with everyday life. They show how to get on with other people and give insights into the way various individuals think. It is important to distinguish the aims and content of a programme from the style of presentation.

Music

The popular music scene is a big part of the media world and has a great influence on young people. In shops, music is used to control people's mood. It is part of merchandising. The purpose is to encourage the public happily to buy more goods. Most Christians have no real objection to music as such. In some countries there is a strong musical tradition associated with Christian worship but there have always been mixed feelings among Christians towards popular music and the other performing arts, dance and drama.

Activity

2 What views might a Christian have about a soap opera that shows people drinking in order to cope with their problems?

Research task

Research the life of the footballer Paul Canoville (you could start with the article on the *Daily Telegraph*'s website 'Paul Canoville's ruin and redemption', 19 April 2008).

- Paul Canoville was Chelsea's first black player
- He partied, took drugs, was unfaithful and promiscuous and used violence.
- He has fought drug addiction and is now clean
- He has twice beaten cancer and come through many problems in his life

Do you think Paul Canoville is a good role model? Or do the bad things in his life mean that he cannot be a role model to others?

▲ Paul Canoville: a good role model?

Choral singing is an important part of many services. ▶

One of the reasons the early Christian Church chose to celebrate Christmas in December was that they hoped to clamp down on rowdy winter celebrations and replace them with a more solemn ceremony. Saint Augustine (354CE) declared, 'If they must have songs, let them sing the music of the church':

> The devil should not have all the best tunes.   (Reverend Rowland Hill)

In the present day, most secular popular music continues to be about love and all the sentiments that go with finding love and losing love. Some Christians feel that popular songs trivialise relationships, are too obsessed with sex and may lead to lustful thoughts and bad behaviour.

> But I tell you that anyone who looks at a woman lustfully has already committed adultery with her in his heart. If your right eye causes you to sin, gouge it out and throw it away. It is better for you to lose one part of your body than for your whole body to be thrown into hell. And if your right hand causes you to sin, cut it off and throw it away. It is better for you to lose one part of your body than for your whole body to go into hell.   (Matthew 5:28–30)

All societies accept that music is a powerful force and can be used to express people's deepest feelings. Individuals may find their own sense of identity when they recognise others who share their taste in music. Songs can unite protesters and give them a sense of solidarity. Music can be the sound of rebellion and might be used to undermine established authority. It is no wonder that music has an influence on young people in particular and that new music may seem threatening to older generations.

In the 1950s in the USA, rock and roll culture brought condemnation from religious leaders, government officials and parents' groups. It was called the devil's music by some people.

Attitudes towards music and popular culture have relaxed among many Christian denominations over the years. Churches use popular musical forms and styles in worship. Most Christians listen to pop music just like anybody else and many Christians work in the pop music industry and in other areas of the performing arts.

Some Christians feel that another important issue for all religions concerning the influence of the media is the popularising of New Age

Activity

In pairs, think of the words of four songs which are popular at the moment. Write down as many of the words as you can. Now discuss what these songs are about.

▲ A crowd of screaming teenage girls reach for Elvis Presley as he sings on stage, 5 July 1956.

ideas. Ever since the hippies of the 1960s, popular culture and the media have retained a nostalgia for 'flower power' ideas. Many people share the concern for peace, love, nature and the environment. There is wide interest in spirituality, mysticism, meditation and alternative holistic approaches to medicine and lifestyles. Some religious people, however, fear that the articles and programmes may give confusing or misleading ideas. Presenters and reporters often mix and match anything about spirituality from various religions. Programmes looking like genuine documentaries try to spice up poorly researched theories about vaguely religious topics.

Astrology is big business and features in most newspapers. Despite the wise men following the star, Christians tend to think that basing your life on any sort of fortune telling is silly or wrong. Most Christians are uneasy about media themes which they think may lead impressionable people to dabble in the occult and some are concerned at the number of programmes which, as a source of entertainment for young people, feature vampires, witches, wizards and zombies.

▲ Tarot cards are used for fortune telling.

Exam practice

Explain Christian attitudes towards the way lifestyles are shown in the media. *(6 marks)*

In answering this question you need to make sure that you do not run out of time because there is so much you could write. Also, remember that Christian attitudes vary a great deal and so do not say that 'all' Christians would respond in a particular way. You should describe some of the attitudes towards lifestyles and then explain why Christians might respond in a certain manner. This could include biblical and church teachings as well as general ideas of how people should live.

Portrayal of Christianity in the media

This topic will help you answer questions on:

- The portrayal of Christianity in the media
- The portrayal of important religious figures
- Responses and attitudes towards films, books and comics which focus on religious/philosophical messages
- Using the media to represent Christianity and to educate both Christians and non-Christians

The portrayal of Christianity in the media

Christianity has no united policy about the media. For example, there are some Christian sects such as the Amish, Mennonites and Exclusive Plymouth Brethren that do not approve of almost any type of secular entertainment, while there are individual Christians who have built up huge media empires. However, there are many ways in which Christians use the media to present a positive and accurate representation of their religion.

JESUS HEALS PEOPLE
...DAUGHTER, BE OF GOOD COMFORT; THY FAITH HATH MADE THEE WHOLE. AND THE WOMAN WAS MADE WHOLE FROM THAT HOUR.
MATTHEW 9:22

EVERYWHERE JESUS GOES, A CROWD GATHERS. MANY ARE SICK PEOPLE.

LET ME THROUGH! I MUST SEE JESUS!

IF I CAN ONLY TOUCH HIS ROBE...

COME ON, MASTER, WE'LL PROTECT YOU FROM THESE SICK PEOPLE!

NO, PETER, I'M HERE TO HELP THEM.

▲ Religious comics are used to teach children about Christianity.

Greenbelt started in 1973 as a small pop festival run by Christians. About 1500 young people turned up. Now the pop and arts festival caters for all age groups, takes over the Cheltenham racecourse for a week and is sponsored by organisations such as Christian Aid and the YMCA. ▶

Some Christians prefer simplicity in their worship and surroundings so as not to distract them from God, such as the Religious Society of Friends (the Quakers). But the Religious Society of Friends do have a drama group called the Leaveners that runs workshops for young people interested in drama; this shows that almost all Christians look to engage with the wider community in lots of different ways, including using the media to do this.

Evangelical Churches often use drama, dance and art especially when leading campaigns for young people. They believe that Christianity is exciting so they should use appropriate media to convey this message. For example, comics for children which retell stories from the Bible or the lives of famous Christians are also seen as a way of spreading the message of Christianity in a way that makes most sense to young people. And many Churches use big musical events like music festivals to get together and celebrate their beliefs with a wider community. These are not 'traditional' ways in which the Church communicates its message, but the view is that in the modern world Christianity needs to engage with people on their terms, so that people can see that Christianity is relevant to them and their lives right now.

The portrayal of important religious figures

Religious people sometimes feel uncomfortable at the representation of important religious figures in drama. For example, some Christians think that God or Jesus should not be acted by an ordinary person. They would say that actors could never play the roles well enough so the performance might be disrespectful as well as being inaccurate. The same would apply to artists trying to paint or sculpt important religious people.

Some Christians are not only against the representation of important religious people but also of any person and all living creatures. This point of view is shared by many Jews and most Muslims. It is based on the first two commandments given by God to the prophet Moses. The first commandment is about not having other gods besides the one God. The second commandment says:

You shall not make for yourself an idol in the form of anything in heaven above or on the earth beneath or in the waters below. You shall not bow down to them or worship them ... . (Exodus 20:4–5a)

Exam tip

Remember that different Christian denominations often have quite different views about the media and about its use.

Activity

1 Discuss the quotation from Exodus on the right. What do you think it means? Does it apply to the media and if so, how?

Challenges to traditional ways of representing religious people

In the West, the 1960s saw a big change in the way many people regarded traditional views on beliefs and behaviour. These new, liberal ways of thinking had a very wide impact due to the influence of the media. Challenging accepted views also meant opposition from conservatives who wanted to keep things as they were.

This all meant that long-established traditions about the representation of religions were challenged too. The Bible has had a huge effect on Western culture and many thousands of books have been written drawing on biblical and Christian themes. So it was inevitable that traditional ways of viewing Jesus and the implications of his teaching would be interpreted differently and sometimes radically. For example, *Joseph and the Amazing Technicolor Dreamcoat* (1968) and the rock opera *Jesus Christ Superstar* (1970) had enormous impact, as did the American musical *Godspell* (1971). These musicals did not criticise Christian teachings but they represented religious people in completely new ways. At first many Christians were shocked by rock musicals on biblical themes but most Christians and Churches who are not against using the media have accepted these musicals and watch them on television or on the stage. Some take part and send schoolchildren to be the chorus in big theatre productions. Now many Christians would say a musical like *Jesus Christ Superstar* gets people interested in Jesus who might never otherwise have thought his teachings had any relevance to them.

While some representations of religious people were about retelling familiar stories in new and exciting ways, other approaches have been more directly critical or controversial. Books, plays and films have used themes from Christian teachings in ways that are very different from the Bible account, and in some the use of sex and violence, or humour, has appalled some Christians. While some Christians might say 'this is just a story' others believe that anything which does not show respect when dealing with Christianity is wrong.

Films

There are many films about biblical stories and people. The first was made in 1897 and was a film of a Passion play – the story of Jesus' death and resurrection. Some are simply dramatic versions of the stories in the Bible which are designed to educate and entertain. Others such as *The Last Temptation of Christ* (1988) are very controversial because they include fictional accounts of Jesus' life which many people found offensive. Another example would be the film *Monty Python's Life of Brian*, which was released in 1979. This tells the story of 'Brian', who is swept up in the opposition to Roman rule over the Jews in first century Judea and becomes a messiah figure to the Jewish people, but is then crucified (alongside Jesus). The film pokes fun at religious belief and while Brian is not supposed to be Jesus, it undermines key messages of the traditional Christian story. Many people were simply appalled by the film when it came out and wanted it to be banned. There was a lot of concern that it would mislead people about Christianity, and it was seen as blasphemous and therefore offensive to God.

Activity

2 Have you seen a musical or a film about Jesus? What did you think of it? What things did you enjoy and what things put you off?

Research tasks

1 Find out what happened when *The Last Temptation of Christ* was first shown. Do you think that people would react in the same way today?

2 Compare that reaction to the reactions to the *Da Vinci Code* and to Mel Gibson's *The Passion of the Christ*.

▲ A film poster for *The Passion of the Christ*, 2004.

▲ Victorian pictures of Jesus made him look very English.

▲ In this picture Jesus is black: this is a detail from a painting by Pap'Nemma, an artist from the Democratic Republic of Congo.

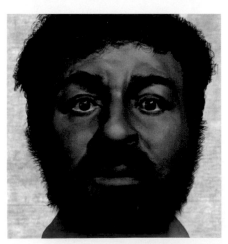

▲ This picture is based on what experts think Jesus might have looked like, based on his age and where he came from.

Books

In recent years there have been many popular books about Christianity and the Church. Perhaps the best known is *The Da Vinci Code* by Dan Brown, published in 2003. The story is about someone trying to solve a murder in the Louvre museum in Paris who uncovers 'evidence' that Jesus and Mary Magdalene had a child together. This book, and the film of it which followed in 2006, made millions of people think more about Christianity and the Church – but not perhaps in ways that the Church really appreciated. This is a quote about *The Da Vinci Code*:

> Reporters have asked whether even a bestselling novel can seriously damage a Church of one billion believers. No, in the long run, it cannot. But that is not the point. The pastoral concern of the Church is for each and every person. If only one person were to come away [from *The Da Vinci Code*] with a distorted impression of Jesus Christ or His Church, our concern is for that person as if he or she were the whole world.
> (United States Conference of Catholic Bishops' Department of Communications)

What did Jesus look like?

While books, plays, films and musicals started to reinvent how Jesus has been portrayed after the 1960s, in fact there has been a very long history of changes in representation of Jesus.

Obviously there are no photographs of Jesus Christ. The first images of him which still exist are from the third century (300 years after his death) and were found in the catacombs in Rome. Fifth century mosaics at Ravenna look more like the Greek and Roman god Apollo and show Jesus as a clean-shaven young man. While it seems that most Romans were clean-shaven, as a Jew, Jesus would not have cut his beard.

In England during the civil war (1642–51) the Roundheads and Puritans smashed stained glass windows because they wanted to cleanse the churches of idolatrous images (see the passage from Exodus 20 on page 186). They thought that the Christian Church had grown corrupt and was full of superstition and so they knocked the heads off statues and carvings.

The Roundheads were not the first people to smash images because of religious belief. Art and religion in the Byzantine Empire were disrupted by iconoclasm (the destruction of religious images) between 726 and 843CE. Some Christians felt that the expression of spirituality in art looked like idolatry, especially the mosaics and icons showing devotion to the Virgin Mary as Theotokos. This is the Greek for 'God bearer' and describes Mary in her role as mother of God.

In the UK, Victorian paintings of Jesus and illustrations in children's Bibles showed Jesus as blonde and blue eyed. Today such paintings are considered unacceptable by many Christians. They are inaccurate because Jesus was Jewish. However, Christians around the world have painted pictures of Jesus throughout Christian history in a variety of different ways to express their beliefs about him. Often they wanted to link Jesus with their own cultures and causes.

Discussion point

Do you think images of Jesus should try to show him looking like someone from his time and culture, or is it more important that people relate his teachings to their own time and their own particular culture?

Discussion point

'*The Da Vinci Code* is offensive to Christians and should not have been published.' Do you agree or disagree?

Exam practice

'Religious figures should never be represented in the media.' Discuss. Remember to give your own opinion and to support it.

(12 marks)

In your answer you may want to start with the fact that probably all religious figures have been represented in the media at some time. You need to consider that some representations might be accurate while others may not. In relation to Christianity you should discuss the teachings of the second commandment and consider the view of some Christians that this forbids any portrayal of religious figures because to do so would be idolatry. You might then consider the views of other Christians who might welcome accurate portrayal. From a secular viewpoint you might say that the representation of religious figures does not matter if you do not believe in them as being sacred and you could also consider whether this is a matter of showing respect for the beliefs of others.

Christian attitudes towards censorship and freedom of speech

This topic will help you answer questions on:

- The concepts of censorship and freedom of speech
- Beliefs and attitudes towards the portrayal of violence and sex
- Attitudes and responses to issues raised by freedom of speech

In most countries, there are laws of **obscenity**. Some countries, like Ireland and Italy, are stricter than others. The same applies to some states in the USA.

The word 'obscene' is used to describe material which is likely to deprave and corrupt the public. In the UK, when the publishers of *Lady Chatterley's Lover* were acquitted of obscenity in 1960 for what might now be considered some fairly mild descriptions of sexual activity, it started a gradual process of society becoming more broad-minded. **Censorship** of the theatre more or less faded away by the end of the 1960s. Prosecutions for obscenity today are mainly confined to the display of photographs and graphics. The law extends not only to matters of sexual morality but to publications about violence and drug taking. The intention of the material is not considered. The offence depends on the effect on the audience or readership.

Fact box

Censorship usually involves someone in authority deciding what other people can read or see. The word comes from the job of the censor, which existed in ancient Rome from 443 to 22BCE. Two censors used to preside over the rules for city life.

Exam tip

Make sure that you can explain what is meant by 'freedom of speech' and 'censorship'.

Censorship can be a difficult issue. On the one hand people want to protect vulnerable members of society. They are concerned, for example, that young children may be influenced to copy bad things they have seen. On the other hand there is the danger of taking away people's individual freedom.

Freedom of speech is the right of people to say what they think without censorship. Together with freedom of the press, these are important means of making sure that countries do not become dictatorships or police states. However, there are many countries which do not permit these freedoms and even those which do, such as the UK, still place some limitations on what can be said or published.

The media has to do a delicate balancing act. Newspapers and television programmes need to provide what their readers and audience want, but they must not offend other people. In the UK, some people campaign against sex and violence in the media, especially on television, and the 'watershed' is a sort of compromise. The watershed, which is nine o'clock at night, marks the time after which more explicit material can be shown on television. The idea is that children should be in bed by that time and adults are capable of turning off the television if a programme causes offence.

Attitudes to the portrayal of violence and sex

Gratuitous sex and violence means portraying sex and violence in a way which is not necessary for the plot of a film or programme but which will attract a bigger audience. Many people are now more liberal minded than those of previous generations and will happily watch scenes which might have shocked people 50 years ago. In 1930s films, for example, the hero and heroine never got in bed together without leaving one foot on the floor. However, most people still feel that gratuitous sex and violence is not acceptable in mainstream media.

In the New Testament Paul says:

Finally, brothers, whatever is true, whatever is noble, whatever is right, whatever is pure, whatever is lovely, whatever is admirable – if anything is excellent or praiseworthy – think about such things.   (Philippians 4:8)

Many Christians are concerned about the amount of violence and sex in the media.

Violence

Some films and computer games seem to glorify war, and scenes of destruction and violent action are often justified as essential to a storyline. Television news programmes report on the violence in the world every day. The pictures are censored by the television companies themselves so that viewers are not too distressed by what they see, but wars, terrorism and violence have to be reported if they are part of the day's news. Even documentaries and films which have anti-war themes still bring the subject of violence into people's homes. Comedy programmes and children's cartoons have characters hitting each other as slapstick humour.

▲ *Tom and Jerry* first came to television in 1960.

Some people feel that the media encourages violence while others disagree, but there is another important issue. It is not just that people might copy the abusive behaviour and bullying tactics they have seen, but the danger that frequent exposure to violence in the media results in the public becoming **desensitised**. People begin to accept that the world has always been a violent place and are no longer shocked by the physical or verbal abuse of vulnerable members of society. It may be that, as a result, more people become victims of violence, particularly women and children, and the public does less and less about it.

Christians might criticise the media about particular films and can boycott them by not going to see them.

Some Christians are pacifists but on the whole Christianity is not a pacifist religion. However, even in a situation of war, the aim of Christianity is to establish peace.

Sex

The same situation as with violence applies to the emphasis on sex in the media. The rising numbers of cases of rape, murder and sexual abuse of women and children which are reported are often blamed on the media and it is claimed that people copy what they see.

Christian teaching reflects and reinforces traditional family values. Christian Churches generally teach that sex outside marriage is wrong. In the past, most people would have agreed with them. Society was much stricter about sexual morality mainly because people were afraid of some of the consequences such as sexually transmitted diseases and unwanted pregnancies.

All Christians are likely to agree that casual sex is not a good idea, but they may have differing attitudes towards what is acceptable in relationships and sexual behaviour. However, many Christian Churches are likely to condemn the media for any material which seems to condone promiscuity, premarital sex, adultery and homosexuality. Christians believe that each person is made in the image of God so each human being is unique and special. Every individual should be treated with respect. Christians also believe that sex is a gift from God and should be part of a loving relationship. To Christians, love is different from lust and it is not just a temporary infatuation.

Love is patient, love is kind. It does not envy, it does not boast, it is not proud. It is not rude, it is not self-seeking, it is not easily angered, it keeps no record of wrongs. Love does not delight in evil but rejoices with the truth. It always protects, always trusts, always hopes, always perseveres. Love never fails. But where there are prophecies, they will cease; where there are tongues, they will be stilled; where there is knowledge, it will pass away. (1 Corinthians 13:4–8)

Pornography

Pornography is the explicit description or showing of sexual activity to stimulate sexual excitement. The term comes from the Greek words for prostitute and writing and originally referred to works of art and writing describing the life of prostitutes.

Discussion points

1 There is no censorship for the internet, so is there any point in having it on other forms of media?

2 Do violent video games make people more violent?

Exam tip
Remember that there are different Christian views about many of these issues so do not simply say 'Christians think that …'.

▲ Sexual images are often used in advertising.

According to Christians, pornography is wrong because it can give the impression that women exist to be used by men and it demeans sex. It exploits women as sex objects rather than treating them as human beings. Western society is far more permissive than it was in the past and people are not so easily shocked, but many Christians feel that the media often gives a false message that sexual freedom will bring happiness.

Although pornography is wrong in the opinion of some people, not only Christians, changing social attitudes now mean that it is no longer a criminal offence in most Western countries. Many films and television plays contain soft-core pornography. Sometimes different versions of films are made for countries where it might be possible to get a more explicit or more violent uncut version past the official censor. Some newspapers and magazines push their material as far as they can in the attempt to have more sensational articles than their rivals.

Many pressure groups, including some feminists, say that the law on obscenity is too vague and they want a return to stricter censorship of pornography. Religious people including Christians of many different denominations support such views.

Issues raised by freedom of speech

The term 'Big Brother' was first used in the book *Nineteen Eighty-Four* by George Orwell. It was published in 1949 but it was set in a fictional nightmare future where there was total invasion of privacy. Everywhere there were posters with pictures of the leader of the party in power. The slogan was, 'Big Brother is watching you'. There was a two-way television screen in every room and the state tried to have complete control even of people's thoughts.

One of the reasons that people in the Western world are suspicious of censorship is because of Nazi propaganda in the 1930s and the censorship in communist countries such as the former Union of Soviet Socialist Republics where atheism was the established view and there was a one-party state.

In most modern democratic countries it is generally accepted that religious belief and worship are a private matter and people should not be stopped from holding public office because of their religion. In the UK, the situation is complicated by the fact that the Church of England remains the established Church.

When thinking about Christian views on issues of censorship, it is important to distinguish between crimes and sins. Crimes break the laws of the state. Sins break commands which people believe came from God. Some actions, like murder, are both a sin and a crime.

In the UK in the 1960s, a committee under the chairmanship of Lord Wolfenden considered how far it was acceptable for a society to pass laws governing moral behaviour. It concluded that, unless we were to say that there is no difference between a crime and a sin, there must remain an area of our private lives that is 'quite simply not the law's business'.

▲ A scene from a 1956 film version of Orwell's *Nineteen Eighty-Four*.

Burning books

The most dramatic censorship of written material is perhaps when books are burnt. Burning books has become a symbol of a society trying to control the people. In 2000 years of Christian history the Church has often been involved with censorship. Sometimes Christians have been the victims of this and sometimes they have been the ones suppressing the opinions of other people:

Discussion point

Is censorship necessary to prevent people from being influenced by dangerous teachings or opinions?

- In Acts 19:19, Paul's converts at Ephesus burnt their books of sorcery. This is sometimes described as the first example of Christian censorship but in this situation the books belonged to the people who burnt them. They burnt them in order to put away the past and make a fresh start.
- For 300 years Christians were persecuted by the Roman state. Sometimes Christians were killed and sometimes their books were burnt.
- The Roman emperor Constantine ruled that Christianity was allowed but less than 20 years later he ordered the burning of the books of the Greek theologian Arius. This time his aim was to suppress heresy.
- When Theodosius I became emperor in 392BCE he made Christianity the established religion of the Empire but both the Roman government and the Church then began to persecute pagans and Christian heretics. Any books that contained teachings that were different from the official views of the Church were prohibited and their authors punished.
- In 496BCE the first catalogue of forbidden books was issued by Pope Gelasius.
- Much later, in 1231BCE Pope Gregory IX set up the Inquisition in order to enforce religious censorship. In the fifteenth century, the invention of printing enabled ideas to be spread very quickly but censorship soon regained control. Pope Innocent VIII introduced pre-publication censorship in 1487 and in 1559 Pope Paul III first issued the *Index of Forbidden Books*. The last edition of this was published in 1948.

The Reformation in England

The Protestant Reformation of the sixteenth century was about freedom of religious belief but brought about the persecution of Roman Catholics, people accused of being witches and Protestants with different opinions.

Under the Act of Supremacy of 1534 King Henry VIII ordered English copies of the New Testament to be burnt. It was not until the reign of King James I in 1611 that the Authorised Version of the Bible was printed in English so that people could read it for themselves. However, not being part of the Church of England was punished as treason. The Religious Society of Friends (Quakers) was one of the groups formed in the seventeenth century and they suffered persecution for following their conscience.

In the seventeenth century Oliver Cromwell set up a licensing system for books and newspapers and there was censorship of anything 'contrary to good life and manners'. This was abolished in 1695.

An Indian Muslim wears a mask of author Salman Rushdie as he displays a placard condemning Rushdie. ▶

Blasphemy

One of the important issues concerning censorship in the UK has been the laws against blasphemy. Blasphemy consists of offensive or abusive remarks about God.

In the 1970s the newspaper *Gay News* published an illustration and a poem by American writer James Kirkup which suggested that Jesus might have been homosexual. The court case established that there was a crime of blasphemy in common law and the editor of *Gay News* was prosecuted. In the 1980s, when Salman Rushdie wrote *The Satanic Verses* which caused offence to many Muslims, the courts decided that, in England, blasphemy only offered protection to Christianity and possibly only to the Church of England.

Many people, not only Muslims, felt that this situation was unfair. They believed that the blasphemy law should apply to all faiths or none.

Exam practice

'Religious people should ignore the media if they don't like it.'
Discuss. Remember to give your own opinion and support it.

(12 marks)

In your answer you need to consider to what extent people can 'ignore the media'. While it is true that people can turn off the television and not read certain books or watch particular films, this does not mean that they will not be exposed to things that they do not want to see or hear. You might consider whether Christians would support the freedom of the media to publish whatever they want or if they think that some things are offensive and should not appear in the media. You might also give a secular view and consider what a non-believer would say about the media.

Religion and the media: Looking at Exam Questions

Each question has **five** parts (a–e), and you need to answer all the parts.
You will only answer **one** question on each topic. There is a total of
24 marks for each question.

(a) **What is meant by 'the media'?** *(1 mark)*

*In your answer you might say that an example
of media is television, radio, film, newspapers or
the internet.*

(b) **What does 'freedom of speech' mean?**
(2 marks)

*Here you might say that it is the belief or
principle that people have the right to speak their
mind or say whatever they want.*

(c) **How is Christianity portrayed in the media?**
(3 marks)

*For this question you need to give different
examples. Depending on the media you might
say that it is portrayed positively or negatively
and you might give examples such as religious
work for the poor and suffering or the way in
which the media sometimes react to statements
which can be controversial like some of the
statements made by the Pope.*

(d) **Explain Christian attitudes towards the
portrayal of violence in the media.** *(6 marks)*

*In this question you are being asked to 'explain'
Christian attitudes not just list them. You might
say that some Christians feel that portraying
violence for its own sake or for entertainment is
not acceptable but that if it is shown to educate
people then it might be justified. You might give
examples of different kinds of violence and
explain how Christians might respond to them.*

(e) **'People should never be allowed to make fun of
religion in the media.'**

**Discuss this statement. You should include
different, supported points of view and a
personal viewpoint. You must refer to
Christianity in your answer.** *(12 marks)*

*In your answer you might want to start by
considering what is meant by 'fun'. You might
say that, as with all other aspects of life, you can
find humour in religion and religious practices.
In relation to Christianity you might say that
some jokes are acceptable but that actually using
the media deliberately to make fun of religion
and what people believe is not acceptable. You
could say that people should always show
respect for other people's beliefs.*

Glossary

Abortifacient a drug or device that causes an abortion

Absolute morality something which is moral in all circumstances

Active euthanasia when action is taken to bring life to an end

Adoration worshipping God for who he is and what he has

Affective poverty when someone can separate themselves from any money or possessions which they have

Agape selfless love, taught by Jesus of Nazareth and felt by Christians for their fellow human beings

Agnostic somebody who believes that it is impossible to know whether or not God exists

AID artificial insemination by donor

AIH artificial insemination by husband

Altar the table or other raised structure in a Christian church on which the bread and wine of the eucharist are prepared

Anglican Church (Church of England) The Church of England is part of the larger Anglican Communion

Anglican tradition the teachings and tradition of the Anglican Communion

Annulment a declaration that a marriage was never a proper marriage in the eyes of a church, e.g. because one of the parties was not completely committed to it

Anointed one see Messiah

Anselm of Canterbury, St (1033–1109) an Italian philosopher and theologian who was Archbishop of Canterbury from 1093 to 1109

Anthropomorphism the attribution of a human form, characteristics or behaviour to non-human things

Apartheid a political system in South Africa from 1948 to the early 1990s that separated the different peoples living there according to skin colour and gave privileges to those of European origin

Aquinas, St Thomas (1225–74) a Roman Catholic priest from Italy, and a very influential philosopher and theologian

Artificial insemination sperm is collected and placed in the woman's uterus artificially

Assisted suicide another term for voluntary euthanasia

Astrology the study of the positions of the moon, sun and other planets in the belief that their motions affect human beings

Atheist somebody who does not believe in God

Atonement the Christian belief that the death of Jesus Christ brought about a reconciliation between God and humanity. Jesus was the Saviour or Redeemer of the world

Avarice greed for wealth

Baptist Church the Baptist Church grew out of the Anabaptist movement during the sixteenth-century Reformation

Believer someone who believes

Bible the sacred book of Christianity

Big Bang theory scientific theory which suggests that there was a massive explosion about 18 billion years ago and that this led to the creation of the whole universe

Canon a collection of religious writings

Celibate unmarried, especially because of a religious vow

Censorship the suppression of all or part of a play, film or book considered offensive

Charismatic form of Christian worship where people try to open themselves to the Holy Spirit and be inspired by it

Cohabitation to live together, especially without being formally married

Confession people saying sorry for things that they have done wrong and asking God's forgiveness

Consubstantiation the belief that the bread and wine consecrated at the eucharist coexist with the body and blood of Jesus

Contraception the prevention of pregnancy by using artificial methods such as condoms and contraceptive pills or natural methods such as avoiding sex during known fertile periods

Darwin, Charles (1809–82) the founder of evolutionary theory who, in 1859, published *On the Origin of Species by Means of Natural Selection or the Preservation of Favoured Races in the Struggle for Life*

Dawkins, Richard (b.1942) British evolutionary biologist and prominent atheist

Denomination a religious group within a faith

Desensitise to make somebody or something less sensitive

Discrimination unfair treatment of one person or group

Doctrine of double effect Roman Catholic doctrine which says that if doing something morally good has a morally bad side-effect, it is right to do it providing the bad side-effect was not intended

Eternal existing through all time

Eucharist a Christian sacrament that commemorates the Last Supper, with the priest or minister consecrating bread and wine that is consumed by the congregation

Euthanasia a gentle or easy death; helping someone to die

Exorcise using prayers and rituals to drive away an evil spirit believed to be possessing a person or place

Finite limited

First Cause the reason behind the existence of everything, usually applied to God

Font a large container in a church containing the water for baptisms

Free Churches churches which are separate from government and the 'established church' (Church of England)

Free will human ability to decide what to do for themselves

Freedom of speech the right of people to say what they think without censorship

Fundamentalists Christians who say that every word of the Bible is absolutely true and there are no errors or mistakes in it

General Judgement the Last Judgement when God will pass his final sentence on the whole of humanity as well as on the soul and body of each individual

Gospel music emotional and evangelical vocal music that first appeared around 1870 in the USA

House groups informal, small groups that meet locally for friendship, Bible study and prayer

Hymn a song of praise to God

Icon a holy picture of Jesus Christ, the Virgin Mary or a saint, usually an oil painting on a wooden panel, found mainly in Orthodox churches

Idol an object of worship other than God

Immanence God is within all

Immanuel title given to Jesus of Nazareth which means 'God with us'

Impersonal not being like a person

Incarnation God taking human form as Jesus Christ

Infinite without limits

Intelligent design a theory which says that life is so complex that it must have been designed by a higher intelligent being, and did not evolve by natural selection

Involuntary euthanasia when other people decide that it would be for the best if someone's life ends, because he or she is not able to make that decision independently

IVF in vitro fertilisation; IVF involves the egg and the sperm being brought together in a test tube

Jesus Jesus of Nazareth, part of the Holy Trinity, the Son of God

Judge belief that, on the Day of Judgement, God will judge everyone according to how they have lived

Lectern a reading stand used in churches to support the Bible

Liberal a belief that the Bible need not be understood literally but can be interpreted

Liturgy (1) a formal arrangement of worship; (2) name for the eucharist in the Orthodox Church

Media means of mass communication

Meditate to empty the mind of thoughts, or concentrate on one thing, in order to aid spiritual thoughts

Memorialism a belief that the eucharist is a memorial of Jesus' acts and words at the Last Supper

Messiah title given to Jesus of Nazareth. Messiah means 'Anointed One' as kings, prophets and priests were anointed in the Jewish religion

Methodist Church a Protestant movement with a total of approximately 70 million followers worldwide. Methodism arose from the work and preaching of John Wesley, an Anglican clergyman

Missionaries people who are sent to another country by a church to spread its faith or to do social and medical work

Monotheists people who believe in one God, such as Christians, Jews and Muslims

Natural selection theory that tiny differences and genetic mutations between creatures of the same species can sometimes make one individual slightly better suited to their environment than others. This means that it survives longer and has more offspring who inherit that trait

Necessary being theory of Thomas Aquinas that God must exist because he cannot not exist

New Testament the second part of the Christian Bible containing the Gospels, the Acts of the Apostles, the Epistles and the book of Revelation

Newton, Isaac (1642–1727) one of the first modern scientists, he argued that the human thumb was so intricately designed and unique to each person, that it had to have a designer

Nicene Creed statement of Christian faith adopted at the Council of Nicaea in 325CE

Numinous a mysterious power that suggests the presence of a spirit or god

Obscenity something that is disgusting or morally offensive

Old Testament the first part of the Christian Bible, originally the Tenakh – Jewish Scriptures

Omnibenevolence, omnibenevolent all-good

Omnipotence, omnipotent all-important

Omnipresence, omnipresent all-present

Omniscience, omniscient all-knowing

Original sin the sin which Eve brought into the world when she picked the fruit from the Tree of the Knowledge of Good and Evil in the Garden of Eden

Orthodox Churches the Eastern Christian churches that are in full communion with the Ecumenical Patriarchate of Constantinople and with each other

Otto, Rudolph (1869–1937) a German theologian Rudolf Otto who explain the concept of the numinous in *The Idea of the Holy* (1917)

Our Father prayer originally taught to his disciples by Jesus of Nazareth (Matthew 6:9–15)

Paley, William (1743–1805) used the idea of a watch to explain that the world did not appear by chance

Palliative care coping with the major aspects of keeping severe pain under control

Parousia (second coming) the anticipated and prophesied return of Jesus Christ to judge humanity at the end of the world

197

Particular Judgement the judgement given to every soul when a person dies

Passive euthanasia when a decision is made to stop giving a dying person further treatment, even though death will be the result

Penitent somebody who feels regret for their sins and confesses them

Personal being like a person

Proselytising to try to convert somebody to a religious faith

Protestant traditions the churches which follow the teachings and principles of the sixteenth century Protestant Reformation

Public registrar a local official responsible for maintaining an index of births, marriages, and deaths in the area under his or her authority

Pulpit a raised platform or stand in a Christian church that is used by the priest or minister for preaching

Purgatory Roman Catholic belief that after death many souls go to Purgatory where they are prepared to go to heaven

Quakers see Religious Society of Friends

Quality of life the consideration of how happy someone is and whether they are suffering

Receptionism belief that the bread and wine consecrated at the eucharist become the body and blood of Jesus when they are received by a believer

Reconciliation the ending of conflict or renewing of a friendly relationship between disputing people or groups

Redeemer title given to Jesus of Nazareth (see atonement)

Relative morality the belief that moral rules can change according to particular situations

Religious Society of Friends 'Quakers', a Christian denomination founded in the seventeenth century

Resurrection when Jesus of Nazareth rose from the dead on the first Easter Sunday

Revelation 'unveiling' – when something which was previously hidden becomes known

Role model a person who is an example for other people

Roman Catholic Church the world's largest Christian Church which is governed by the Pope

Roman Catholics members of the Roman Catholic Church

Sacrament an outward, physical sign of an inward, invisible grace

Salvation Army a Protestant denomination founded in 1865 organised in a quasi-military way and known particularly for its charitable and social work

Samaritans an organisation that was started in 1953 which provides emotional support to anyone in distress or at risk of suicide

Sanctity of life the belief that there is something special or holy about life

Sanctuary the east end of a church and the traditional place for the main altar

Saviour title given to Jesus of Nazareth (see atonement)

Service of the Word a church service, or part of one, consisting of Bible readings and preaching

Sexism discrimination against women or men because of their sex

Speaking in tongues 'glossolalia', one of the 'gifts of the spirit', the making of sounds that are not recognisable as any known language

Stained glass windows originally used in churches as a way of telling Bible stories

Stations of the Cross a series of fourteen pictures or plaques found around the walls of some churches which recall events in the last days of Jesus' life

Stem cells single cells which have the potential to be 'reprogrammed' to develop into any type of cell in the body

Suicide the act of deliberately killing yourself

Supplication prayers in which people ask God for their own needs and those of others

Tabernacle a box or case in which the consecrated bread of the eucharist is kept

Teetotal completely abstaining from alcohol

Thanksgiving a prayer or act which gives thanks to God

Therapeutic cloning a medical procedure where single cells would be taken from a person and 'reprogrammed' to create stem cells, which have the potential to develop into any type of cell in the body

Transcendent, transcendence God is above all

Transgenic an animal or plant that contains genes from a different species

Transubstantiation the doctrine of the Roman Catholic and Orthodox Churches that the bread and wine of the eucharist become, in substance but not appearance, the body and blood of Jesus Christ at the consecration

United Reformed Church the result of a union between the Presbyterian Church of England and the Congregational Church in England and Wales in 1972, the Reformed Association of Churches of Christ in 1981 and the Congregational Union of Scotland in 2000

Vatican II the Second Ecumenical Council of the Vatican (Roman Catholic Church, 1962–5)

Verbal inerrancy the belief that every word of the Bible was inspired by God's guidance of the writers through the Holy Spirit

Voluntary euthanasia when someone asks for the end of his or her own life but is unable to commit suicide without help

Word of God the belief that the Bible is the revealed word of God

Worship to honour a supernatural or holy power by adoring or venerating it

Index